THE COURAGEOUS STATE

RETHINKING ECONOMICS, SOCIETY
AND THE
ROLE OF GOVERNMENT

By Richard Murphy

Searching
finance

Published under licence 2011 by Searching Finance Ltd, 8 Whitehall Road, London W7 2JE, UK

ISBN: 978-1-907720-28-4

Typeset by: Deirdré Gyenes

THE COURAGEOUS STATE

RETHINKING ECONOMICS, SOCIETY
AND THE
ROLE OF GOVERNMENT

By Richard Murphy

About the author

Richard Murphy is a chartered accountant and economist. He has been described by the Guardian newspaper as an "anti-poverty campaigner and tax expert". A graduate in Economics and Accountancy from Southampton University he was articled to Peat Marwick Mitchell & Co in London. He subsequently founded a firm of accountants in London which he and his partners sold in 2000. In parallel with his practice career Richard was chairman, chief executive or finance director of more than 10 SMEs.

Since 2003 Richard has been increasingly involved in economic and taxation policy issues. He was a founder of the Tax Justice Network and is director of Tax Research LLP which undertakes work on taxation policy, advocacy and research for aid agencies, unions, NGOs and others in the UK and abroad.

As principal researcher of the Tax Justice Network from its inception until 2009 Richard helped put the tax haven issue on the international agenda as principal author of such works as 'Tax Us If You Can', 'Closing the Floodgates', 'Creating Turmoil' and the extensive analysis underpinning TJN's Secrecy Jurisdictions website and its Financial Secrecy Index.

Richard's work for the TUC, PCS and others on the tax gap in the UK has also put this issue on the UK tax agenda. Richard is also a principal author of many of the proposals made by the Green New Deal group in the UK, and has written extensively on tackling the UK's deficit without imposing cuts on the most vulnerable in society.

Richard has written widely, and blogs frequently. He has appeared in many radio and television documentaries on taxation issues. He has also presented written and oral evidence to select committee committees of the House of Commons and House of Lords.

Richard has been a visiting fellow at Portsmouth University Business School, the Centre for Global Political Economy at the University of Sussex and at the Tax Research Institute, University of Nottingham.

Richard was voted the seventh most influential left-wing thinker in 2010/11 in a Left Foot Forward poll, making him the highest ranked UK based economist on the list.

About Searching Finance

Searching Finance Ltd is a dynamic new voice in knowledge provision for the financial services and related professional sectors. Our mission is to provide expert, highly relevant and actionable information and analysis, written by professionals, for professionals. For more information, please visit www.searchingfinance.com

CONTENTS

CONTENTS

CONTENTS

PREFACE

The Courageous State is a book written in a hurry. I'll get the apology in straight away in case it shows. I would have liked to have spent more time on it, but when Ashwin Rattan of Searching Finance approached me in June 2011 to write a book on tax I realised that, much as that might be fun (trust me, I mean that), there was a more pressing issue to address. That more pressing issue was the oft-documented absence of ideas for an alternative economic strategy, let alone an intellectual base on which to build one. The result is that, in the space of just three months, The Courageous State was written.

If that haste means this book might need to change and develop over time, so be it. What is clear is that the economics profession has failed us. I can't and won't pretend to have all the alternative answers that are needed. I just want to stimulate debate on what an alternative economics – not just in practice but quite unusually also in theory – might look like. That's what created my sense of urgency about this project.

That said, I did not, of course, come up with all the ideas in this book over the three months it took to write. Some date back to my undergraduate days when I realised what a lot of nonsense I was being taught during my economics courses. Other ideas arose during my career as a chartered accountant in both practice and commerce. What I know about business I learned from doing it. It's an invaluable learning method. And some ideas have, of course, come from thirty or more years reading on economics, accountancy, tax, ethics and other issues. Doubtless I have not referenced many sources of ideas I use in this book as a result. If I have not, I apologise: the oversight is not intentional.

Most of the ideas to be found here have, however, developed over the last decade as I have increasingly worked on issues relating to tax justice, tax havens and the resulting economic impacts of tax systems on the world and the well-being of the people who live in it. I have never pretended that such work was an objective assessment of the problems tackled. It has always been motivated by an overt bias to the poor. This has meant that the work in question has been both the most exciting and toughest part of my career and much of the thinking that has underpinned my approach to that work, and which has also resulted from it, is reflected in this book. As a result there is no doubt that I must begin my notes of thanks with those with whom I have worked on tax justice issues.

John Christensen rightly comes first in this list of thanks. Over the last nine years we have worked together day in and day out on tax justice issues. It's been the most fruitful working relationship I have ever enjoyed. I am immensely grateful for the countless hours we have spent working out how to tackle the economic, accounting, taxation, social, development and other concerns that have mutually driven our work. Those discussions influenced much that is in this book.

Others working on tax justice issues have also had real impact on my thinking. I was influenced by Professor Prem Sikka for many years before I met him, and before he introduced me to John Christensen. I continue to admire his work and enjoy his friendship. If anyone epitomises courage, it is Prem.

Alex Cobham of Christian Aid has helped my thinking enormously, and made enormously useful comments on drafts of this book. Professor Ronen Palan of the University of Birmingham, with whom I have co-authored, has been a consistent influence. Raymond Banker, Jack Blum and Tom Cardamone have added a US dimension to my understanding, whilst Markus Meinzer added in a German perspective. Nicholas Shaxson saw the issues John and I were seeking to address from a journalist's perspective, and changed our view of it as a result. Nick Mathiason assisted that process.

Beyond tax justice, Dennis Howlett introduced me to blogging. I have to thank and blame him for the countless hours I've spent blogging ever since that fateful first blog back in 2006.

Outside the tax sphere I have been privileged to work with Colin Hines for almost as long as I have been involved in tax justice issues. Colin is a tireless environmentalist, localist and campaigner. Through Colin I was introduced to the Green New Deal group. Many of its members, including Ann Pettifor, Andrew Simms, Larry Elliott, Geoff Tily, Jerry Leggett and Ruth Potts have been significant influences on my thinking. My thanks to them all for that and for their company on many occasions.

In the broader sphere of left of centre thinking, Neal Lawson and Howard Reed have been influential. Howard offered some invaluable comments on parts of this book, for which I offer thanks, but as with all others with whom I have discussed it, the errors that remain are mine alone.

More broadly I have to thank my oldest friend, Jack Ray, for introducing me to a love of writing when I was in my early teens. He told me, long ago, that writers and thinkers can be more influential than politicians. He may not recall doing so, but it had a powerful impact on me, and my career.

I also owe a debt of thanks to the Quakers and to Wandsworth Quaker Meeting in particular. Whilst a member of that meeting I realised that I was meant to do something more practical about issues of social justice. As a result it has been especially pleasing that I am now funded in no small part by the Joseph Rowntree Charitable Trust, a Quaker charity. This book would not have been possible without their assistance.

I should also offer a note of thanks to others who have helped fund my work over recent years including the Trades Union Congress, the Public and Commercial services Union (PCS), the Task Force on Financial Integrity and Economic Development (and behind them, the Norwegian and Spanish governments), the Greenpeace Charitable Trust and others. You are in no way responsible for this work, but I am grateful for the support that has enabled it to happen.

I wonder what my mother, who died over twenty-five years ago would have made of this book. My father has followed my development on these issues with interest and taught me that parenting never ends. I'm grateful for that.

But most of all my thanks go to my wife, Jacqueline, and my sons. Jacqueline has been the strongest supporter of what I do, whether practically, intellectually or emotionally, that I have ever had. More hours have been spent with her discussing the issues addressed in this book than with everyone else combined. I could never say thank you enough. And then there's James and Thomas. Aged ten and nine they've been constant companions as my work on tax and related economic issues has developed and they've got used to a father who spends too much of his time wedded to a keyboard. All I can say is that this book is really for them. When I became a father I could no longer accept the world as it was, or the risk that my children might inherit the mess that was being made of it. I had no choice but try to make a better world for them to live in. This book is part of my contribution to that goal. Which is why this book is dedicated to Jacqueline, James and Thomas, with love.

Richard Murphy

Downham Market
Norfolk
October 2011

CHAPTER 1

INTRODUCTION

In October 2008 the world's economy nearly fell over. It didn't just suffer a problem from which it has since recovered a little, although that has happened, as we all know. I mean it nearly fell over. To put it another way, it nearly collapsed.

Over the weekend of 4–5 October 2008 emergency meetings took place in the Treasury in London because the managers of Royal Bank of Scotland knew they could not open for business on the following Monday morning. They were for all practical purposes bust. They had reached the point where they weren't sure they could put money in their cashpoint machines: they were no longer sure that they had any.[1]

That wasn't a minor embarrassment, or even a serious economic crisis: that was risk at level 10 on the economic Richter scale. To explain the seriousness of the situation, on average it is reckoned that most households in the UK have three days' meals in their store cupboards. After that their food begins to run out. As a result we are nine meals from the breakdown of society at any moment.[2] If as a result of a bank's failure there was sudden inability on the part of large numbers of people to pay for food, or inability on the part of a major supermarket to take people's cards, or inability on the supermarket's part to pay for new supplies then any one or all of these things could have brought the food chain crashing down, with all the resulting massive social consequences that would have followed. That's how close we got to major civil disruption;

1

to the mass breakdown of law and order and to the end of the current structure of the economy.

The day was saved: Alastair Darling may one day get the credit he deserves for his cool action in the face of this potential calamity. Gordon Brown also deserves a fair share of credit. And yet, after a brief renaissance of Keynesian economics in the aftermath of the crisis when it seemed just possible that a combination of sound thinking in the UK and strong action in the US might prevent global meltdown, everything has gone wrong again. Across Europe governments have abandoned intervention in the economy. David Cameron and George Osborne led the way in the UK when, without an electoral mandate, they secured power and declared to the surprise of the followers of their coalition partners that the only way to deal with the economic crisis was for government to walk away from the problem.

That is precisely what Cameron and Osborne, with their allies Nick Clegg and Danny Alexander, have done since then. These two have become the apotheosis of something that has been thirty years in the making: they are the personification of what I call the cowardly state. The cowardly state in the UK is the creation of Margaret Thatcher, although its US version is of course the creation of Ronald Reagan. It was these two politicians who swept neoliberalism into the political arena in 1979 and 1980 respectively following the first neoliberal revolution in Chile in 1973 that saw the overthrow of the democratically elected Allende government by General Pinochet. Since then its progress has been continual: now it forms the consensus of thinking across the political divide within the UK, Europe and the US.

The creation of the cowardly state

The economic crisis we are now facing is the legacy of Thatcher and Reagan because they introduced into government the neoliberal[3] idea that whatever a politician does, however well-intentioned that action might be, they will always make matters worse in the economy. This is because government is never able, according to neoliberal thinking, to outperform the market, which will always, it says, allocate resources better and so increase human well-being more than government can.

That thinking is the reason why we have ended up with cowardly government. That is why in August 2011, when we had riots on streets of London we also had Conservative politicians on holiday, reluctant to return because they were quite sure that nothing they could do and no action they could take would make any difference to the outcome of the situation. What began as an economic idea has now swept across government as a whole: we have got a class of politicians who think that the only useful function for the power that they hold is to dismantle the state they have been elected to govern while transferring as many of its functions as possible to unelected businesses that have bankrolled their path to power.

This, it should be said, has not just been an issue within the Conservative party. Thatcher arrived in power with what was, in retrospect, a remarkably timid manifesto for change, and although she became bolder as her career as Prime Minister progressed she retained a strong belief in the power of government regulation over the businesses that she privatised. Her legacy was regulated capitalism: ownership in private hands, with some power to control those sold-off enterprises retained by state-appointed regulators that were one stage removed from the ministers who appointed them.

John Major oversaw a collapse in the credibility of government, and something more besides. It was on his watch that the Private Finance Initiative (PFI) began, and it was on his watch that some of the more absurd privatisations, such as that of the railways, were undertaken. It was John Major who began the process of outsourcing. A weak Prime Minister ran away from his responsibilities: the cowardly state was by now in full flow.

Tony Blair continued the process. It was he who promised the 'The Third Way', not that anyone knew what it was, any more than anybody now knows what David Cameron's 'Big Society' might be. Both, however, have a hallmark in common: they meant 'anyone but government', and that was the intention. These were prime ministers in common in that they believed that whatever one asked for it was not the state's role to supply it.

Based on this belief, Blair pursued outsourcing as if it was the solution to all the government's problems. Despite having opposed PFI when in opposition PFI became Labour's favoured form of government finance until we have ended up in the absurd situation that the building in which the Treasury is located is now owned by an offshore company.[4] And everywhere the message was given that light touch regulation of finance was to be the Labour mantra, 'liberated' as it had been by Thatcher from the constraints that had previously made it responsible in her 'Big Bang' reforms in 1986. This was perhaps the most cowardly act of all, for from that 'liberation' and subsequent failure to regulate sprang a finance sector that has now dragged us to our knees. Gordon Brown may have saved the day in 2008 and had a moment of glory in the April 2009 G20 summit, but for his role in allowing finance to take over the UK economy he too takes his share of the blame for creating the cowardly state.

What the cowardly state represents

- This is the state that now argues that in the face of mass unemployment the government's only choice is to sack more people.
- And this is the state that says when there is no hope of the market generating new jobs, new investment, new innovation, new skills and new prospects then the government must cuts its spending and so remove any prospect of recovery from the economy.
- This is the state that says that those who never created this crisis must pay for it while the rich and powerful who did create it from within the banks must have tax cuts.
- This is the state that failed to stand up to bullying and abuse from the media.
- This is the state that is failing its young by putting them in debt for what may be the rest of their working lives to secure an education that previous generations enjoyed for nothing.

- And this is a state that does not have the courage to provide its young people with jobs, its old people with secure care, its population with protection against unemployment and the unforeseen and its children with decent schools.

This is a cowardly state: a state that sees responsibility and runs away from it. This is a state that now exists solely to facilitate the looting of its power to tax for the benefit of an elite who want to own its assets through the PFI scheme, and be guaranteed a high and risk-free income for doing so. It is a state that wants to privatise its education system through 'free schools' – free only because yet more tax goes to the private sector in the process. And it is a state that wants to hand control of one of the UK's greatest achievements – the National Health Service – to the market so that we can copy the US healthcare model and double the cost of provision in exchange for worse healthcare outcomes – all so that a few can cream off from the tax revenues a wholly undeserved and excessive risk-free return for being in the right place at the right time, somewhere near their old school friends who might now be in power in Westminster.

No wonder we're in a mess. And no wonder the world's markets are teetering on the brink of collapse. After all, why invest in businesses when something so much more attractive – the outsourced tax income stream of a government as anxious as possible to give it away – is waiting to be claimed just around the corner?

The result is that private industry has discovered that rather than trying to innovate new products in an uncertain consumer marketplace it is much easier to make profits from the certain commodities that people are always going to need, such as health, education, local government services, the utilities and so on that were once the preserve of government. So not only are these services now more costly because a profit margin has been or is being added into their cost structure, it can also be argued that their transfer into the private sector via outsourcing actually weakens the incentive for companies to invest in new technologies which might be useful to meeting people's needs.

Meanwhile, in the financial markets speculation has replaced real investment. This is logical because investing in new technologies in manufacturing or services is a much less safe bet for individual businesses than just getting on one of two gravy trains, the first being public sector outsourcing and the second financial derivatives.

In that case no wonder faith in government itself – and its ability to control anything – has been shattered, as recent rioting has shown.

As commentator after commentator has said, we now have weak governments led by weak politicians who are bereft of any idea apart from dismantling the mechanisms of state that they have been elected to manage for the benefit of the private sector.

This is what neoliberalism has brought us to. This is the legacy that Thatcher has delivered to us. This is what happens when government is run by cowards who believe that there is nothing they can do but acquiesce to the demands of the market.

The need for a Courageous State

And yet it need not be this way. As I argue in this book, we could have a Courageous State. A Courageous State is populated by politicians who believe in government. They believe in the power of the office they hold. They believe that office exists for the sake of the public good. They know what that public good is. They think it is their job to help each and every person in their country to achieve their potential – something that is unique to each person and which at the same time is a characteristic we all have in common. And they believe they can command the resources to fulfil this task – whether through tax or other means – and that they should command those resources so that we as a country can each achieve, both individually and collectively.

We have not had politicians like that for a long time. These are politicians with the courage to work out when the market is absolutely the right mechanism for delivering what society needs – and which backs those who wish to partake in that market openly, honestly and accountably by providing them with the environment they need so that they can flourish, while delivering all the resources required to curtail those intent on market abuse.

6

And they are politicians who are as capable of deciding when the market can never deliver – because it is wholly unsuitable for the task in hand – meaning that it is the job of the state to ensure that what society needs and wants society shall get, at the lowest possible cost for the highest possible outcome for the benefit of all involved.

These are politicians of integrity. Who will carry their conviction with pride. Who will stand up to those who get in their way, not by ignoring them and not by bullying them but by presenting them with reasoned argument that shows that these politicians have worked out what they are doing, and why, and how they mean to achieve it.

I suspect a great many of us want such politicians. Politicians who are strong and effective; people we can believe in and who inspire but who we know we can hold to account through the democratic process. Politicians we can hold up as examples. Politicians with the ability to admit mistakes and move on. Politicians who we are willing to follow. Politicians of the stature of those who built the post-war consensus in the UK, for example, which proves that such people can exist.

But that's the problem with this vision. That consensus was built on the basis of a very different political viewpoint to that which now prevails. It was built on the political logic of John Maynard Keynes. Keynes was a Cambridge professor of economics and a former civil servant. He realised that markets do not work as most economists, including the neoliberal economists who dominate current thinking, argue they do. He had a profound insight that neoliberal economists do not share. He realised that markets, just like the rest of us, often have little or no clue at all about what is going on. That might sound like a statement of the obvious, but as I will explore in this book, neoliberal economics – and all that follows on from it, including the crashes we have had and are facing – is built on a very different logic. Neoliberal economics assumes that there is nothing markets do not know, and therefore nothing they have not already built into the prices that they charge. Neoliberal economists assume – quite extraordinarily – that markets know everything but that as mere human beings politicians are error prone and therefore are bound to get things wrong.[5] Which is why, neoliberals say we must trust markets and not politicians. And despite the absurdity of this claim – for that's all it is – the politicians of the cowardly state think this is true.

This, at its core, is the difference between a Courageous and a cowardly politician. A Courageous politician knows that there is a great deal that he or she does not know, and knows that despite that they will have to act. A cowardly politician believes that the market knows everything and that in that case they had better do nothing. But of course, as Keynes realised, for reasons that I will explore, markets cannot know everything. In that case they're not infallible and to be followed on all occasions as the likes of George Osborne following in the wake of Margaret Thatcher believe to be the case. Markets actually get things profoundly wrong.

Where markets go wrong

That glaringly obvious insight is not hard to reach. Markets are, after all, made up of human beings, and not one of us individually knows everything. It's hardly surprising that collectively we do not either, a point that was fundamental to the developments in economics that Keynes pioneered. Indeed, it would be surprising if that were the case even if human beings did in each and every case know everything, as nothing would overcome the fact that we would remain appalling communicators of that understanding.

Precisely because the politicians who would populate the Courageous State would know that markets fail they would also know it was their job to exercise the judgment for which they had been selected, and to do so on our collective behalf, empowering them to intervene when necessary to counter the excesses and deficiencies of the market, while also ensuring that those things the market cannot do are delivered as required.

However, that requires them to have a framework for decision-making that they can use when exercising that judgment. That same framework could, of course, also be used to communicate their intentions, to elicit broader understanding of them and to ensure that those who were instructed to act on their behalf knew why they were doing what was asked of them. And that's where we have a problem, because we do not have that framework.

Neoliberalism clearly is not it: it is the framework for the current failure of thinking. And unfortunately Keynes's thinking has been greatly abused since his profound insights helped save the world from recession in the 1930s. Keynes dedicated himself to practical matters and the war effort from soon after the time he published his magnum opus 'The General Theory of Employment, Interest and Money' in 1936. As a result, and as I discuss below, his ideas were never fully developed by him and those who came in his wake delivered something that approximated to them which was, however, based on the same assumptions of neoclassical economics that also underpin neoliberal thinking.

Neo-Keynesian thinking therefore shares the assumption that the market knows best, and that a market solution will always, eventually be optimal. The only difference, as I note when addressing this issue, is that neoliberal thinkers believe that the markets are so powerful they not only know everything, but also anticipate everything, so that the move from one optimal state to another is instantaneous, whereas neo-Keynesians think there is a delay between the two situations, justifying government intervention while a transition takes place if there are adverse impacts of change in the meantime. Unfortunately, one market it seems the neo-Keynesians did not think might suffer from such imperfections was that for finance. As a result they were as unprepared in 2008 as the neoliberals.

The consequence of the similarities between neoliberal and neo-Keynesian thinking is that the decision-making framework for a Courageous State does not exist at present. That means that while we all know that the market does not know everything, and that there is a very clear role for the state, and that the state has an absolute right to raise taxes (even though neoliberals challenge this on the basis of logic that I show to be completely wrong) there is at present no theoretical basis for what I describe as a 'cappuccino' economy.

The cappuccino economy

A cappuccino economy is the mixed economy that exists within society (the cappuccino cup) with the state being represented by the strong back coffee that underpins the whole edifice, while the private sector is the hot frothy milk that is added to that coffee to work in combination with it to make the final product. The luxuries paid for out of our limited disposable incomes that add the gloss to the private sector are represented by the nutmeg or chocolate that float on top of the hot milk which represents the private sector as a whole. The spoon represents democracy that determines the mix between the coffee and milk, with sugar representing the sweeteners necessary to ensure that almost all accept the eventual outcomes determined by government.

The metaphor can be pushed a lot further: the saucer represents the welfare state that stops people falling out of society; the barista has the skills society needs and must perpetuate, the coffee-making machine and indeed the coffee shop in which most cappuccino is drunk are both representative of the infrastructure that is essential in any society, while the recipe is based on our wisdom and tradition of accumulated knowledge. The fact that cappuccino is very often drunk in a social environment is indicative of the fact that it is the exchanges within society that actually fulfil us as people and are the way in which we understand our purpose.

Most people I have ever described this metaphor to can instantly relate to it: this is the world in which many people live and it is the world that they understand. And yet there is no economic theory currently in use that describes this economy. And that, I suggest, is the real problem we face right now, and is the reason why we are in a mess. It is also the reason why having explored all the issues I have noted so far in this introductory chapter in more depth in Part 1 of this book, I then move on in Part 2 to offer an entirely new perspective on economic theory.

I am, of course, aware of the preposterousness of doing so. I know that millions of people around the world have invested vast amounts of time and effort into developing, learning, teaching and using the methodologies promoted by neoliberal economics, and to a lesser degree those of neo-Keynesian economics. Of course that is the case, and despite that I say that all that effort has been in vain; much of that effort has been made to simply perpetuate a system which most of those who engage with it know deep down to be fundamentally flawed and that there simply has to be something better on offer.

Why this book needed to be written

I have waited more than thirty years for that 'something else'. I realised how absurd conventional economics was during my first year as a university undergraduate. Being asked to believe in a myth as absurd as the one I have just outlined was a demand too much for me, which was one reason why I also chose to go out and take part in the real economy as an accountant and business person rather than stay in academia, as no doubt I could have done.

Well, I am bored with waiting for that something else to come along, because so far it has not, even if some very effective critiques of existing economics are now available, and are referred to in chapters that follow. That's why I have now written down, for the first time, a summary of the ideas that have informed my own thinking, which has persuaded me to work for major economic reform for most of the last decade. I stress it is only a summary: this is an exploration of these ideas and some massive leaps are made during the course of their development in this book. If they appeal to some then more work might be required on them. I am completely relaxed about that: I make no claim, as neoliberal economists do through their modelling, to be omniscient.

I am equally well aware that many people will reject what I write as being completely wrong, absurd and much worse than that. I have become well and truly familiar with such claims over the last five years while producing what has now, according to independent sources,[6] become the Number 1 economics blog in the UK at http://www.taxresearch.org.uk/Blog/. Perhaps I needed to withstand the abuse of so many (mainly from the right wing extremes of the economic blogosphere) for so long before taking the risk of putting forward the ideas contained in this book. What I do know is that the time for an alternative has arrived, and I can wait no longer.

A new way of economic thinking

The way of thinking about economics I propose is very different from the economics we have endured for too long. I stress, it's so different I don't even call it a model because it isn't in the way the neoliberals describe their models, not least because it may be quite hard to explain it mathematically. It even looks different to neoliberal models – and that too is deliberate. It occurred to me long ago that if the curse of neoliberal thinking was to be driven from our economy then it had to begin with a new set of diagrams that can be taught in schools, to first year undergraduates and to professional trainees, all of whom have for decades endured an almost unvarying diet of graphs that are predicated on the belief that human beings' behaviour is solely focused on maximising their own individual returns; that businesses maximise their profit and that everything that indicates success in life depends on consuming more of what is (after the first hour or two of instruction) available in the cash economy.

Of course I am grossly simplifying all that conventional economics has to say by stating things in this way. I know that vast amounts of work have been done to explore situations where these assumptions do not hold true. But none of that work changes the meta-narrative of neoliberal economics that now holds sway. That meta-narrative is that only the market works, and that meta-narrative is dependent upon these assumptions, gross caricatures as they might be, just as it is also dependent upon the already noted assumption that markets know everything not only now but for all time to come, and that each and every one of us is an equal and full participant in those markets with full access to all it has to offer. These things are not true, so I have to offer something else in their place.

Part 2 of the book does this over many words and about fifty diagrams. It would be pointless duplication to repeat it all here and yet the core ideas can be presented now as the foundation for what is to come. It would also be pointless to pretend that this section is the easiest part of the book to read: it isn't and I know that. Take comfort, though. If you really can't face it Parts 1 and 3 can be read in isolation and leave Part 2 aside: that is possible.

The way to achieve our potential

In choosing a focus for what I think motivates economic activity I suggest that people seek to achieve their potential. We all have potential to achieve: our goal is to find what that potential is and to get on and achieve it to the extent that we wish. I make no presumption that we will actually maximise: indeed, as a matter of fact I assume that most of the time we will fall short of our goal. We are human after all. That sheer humanity also means, however, that we all have potential in common. In that sense we are all equal.

Equality matters to me. It has often been said that since equality of outcomes in an economy – in the sense that we all have equal material well-being – is not only undesirable (because it massively over-emphasises the importance of material consumption which is of varying significance to different people) but is also not achievable (due to issues like geography that are bound to distort the way in which resources are used) then equality of opportunity is what matters. I do not agree. This pre-supposes equal access to material, social and intellectual resources as much as does equality of outcome, while excusing differing outcomes on the basis of this materialistic measure. And in any event, it has never as far as I know ever been built into any economic modelling, removing it from all likelihood of achievement. Potential, on the other hand, I can illustrate.

Because we are all finite, because the world is finite and therefore everything within it is finite our potential is limited – which is why I show it as the circumference of a circle. The resulting way of thinking about economics is as a result inherently green.

That is also reflected in the fact that our potential is not, of course, just to consume. Far from it in fact: I suggest that first we have potential to produce and commune materially, second to undertake emotional relationships in community with others, third to further our understanding within society, and last to realise our purpose and so help create our communal identity. We can succeed or fail individually in each of these areas, as we can in each of these areas as a nation state as a whole.

An approach to poverty

There's nothing very radical about this: many management, motivational and psychological techniques will have broadly similar approaches, but I explicitly bring them into economic thinking where they are almost forgotten. In so doing I point out that failure means we are in absolute poverty: where we either cannot feed ourselves, or our relationships have failed, or we cannot integrate into society or we believe we have no purpose. Each is life-threatening in its own way. And as such we dedicate our resources individually and collectively to avoiding these situations because they are harmful.

That perception of poverty is not restricted to the person who is actually suffering it. Although economics seems to have never recognised the fact we are empathic beings. We are not just motivated by personal gain. We care for others. As such another person's poverty demands action from us: not for our own personal gain and not to salve conscience as neoliberals argue, but for purely altruistic reasons. We can and do act wanting nothing in return. Therefore we want to alleviate the poverty of those who face real risk as a result of the situation they are in – and do so individually, collectively and as a society through the agencies of government that we empower through the democratic process to act on our behalf.

And that is not just true in the case of absolute poverty: it is true of relative poverty too, which we also wish to alleviate. If we did not, the whole fabric of modern society would have collapsed long ago and our whole model of government would have been rejected many times over in election after election because we have, without doubt, set out not just to alleviate absolute poverty but to alleviate relative poverty too.

So what is relative poverty? I define it empathically. It's that state where absence engenders sufficient concern that others wish to alleviate it. And yet that idea of relative poverty is now rejected by neoliberals: let the poor get on with it, they say.

That is the coward's approach to government and is not that of the Courageous State. Courageous politicians recognise the need to help and sustain others and that we have a capacity to do so when they are in need because there is a collective awareness that we are all better off when we do just that. Of course our perception varies as to when the moment arrives that assistance is no longer required: it is for the Courageous politician to decide when empathy has run out. That occurs when relative poverty ends and the beginning of abundance is reached. There is no doubt that this happens. And there is also no doubt that politicians are not alone in being able to assess when this point is reached: we call can do so.

In that case, as I show, there are very strong reasons for thinking that, once that point of relative abundance has been reached, a balanced life is better than an unbalanced one. By balance I mean that we seek to organise our lives so that the time and resources dedicated to consumption, work, family, friends, learning, understanding and our ultimate purpose and meaning are balanced. It is not a difficult concept to understand: most of us know we struggle with it daily. Of course there are assumptions implicit in reaching this conclusion, and yet most of us have a strong instinct that this understanding is true, just as most of us have equally strong instincts that excess is harmful to our well-being.

The effect of money on well-being

Despite that, when money is introduced into the economic equation I show that there are powerful forces seeking to unbalance our world view. Although we can never exceed our potential to have emotional relationships, to fulfil our intellectual potential or to determine our purpose it is entirely possible for us to consume more than we both need and can sustainably consume. Sustainability is, I argue, in this context a variable: if we assume the world will end next week, anything goes as far as consumption is concerned. If, more realistically and more reasonably, we presume both the world and human life on it are to have a long-term future then the world is not just finite, it is also subject to entropic decay. That means that unless we can expand the possibilities for using resources better by applying our intellect better – and on occasion that is clearly possible, which more than justifies my argument that we should invest heavily in such activity

– there are not only real limits on what we can consume but they might decline over time.

Money subverts this process. Money has its own power. Money is unequally allocated. And money can be used to distort that inequality still further. Advertising has a particularly pernicious role in this process.[7] Advertising has, I argue, just one goal: to breed dissatisfaction. Advertising then suggests that dissatisfaction can be relieved by new consumption, the benefit of which advertising then seeks to destroy by implying what was consumed was still not the nirvanic experience that was desired, but which further new consumption might just provide, with the process being repeated endlessly.

An endless repetition of the consumption cycle does, however, have a goal which, I argue, is to encourage cycles of debt and interest payment that ensure there is a steady transfer of power within the cash economy. This has two marked impacts on well-being.

First, we over-consume compared to our capacity to do so, but since we are finite that excess consumption comes at a cost. One cost is to the planet that supports us: we are very obviously abusing it to its limits. There is, however, a further cost and that is to our emotional and intellectual well-being, to our balance and in turn to our ability to achieve our purpose – that reason for which we really live. Our capacity to achieve all these things is actually reduced by our focus on excess consumption. I argue that our current patterns of consumption do not make us better off: it positively hinders the well-being of those who do it.

Second, as the distortionary power of the cash economy grows there is an accumulated debt established that then grows exponentially. And since money, I suggest, only has value because it represents the power of transactions yet to be completed – since it is the implicit promise to complete an exchange that affords money its value in the first instance (a fact that is prominently displayed on our bank notes, anachronistically to many but more truthfully than most of us realise) –this accumulation of incomplete transactions must mean that if one party can afford to accumulate this cash it must be at cost to another party who is waiting in vain for the promised transaction to complete.

This distortionary process has real consequences. Wealth is shifted by it. The incomes of those waiting in vain for transactions to be completed – who are mainly those, by definition, on lower cash incomes – lose out on the promise of transactions that add value to them because that promise is not fulfilled by those who can hoard cash in what I call the financial / speculative economy where the accumulation of cash is in itself the goal for the power it represents. That power is explicitly inherent in the ability of those who accumulate this cash to prevent completion of real transactions in the real economy that would represent income if those transactions were completed for the benefit of those who have not been able to accumulate cash wealth.

This process of withholding income explains why real wages for most have stagnated. Those who hold cash instead visibly reinforce their power by encouraging consumption (through the use of advertising) on the basis of borrowing and not income. This borrowing is undertaken on contractually onerous terms that are imposed (through mechanisms such as student debt) on as many people as possible. The result is that those with cash retain their power of ownership of money instead of transferring it; their incomes are reinforced by the payment of interest that transfers value from the real economy into the financial / speculative economy, which grows exponentially beyond the limits of the real economy in which transactions for real value occur to sustain it.

The result is that the financial / speculative economy that represents the market for money exists outside the real economy. This is now all too apparent. Its transactions take place in the City of London and in tax havens. Those places extract value from the real economy. The inequality they give rise to is all too obvious, as it its impact. And without correction by the Courageous State this impact would grow to the point where the excess of this advertising-driven, loan-financed, interest-laden economy would produce apparent worth for a few who dominate the financial / speculative economy that is beyond any need they might ever have, while in the real economy too many would be in real poverty and very large numbers would be in relative poverty, with the likelihood of the numbers increasing over time. This is the situation I think we have begun to approach in 2011.

The right of the state to intervene

All this has happened despite the intervention of government to date. It would be so much worse if government had not been willing to intervene. Neoliberals, of course, think government should not intervene, and that is why we have the cowardly state. Theirs is a policy to reinforce the wealth of a few. They seek to achieve this by arguing that the state always acts to allocate resources worse than individuals would do if only they kept their own money and did not pay tax to the state. In this belief is found the whole basis of the 'tax is a bad thing' argument that so pervades modern politics that we have a generation of politicians now frightened to exercise one of the most fundamental rights a government has, which is to collect tax.

As I argue in Chapter 7, that right to tax is absolute and a prerogative of government. It is as strong as, if not stronger than the right to hold private property. And government does not hold this cash as an agent for taxpayers: tax revenues are the property of government and no one else. As a result politicians do not, except for the constraint of needing to seek re-election, have to spend their lives tediously referring to 'the taxpayer's money'. The government's revenues are its own. They belong to government, and always do because it is the government that determines the right to own property in a state and it is the government that makes that right entirely conditional on tax being paid as a condition of owning most property.

This point that paying tax is an absolute condition of acquiring, owning, buying, selling, transferring, occupying or using property, and that those rights are necessarily foregone if the tax due is not paid, might appear pedantic or even semantic but it is more than that: it is also liberating. Because this is true politicians can have the confidence to claim the tax that is due to government, something that appears beyond the wit of too many at present.

Having claimed that tax they are not then beholden to the higher-paid, well-off tax payer or the large corporation for the use of those funds, at least no more than they are to the individual who just pays indirect consumption taxes out of their very low income. The politician is no more accountable to either because neither has a greater claim on the cash the government has to spend, for that tax is the government's and no one else's.

That said, it has to be remembered that there is a proper mechanism for holding the politicians to account for their use of tax and that is the ballot box. As I argue, in this respect tax also has a special role to play since visible and transparent tax systems are usually associated with enhanced democratic accountability. This, however, is a relationship in which all individuals should be equal and not one where the amount of tax paid affords special rights, and it is also one that recognises that through the taxpayers' participation in the democratic process they grant the state the right to spend as it sees fit the money it raises in accordance with its mandate.

Given that is the case the Courageous State is then liberated by the democratic process to intervene in the economy – as it is duty bound to do. Its objectives flow from the way of thinking about economic behaviour that is developed in Part 2 of the book, as outlined above. It has duty to constrain the feral activity of the financial / speculative economy that exists over and beyond the constraints of the real economy in which real needs are met. And it has a duty to bring back into balance the economy as a whole, meaning it will have to constrain the excess material consumption that currently seriously threatens our long-term well-being. It will at the same time have an increased duty to reduce poverty (and so increase consumption in some cases) but as importantly to invest in the family and communities, in learning and in our collective understanding of purpose and identity.

Finding solutions to the challenges

These are enormous challenges, and I do not doubt the courage that will be needed to face them in the short and long term. Precisely because they are such big issues I dedicate Part 3 of the book to the solutions we need. I find books that simply reach the conclusion that there is a problem intensely annoying. That is why I dedicate a significant part of this book to the solutions that we might need to tackle the problems we have, all of which are intended to address the issues that the theoretical analysis of

Part 2 suggests we face. Some of those solutions are needed in the decidedly short term: they are the big ideas that will save banks, turn the economy around, restore hope, deliver jobs and provide the finance to make sure that all this is possible.

Some are the necessary measures we will have to take to defend our right to take such action in the interests of this country in the face of challenges from the neoliberal establishment and the financial / speculative economy which is going to resist this with all its might. Those measures will include much new regulation of banking and the finance sector, including capital controls and a raft of action required to control tax haven abuse. Financial transaction taxes also play a key role in this task – and in bringing speculation under control. But I argue that all this is to the good: the pretence that we can only afford to run a government if we let finance destroy our well-being is shattered: the wealth of this country is quite clearly based on the people who live and work within it together with the resources they can command. Doing deals plays little part in that. It's time we got the balance right. A Courageous State will do that.

Yet more measures will be needed to control advertising that promotes the pernicious abuse of our planet's ability to sustain the excess consumption of some in the world, all with the intention of ensuring most people are controlled by the yoke of the borrowing they must undertake.

And then there will be moves to restore our long-term balance. There need to be measures that restore communities and make all within them important, and measures that tackle poverty and ensure we can all participate in achieving our potential. We also need initiatives to encourage learning that is appropriate to people's needs, and not just to the tiny elite who want to end up working in the financial / speculative economy; while if we are to curtail that economy we will also need to realise our true worth and build a sustainable economy based on what we can really achieve ourselves – alongside the benefits of sustainable, fair and accountable trade. That will, however, mean investment in new infrastructure, new methods of production and new services – for services will actually be more important to us when we materially consume less, as we must. The mechanisms to finance this investment – not least through massive reform of pensions – are all explored.

And so too are the mechanisms by which other services are supplied. So the NHS must not only remain in state control but end all pretence of imitating market structures, while social housing has to be a significant part of social provision and education (free for all) has a higher priority than now, both for the young and on a life-long basis.

Creating a state of hope

The result is that the Courageous State would build a very different economy from that which we have now, based on a very different idea of what the role of the state is, fuelled by its desire to work on behalf of the people of this country whose potential it seeks to fulfil, sustainably.

This is indeed very different from the economy we have now. What we have is unsustainable. The financial / speculative economy is tottering on the brink and demands ever more resources from the real economy to both sustain it and the wealth of the few who benefit from it. The Courageous State would recognise this is no longer viable. And nor is it viable that we consume our planet while warming it beyond limits that life can endure.

And yet in all this I make clear that my vision for the Courageous State is one of hope.

Is there anyone who does not want to live courageously, or to follow those who are?

Don't we all want to relieve poverty, whether we are in it or not?

Is there anyone who would not feel better if they lived a more balanced life?

Don't we all want the chance to value our friends, families and communities more?

Wouldn't we all feel better is we felt a stronger affinity with the society of which we are a member?

What would we give to understand better why we are here, what we are meant to do and have opportunity to do it?

And wouldn't we all like to make enough to live without being burdened by debt?

What if, in the course of making our living we had the choice to work for ourselves knowing that a level playing field existed on which we had a chance to compete fairly, openly and accountably without cheats getting unfair advantage and without big business removing our chance to take part in the economy to which we all have a claim?

What would we give to know healthcare would be ours for life, open to all equally?

And that education would be provided on the same basis – but that the education in question would not be imposed upon us but would be designed to suit our needs?

How do we value security in old age?

Can anyone describe the value of living in a society where equality is valued and where all make a contribution to well-being based on the ability to do so?

Perhaps most importantly of all, at a time when the prospects for the young seem bleak, what would it feel like to live in a state where the young had hope, and not just for now, but where they could believe that this planet might be available for their children to inhabit in safety as well? That's a prospect my son's children (yet to be born) are being denied at present.

The Courageous State offers this hope; our existing, cowardly, state does not.

There is a choice. We can be courageous. Or we can be cowards. We cannot be both. But only one option is available if we want to both solve our current problems and build a sustainable future. Our only viable choice is to build a Courageous State.

The question is, do you have the courage to do just that?

---

1 Paul Mason's Book *Meltdown: The End of the Age of Greed* provides perhaps the best account of this period , Verso, London, 2nd Edition, 2010

2 This idea was first explored by Andrew Simms of the New Economics Foundation – see http://www.neweconomics.org/publications/nine-meals-anarchy

3 I am aware that the terms neoliberal and neoclassical are technically the same in economic theory – but neoliberal does clearly imply a particular political approach to the issue which explains my preference for the term

4   George Monbiot's book *Captive State: The Corporate Takeover of Britain*, Pan, London, 2001, is good on this issue

5   I am aware that many economists will argue that this is not what they think and technically they may be right. The problem for them is that they assume that the form that uncertainty takes is always predictable and that markets price on this basis. Add these together and you get back to the assumption that they assume perfect foresight.

6   http://www.wikio.co.uk/blogs/top/economy accessed 21-8-11

7   Neal Lawson's book *All Consuming*, Penguin, London, 2009 is recommended on this issue.

PART 1
WHY WE NEED THE STATE

CHAPTER 2

THE CRISIS OF CONFIDENCE

IN THE STATE

As I stated in Chapter 1, we live in a world of frightened politicians. It's extraordinary that the people elected to the highest offices of state seem to have either no idea of what they're to do with the trust that has been placed in them, or, worse still, are in power with apparent intent on misusing their positions to undermine the state in which they hold office.

The result, as I argued, is that we live in what I describe as cowardly state. The rot set in with Margaret Thatcher and has continued unabated since then. Privatisation, outsourcing, the Private Finance Initiative, the Third Way, the Big Society, cuts in the face of recession; all are but steps on the neoliberal path of politicians backing away from their responsibility to exercise the power of government on behalf of us all.

I could spend a long time exploring this thesis in depth. I am not going to because you, the reader, either recognise it and agree with it, or you don't. You either see the decline in voter turnout, the fall in confidence in politicians and the reduced stature of those holding public office as issues that support the hypothesis that faith in government has declined precisely because the faith of politicians themselves in the processes they are meant to manage has declined, or you don't. And candidly I doubt I will change your mind on this issue, however long I write about it and however many other people who share my opinion I might quote in support of my contention.

The simple fact is that right now in 2011 we face an economic crisis; we have weak politicians, with weak public support, using weak policy initiatives which few comprehend and which even fewer have faith in who are, in effect, saying that this is because there's nothing they can do to stop the rot and it's all down to the market to solve the problem while they sit on the sidelines and watch.

And I don't agree with them.

I think they are running a cowardly state and I want to live in a Courageous State.

If you think the market can solve all our ills and government should back off more to let it have free rein, that's your choice. I respect your right to make a mistake just as much as I hope you'll let me suggest that the best thing you can do is stop reading this book now. You'll be wasting your time going further.

For those who do want to go further, my concern is not in showing we have reached this position of weakness because that is self-evident, I hope. I am instead interested in explaining in Part 1 of this book why we reached this position, what is to blame for it and what the consequences are. In so doing I hope to lay the foundations for Parts 2 and 3.

The development of the cowardly state

What is astonishing is that since Margaret Thatcher came to power we have had an unbroken neoliberal tradition of government in the UK that has continued without interruption through all successive premierships (that of Gordon Brown, possibly, being excepted). John Major, Tony Blair, David Cameron and Nick Clegg (in his role as leader of the Liberal Democrats and deputy prime minister) have all shared something quite extraordinary, which is a deep dislike for the state. Gordon Brown takes his fair share of blame for his period of tenure as Chancellor of Exchequer.

Of course there have been differences. Blair and Peter Mandelson called their approach New Labour and the Third Way. Cameron calls it The Big Society; Clegg bases his belief on the Orange Book. But what is unavoidably true is that they all have a great deal in common – much more in fact than any of them would want to admit. This commonality is based on the shared neoliberal belief that government is inept, the market works, and that anything and everything that can be done to deliver the services of the state through the mechanisms of the market is of benefit.

This is a new consensus in British politics. Its existence may have only really become apparent with the arrival of the Coalition government in 2010 and yet although this neoliberal policy seems alien to the conservative tradition of the party of that name, the left-wing roots of the Labour party and the social democracy that many thought the Liberal Democrats believed in, it has become apparent that there is an exceptional hegemony of thinking at the heart of politics in the UK, and maybe elsewhere.

Of course there has been consensual thinking in UK politics before now. So similar were the economic policies of the post-war Labour and Conservative governments (once the near revolutionary impact of the 1945 Labour government had been recognised as irreversible across the political spectrum) that a word – Butskellism – was coined to describe it. Combining the names of Tory Chancellor R A Butler and his long-term Labour shadow, Hugh Gaitskell, the implication was clear: the choice between the two was one of minor difference.

That consensus was built, however, on something that almost anyone with an interest in politics could understand and relate to. The underlying assumption was that the state could deliver a transformation in the lives of the population of the UK, and as a result that policy's coherence with the obvious desire of the politician to exercise power was easily understood.

The new consensus that has now emerged is something very different. In many ways Tony Blair might have thought of himself as the heir to Thatcher but he was really something very different: she had learned and introduced neoliberalism; he lived it. And so do his successors. For all of them the aim is the same: the dismantling of the state is the objective. This goal has always been in a sense at the very core of the liberalism to which each of the political leaders involved might have claimed they subscribe to for their own reasons, and yet it is liberalism with a twist, hence its neoliberalism. It is that twist that is significant because this is liberalism for a particular, and new, elite. It excludes conservatives, with a natural inclination to preserve the state and tradition, and inclined to 'old money'. And it abhors the left, which supports the state and demands equality – which is the last thing this policy is meant to deliver for the elite it is intended to benefit. The difference from all previous democratic British traditions is, however, that this elite do not intend to maintain their position by keeping control of government but intend to do so instead by dismantling the mechanisms of government and rebuilding them in organisations that they can control for their own benefit, especially by securing irrevocable contractual claims over taxation revenues that they will manage henceforth in their own private companies which they claim will undertake the tasks of state so much better than the state could do itself.

If this sounds far-fetched remember that in 2010 we had a proposal for the first 'virtual' council in the UK, when Suffolk seriously suggested the outsourcing of virtually every service it supplied – a policy that admittedly collapsed not long after it was proposed, but which suggests that others will seek to follow, and soon. In that case, can it be long before the government follows the same path?

My argument is a simple one, which is that we did not end up in this situation by chance: this development of the cowardly state represents a seemingly coordinated and certainly consistent pattern of policy that has, despite the changes of political parties in power, continued unabated for an extraordinary period of time. With its genesis in Thatcher, this policy of transferring the processes of the state to the private sector with the intent that they should never be reclaimed can be argued to have been undertaken over a thirty-year period which appears to have been almost uninterrupted by such niceties as the democratic process.

The consequences of the cowardly state

There have been inevitable reactions to the promotion of the cowardly state by almost all political parties (the nationalists and

Greens seeming to be at least partial exceptions to the general rule).

First, there has been an enormous loss of confidence in politicians in the UK. That's an entirely rational reaction by the UK electorate. If the politicians standing for office seem to have no confidence in the processes of government that they wish to run, they're hardly going to present a confident front, or even a competent front, to the electorate. After all, any rational person might wonder why someone is desperate for a job in an organisation they appear to despise and are setting out to destroy. When that opinion appears commonplace among those who have actually secured power across the political divide, the falling turnouts in elections, nationally and locally (where the diminished role of government is even more apparent) are entirely understandable.

This has led to a second reaction: it is possible that there has been a loss in the democratic process itself. Extremist parties have risen in popularity and far right-wing racists have been elected in areas where Labour might have once been thought to hold almost automatic appeal.

The Scots, meanwhile, appear to be rejecting Westminster in favour of a nationalist party that has one thing going for it: an ability to project a reason for wanting power over and above the pure gratification of ego-driven desire. No wonder it has proved popular!

The ramifications go further than that. The contempt in which some politicians hold public servants is so apparent that the best – who almost inevitably have the greatest chance of alternative employment – have left or are leaving. This has been clearly evidenced by the Coalition government's NHS reforms. Although at the time of writing these are not enacted it was still possible for Andrew Lansley, the minister responsible for the reform process, to say, long before the parliamentary progress of his ill-fated bill had even got under way, that the process of reform had progressed too far for it to be reversed. That was probably true: he had put hundreds of thousands of staff on notice that he thought them burdensome to the state and many of them quite reasonably took umbrage and took the first possible opportunity to leave the service of an employer that treated them with such contempt. Democracy had nothing to do with this; indeed, even parliament was ignored in this process. The contempt of a minister for those in the employ of his department was enough to effect the change he wanted.

How did we get a cowardly state?

The outcome is clear: we have politicians whose seeming main aim for being in government is to dismantle it so that the revenues of the state can be passed to the private sector. We have ministers who make clear they have no confidence in their staff, that they do not believe in the services they supply, and would like nothing more than to close down the whole business of government. Unsurprisingly we have an electorate disenchanted with the political process. At the same time we have a private sector unable to provide the economic miracle expected of it by those politicians who have absolute faith in its power to deliver. We've had a recession and look like we might be heading for a depression. Why is anyone surprised?

How did we reach this position? How has the consensus that built our post-war prosperity been replaced by a consensus that built the deregulatory environment which resulted in the near collapse of the UK economy in 2008 – and which treated the mechanisms of state that prevented that collapse with such extraordinary disdain that the status quo of contempt for government, that has resulted in a near universal demand for cuts in public services, come to pass? Why is it we have such a cowardly state, headed by apologists for inaction intent it seems on securing their personal well-being while the offices they hold fall into ever greater disrepute?

These questions need answering, not least because the model of a state without a government now exists: Belgium has survived without the government for more than a year. The process of democracy is under threat, and with it the role of government itself. As a result, the need to rethink the role of the state has never been more pressing. That, ultimately, is the purpose of this book.

CHAPTER 3

THE ECONOMIC MYTHS

We live in a world of frightened politicians who are pulling the state to pieces. As I have argued in the previous chapter, the UK's Coalition government, which definitely fits this description, is simply pursuing a pattern of policies first initiated by Margaret Thatcher but which have been adhered to consistently by almost all her successors, irrespective of political party.

There is an explanation for this extraordinary situation. The thirty-year period that has seen the destruction of the confidence of our politicians has simultaneously seen the rise in confidence of our bankers. Both outcomes are the predictable consequence of the near universal application of neoliberal economic policies throughout this period. It should be added that the previous period of consensus, which lasted from 1946 until 1973 (with the years between 1973 and 1979 being unfairly seen as a period of transition) was the consequence of a similar dominant economic logic, in that case of neo-Keynesian thinking.

The implication is clear: it is not party politics that dominates the policy-making of UK governments, but the prevailing economic consensus. It is therefore to the thinking behind those periods of consensus to which attention must be given.

Perhaps perversely in that case, and even inexplicably for many, both neoliberal thinking and neo-Keynesian thinking are closely related in terms of both being in what is called the neoclassical tradition of economic theory. Much of the criticism of neoliberal thinking that I make below can be equally applied to neo-Keynesian thinking because it is based upon many of the same assumptions as neoliberal thought. However, an important point should be made. While the economics of neoliberalism and neo-Keynesianism appear to be linked, the economics of Keynes himself is far removed in very many respects from neoclassical thinking, and it was Keynes's thinking that gave rise to the post-war consensus, and not neo-Keynesianism. The economists of this period may have been neo-Keynesian and it was their inability to realise the significance of the difference between their prescriptions and the political thinking of those they influenced that in itself created the opportunity for the rise of the neoliberal mantra that has supplanted them in the economic faculties of almost all of the world's universities, but the politicians remained Keynesian throughout this period.

I make the distinction with good reason. I perversely argue two things simultaneously in this book. One is that the details of economic thinking matter a lot and have the power to make or break the well-being of billions of people. The second is that most politicians and commentators do not understand any of that detail and instead subscribe to the very high-level narratives that flow from it.

This distinction is really important. The detail matters because if it is wrong then the big narratives are also likely to be wrong. The big narratives matter because they become the basis for belief that is not necessarily evidence based. Indeed, it is not unfair to say much of economics is more akin to a faith system than anything approaching logic or science. It is the faith system of neoliberalism that has dominated cross-party political dialogue for thirty years. Examination of just some of the detailed logic of neoliberal economics shows that such faith is misplaced. And if that is true it follows that we need another economic logic giving rise to a new economic meta-narrative, which is the issue which most of this book will address. But the faults of both neoliberalism and neo-Keynesianism have to be addressed first.

These faults will be addressed in three stages. The first is to address, in the rest of this chapter, some of the fundamental logical flaws that underpin neoliberal thinking that are not nearly widely enough known.

In the next chapter I will address the reason why markets cannot supply many of the services that must be universally funded by the government if all are to have access to them in the UK, contrary to popular current perception that this is the case. In the last chapter of this section I will explain why the state has an unambiguous right to tax, which is a fact commonly challenged by neoliberal thinking but which, if true, liberates the state to make decisions on spending without having to continually apologise for doing so, which then liberates it to act in very different fashion.

However, I do not pretend for a moment that I am offering a complete critique of neoliberal economics. I have no intention of doing so as there are others who have already undertaken that task better than I could. I would in particular recommend Jonathan Aldred's book 'The Skeptical Economist' which does so, really well. For the more mathematically inclined, Steve Keen does equally well in his book 'Debunking Economics'. Tony Judt's last book 'Ill fares the land' is a broader and more reflective analysis, while Robert Skidelsky's 'Keynes: The Return of the Master' deals with some of the macroeconomics in an accessible way. For some very robust deconstruction of the assumptions underpinning neoliberal economics Paul Davidson's 'The Keynes Solution: The Path to Global Economic Prosperity' is a great read. I would recommend them all.

The fundamental flaws in neoliberal thinking

Those books being noted let me say what the meta-narrative of neoliberalism has been that led to our current crisis. The first point is that markets always know best. The claim is that the price mechanism always allocates resources efficiently and that any intervention in the process is bound to result in a suboptimal outcome for the people of the country where the intervention takes place.

It necessarily follows that it is claimed that all that government does is suboptimal because price mechanisms do not determine the allocation of resources in government activity; human judgment does that instead, and according to neoliberal think-ers those exercising that judgment cannot second guess the better decisions individuals could make if they instead had command of the cash involved.

Third, it follows that tax is a bad thing because it is the mecha-nism that takes people's choice away from them and arbitrarily gives it to government, which then misuses it.

I am aware that these are gross simplifications, but together they form the basis of the common meta-narrative of neoliberal-ism that has driven the belief among politicians that all they do is harmful, that passing over activity to the private sector is always for the best and that tax is something they must always apologise for. In combination, those beliefs have incapacitated government.

Why has that happened? To begin, it must be stressed that the difference between this thinking and that of Keynes which gave rise to the previous period of political consensus is really fundamental. The difference is, perhaps, best explained in easily accessible form by Robert Skidelsky in his book 'Keynes: The Return of the Master'.[1] As he makes clear, neoclassical (and so neoliberal) economics is based upon the belief that everything about the world is measurably probabilistic. What this means is that neoliberal economists believe that, first, we know everything that might happen in the future. Second, they believe that we can attach to each event that might happen in the future a probability that it will occur. So, for example, such economists might say that in 2024 I might move house and the probability of this occurring is 15%. The result is that these economists think that the future is entirely predictable.

However, real life experience shows such a belief is obviously wrong, and Keynes pointed out why. As he argued, the number of circumstances where we can make the predictions neoliberal economists think possible are remarkably limited. He said the future is not probabilistic as they suggest in most cases: it is actu-ally uncertain.

To summarise briefly: the difference between the risk which is assumed to underpin all future behaviour in neoclassical econom-ics (including it must be stressed, neo-Keynesian economics) and the uncertainty that is assumed to exist around all future behaviour in truly Keynesian economics is that in neoclassical economics it is assumed that all future possibilities are known. Keynes said that that is wrong: the future is uncertain and we simply cannot predict what might happen.

Nassim Nicholas Taleb captured the essence of what Keynes argued in his now famous 'Black Swan Theory'.[2] His metaphor is a powerful one: the existence of a black swan was simply unknown and unimagined in Europe until its discovery. Then, something previously unimaginable was known to be possible. This is uncertainty explained: uncertainty is about the unknown that we know must exist, although of course we do not know what it is. All we can say is that because the unknown is possible we cannot predict the future probabilistically, and yet all neoclassical economics assumes that we can. Clearly the consequence is enormous for economics.

That is the case because not only do neoliberal economists say that the future is predictable, they also assume that markets are completely and accurately able to price all the probabilities about future possibilities, so that as a result they always optimally allocate all the economic resources in society if nothing interferes with their ability to do so (such as government). To put it another way, neoliberal economists assume that human beings when engaging in the market place are omniscient: they can clairvoyantly foretell everything that might happen and how likely it is to occur and when.

If someone made this claim of a religious group they would be considered mad. If they said it in any social setting they would be considered likewise. It's as if a significant number of geographers were declaring the world to be flat, or large numbers of physicists declared Copernicus to be wrong after all. But neoliberals have said it often enough in economics that millions of people believe them, including, by implication, all our politicians. I will let you draw your own conclusion.

Keynes said this was wrong. He said we did not know what would happen in the future. And so politicians had to make that judgment, and get it right sometimes and wrong on other occasions. It might sound like a remarkably ordinary thing to say; in economics it was revolutionary. So much so that it is still unacceptable to most to believe it.

In fact, even neo-Keynesians aren't quite sure they can believe Keynes on this issue. Fundamentally they're neoclassicists and make the same basic assumptions as neoliberals, with just one significant twist. The real difference between neo-Keynesians and neoliberals is not that their theories are fundamentally different, but that they believe there is a difference in human behaviour when faced with a change in the economic environment. The pure neoliberal assumption, rationalised in what is called the efficient market hypothesis, is that because the range of all possible future outcomes is already known, with appropriate probabilities already having been attached to all of them, then human beings can react instantly to any circumstance that comes to pass in the present time. There is, therefore, no delay between a circumstance arising and people and markets reacting to it. And because it is assumed by neoliberal economists that the market has already anticipated all possible outcomes, and has therefore allocated resources efficiently in anticipation of them, it will reallocate those resources immediately in the present moment when outcomes actually occur without a requirement for any intervention from an outside agency, such as a government. This, therefore, justifies their belief that the government should leave markets well alone because they always know what is best.

Neo-Keynesian economists, on the other hand, take a different approach. While they too, when all is said and done, believe that the future is known, with probabilities being attached to all outcomes, they do not think that people can react instantly when the situation in the present changes from one foreseeable outcome to another. Therefore, neo-Keynesian economists believe that there can be a time-lag between a situation arising and people and the markets being able to react to it. If during that period there is an unfortunate consequence from that lag, for example high unemployment, they believe that it is appropriate for a government to intervene to correct that situation while people and the markets move to a new optimal outcome, which they assume will arise in due course. That therefore justifies short-term involvement by the government in markets in their opinion until such time as markets undertake their natural correction, which neo-Keynesian economists think they will, in due course. When those short-term adjustments failed in the 1970s neo-Keynesians had no answers to the neoliberal challenge on their position, and the consensus changed.

Keynesian economists do not agree with either of these positions. They argue, quite correctly in my opinion, that because we are unable to know the future we have no prospect whatsoever of anticipating all changes that might occur. As a result, they do not think that we can necessarily rely on the market to efficiently allocate resources and as such intervention by governments is always required to compensate for market failings. That hypothesis underpins this book because to think otherwise defies all logic.

Putting this in context, or why we're in a mess right now

All of this might seem incredibly theoretical and far removed from real life. In a sense, of course, it is. The assumptions underpinning both varieties of neoclassical economics are quite absurd. Even neoclassical economists know it, but they claim that although the assumptions bear no relationship to reality, because they say they work as predictors of actual behaviour we should accept them as being useful theories in practice. That is, of course an argument that might be sustainable if neoliberal economics actually worked, but as we now know that is not the case.

One of the leading neoliberal economists of all time is Alan Greenspan, the once legendary and now notorious former chair of the Federal Reserve in the US. When he was questioned in October 2008 on the reasons for the economic crisis he had to admit that he had been wrong about the assumptions that he had made. He told a US congressional hearing with regard to the failure of major banking institutions, such as Lehman Bros, that:[3]

> "Those of us who have looked to the self-interest of lending institutions to protect shareholders' equity, myself included, are in a state of shocked disbelief."

Representative Henry A. Waxman of California, chairman of the committee asked him:

"Do you feel that your ideology pushed you to make decisions that you wish you had not made?"

Greenspan responded:

"Yes, I've found a flaw. I don't know how significant or permanent it is. But I've been very distressed by that fact. This modern risk-management paradigm held sway for decades. The whole intellectual edifice, however, collapsed in the summer of last year."

Greenspan was not the only regulator to acknowledge this fact. Lord Turner was responsible for a report issued in March 2009 by the UK Financial Services Authority (FSA),[4] of which he was chair, which said:

"But the crisis also raises important questions about the intellectual assumptions on which previous regulatory approaches have largely been built.

"At the core of these assumptions has been the theory of efficient and rational markets. Five propositions with implications for regulatory approach have followed:

(i) Market prices are good indicators of rationally evaluated economic value.

(ii) The development of securitised credit, since based on the creation of new and more liquid markets, has improved both allocative efficiency and financial stability.

(iii) The risk characteristics of financial markets can be inferred from mathematical analysis, delivering robust quantitative measures of trading risk.

(iv) Market discipline can be used as an effective tool in constraining harmful risk taking.

(v) Financial innovation can be assumed to be beneficial since market competition would winnow out any innovations which did not deliver value added.

"Each of these assumptions is now subject to extensive challenge on both theoretical and empirical grounds, with potential implications for the appropriate design of regulation and for the role of regulatory authorities."

It is worth noting this at length because, as the report acknowledged, belief in these assumptions (which replicate those I have noted in a different way, above) gave rise to the regulatory failures that in turn resulted in the 2008 financial crash.

The assumptions noted are those of neoliberal economics. By assuming that the future was predictable, markets were as a result efficient and people were rational, consistent and desired maximum profit (assumptions to be considered in more depth later) neoliberal economists in effect assured us that market crashes simply could not happen. Note that they did not prove any of this: all these claims were based on the implausible assumptions already noted, but such was the almost quasi-religious belief (and it was no more than that) in them Lord Turner's FSA had, like Alan Greenspan's Federal Reserve, assumed that a crash was not possible because the assumptions of neoliberal economics said that such things were not possible.

And that is precisely why we had a crash. By assuming we could not have one, we let a crash creep up on us unnoticed. That happened because bankers were sure the neoliberal economists were right: after all, they had good reason to be as they were the biggest winners from the system they proposed. So bankers traded on the basis of models of risk that assumed they knew the future. Their slight difficulty in actually knowing what the future might hold was easily overcome: they simply assumed that it would replicate what had happened in the past. And as they built their models on the basis of data that did not include a market crash, they presumed that the probability of a crash in the future was so small that they could simply ignore it. Which meant that when it happened they were wholly unprepared for it.

That might sound absurdly simplistic, but that's exactly what happened. Worse still, regulators shared this assumption, as the comments from Turner and Greenspan reveal. Under the weight of that body of opinion politicians of all political parties were persuaded that this was reasonable. So when Gordon Brown declared that boom and bust been abolished what he meant in effect was that because neoliberalism could predict the future we need never suffer boom or bust again. He probably meant it. He was wrong. His error was to believe the economics of neoliberalism: it is for that that he is culpable.

And yet in his culpability he reflected an opinion that had become nearly universally accepted. Never was there a situation where a cry that the Emperor was not wearing any clothes was needed more, and yet there was a collective willingness among most economists to ignore the few who told the truth. As a result, everyone else was left in the dark, including politicians.

That, however, means that it is absurd to blame any one politician or party for this failure. It cannot be said, for example, that the failure of the world's banks can be blamed entirely on New Labour's attitude towards bank regulation. Those other (more right-wing) politicians who have made that claim ignore one simple truth, which is that they adhered and still adhere to the same philosophy that created this crisis. New Labour regulated in accordance with standard neoliberal economic theory that was being taught in every economics department at every university around the world because neoliberal thinking had replaced all critical opposition in every such location. The trouble was that such thinking was fundamentally flawed, as has been shown.

Some excuses and some other flaws

Is there any excuse for this error on the part of politicians and others who were persuaded that neoliberal economics was right? I can only offer one. Until the 1970s it's fair to say that great deal of economics was written in relatively plain English. A politician should have been able to comprehend much of it without special training. Neoliberalism changed all that and mathematics became the language of economics.

One of the objectives, or so it seems, of neoliberal economics is to prove that its market-based ordering of society is as natural as are the findings of the physical sciences. The aim is to suggest that this is the only way in which society can be ordered and that anything else is contrary to natural laws. It is this ambition that has driven the mathematical approach to economics that neoliberals adopt. And this approach is incomprehensible to many.

Now I have nothing against maths. I have struggled and some-times succeeded with it for much of my life, and I'm not averse to using it when the occasion suits (and this book is not one such occasion, you will, no doubt, be pleased to note). But I have a real problem with maths when it does two things. The first is when it distorts the analysis that is undertaken. The second is when that maths is in flat contradiction with the world we observe around us. It's my argument that neoliberal economics fails on both scores.

One very good reason why neoliberal economists are so wedded to their view of future predictability is that Keynes's model of fundamental uncertainty is just so much harder to deal with because it makes the maths of most economics really hard to handle. After all, working out the answers mathematically when the variables in the equation aren't known is always going to be harder than when they are.

And the neoliberal economists' assumption that the future looks like an extension of the past – however illogical that might be – is also designed to make the maths easier because then no one is having to guess what data to use – it's already available from what's happened to date.

However, this overlooks the obvious problem that data is read-ily available for a lot of things, but in very many cases the old maxim told of accountants – that they know the price of every-thing and the value of nothing – really does apply. What I mean is that the things that can be recorded are commonly, first, those things that can be transacted for in cash, and these are very often not the most important issues that relate to the achievement of well-being or people's potential; and second, using that data in isolation necessarily means that massively important issues are then ignored in the analysis undertaken. So, for example, the subjective value of life itself and the relationships that make it worthwhile simply can't be reflected in these calculations. That means that these issues are either ignored or entirely judgmental data has to be added into the equations to allow for them – in which case the whole purpose of using mathematical analysis – which is to supposedly produce impartial analysis – collapses.

But that impartiality is not true in any event because the maths itself has to assume certain things of human beings or it cannot work. So, for example, economists have to assume that people want to 'maximise' their well-being or the maths that they use does not work. But candidly, most of us would not have a clue what maximising our well-being might mean, so the assumption bears no relationship to reality.

And, again, to make the maths work economists have to assume we are rational so that, for example, if we prefer product A to product B and product B to product C we are bound to prefer product A to product C. Except on every Saturday throughout the UK it's easy for anyone to observe that this is not true. People just do not behave like that. Which means that the maths has been adopted irrespective of the reality – and of course the outcomes are wrong as a result.

Moreover, the maths that supports neoliberalism is also on some occasions just shockingly inappropriate. So, for example, the whole model that is used by neoliberal economists to claim that markets always get things right and governments will always get things wrong is based on some quite extraordinary assumptions. One is that we all maximise our well-being and that all businesses maximise their profits. I'll let you decide about the former for yourself but in my experience across hundreds of businesses I have directed or advised I do not know of one that has maximised its profits as economists say they should, not least because they would have had no clue how to. But economists overcome that problem by repeating the assumption already noted that everything knows everything, not just about the present but for all time to come. But even that absurd claim is not enough for them. They also assume that businesses operate in the most bizarre way.

So, for example, they assume that every business sells every product it makes at what is called its marginal cost of production. That means all they want back for the product they sell is the precise cost they incur for making the precise item they have sold. So if they sold you, for example, an MP3 download then they not only should but must, if this model of utopia described by neoliberal economists is to work, charge you just exactly what it cost them to make the MP3 download they sold to you. You can ignore the cost of making the MP3 downloads they sold to anyone else – that does not matter. All that matters is the cost of the MP3 they sold to you. And while the cost of an MP3 download is not nothing (after all, the vendor does have to pay for a little bandwidth to let you have access to their web site) above and beyond that there is no cost to them of letting you have a download – so you should, at most, pay much less than a penny for the product. If you don't, the whole edifice of neoliberal economics collapses. That's what neoliberal economics says. Profit maximisation is not happening in that case. The allocation of resources in the economy by business is wrong and inherently inefficient just because that one MP3 download is priced incorrectly.

I kid you not: the whole edifice of neoliberal economics and the mantra so often repeated that business is more efficient than government is based on this type of logic. And if anyone does not follow it, the claim that business is more efficient is just not provable. I stress, I don't say it's wrong because I can't say that. I am just saying it's not provable. The assessment of whether it is better or worse is a matter of judgment, but it is not a matter of fact.

No wonder therefore that Alan Greenspan discovered that his assumptions were flawed, or that Lord Turner realised that the intellectual foundations on which financial market regulation in the UK have been built were wrong. And yet, a few notable exceptions such as Steve Keen apart, economists have either not noticed that that they have got their maths wrong, or they have persuaded themselves and their students and the Treasury departments of every government of any significance around the world that they are right despite the errors their models include.

The consequences

Two questions do, however, follow. One is to ponder whether this whole edifice of economic theory is in fact a purely political construct that lacks intellectual merit because it entirely lacks the objectivity that the neoliberal economists claim for it. I certainly think that possible. In fact, I would call it a giant con-trick.

The second is to ask why this error did not have consequence during the neo-Keynesian era from 1946 to 1973. It can safely be said that the answer to this second question is that this error did not have harmful consequences because mathematics had not got in the way of sound economic judgment on the part of politicians during much of that period. As a result, they still formed their own opinions, which were no doubt heavily influenced by Keynes himself, even if their advisers were of neo-Keynesian persuasion.

The point is significant: Keynes, as noted above, argued that economic policy must be created in situations of uncertainty where outcomes cannot be known. As such it was the job of politicians to form a judgment on the right course of action to undertake. And, precisely because he said that politicians could not rely upon markets to deliver optimal outcomes, it was their job to decide when government should intervene in the economy to produce those outcomes the politicians thought desirable. Of course, during the postwar period those outcomes revolved around the achievement of full employment, since the memory of the Great Depression was far too painful to allow for the recurrence of the mass unemployment suffered during the prewar period.

The result was that these politicians were empowered by Keynesian thinking to take action. Keynesian thinking gave politicians the final say in determining well-being. The consequence was a Courageous State.

In contrast, neoliberal economics turned much of this Keynesian thinking on its head. Markets now ruled. All that politicians had to do was get out of their way. And that is precisely what they have tried to do. As a result it is not an exaggeration to say that the decline in the role of the government, politics, democracy, and the state is the inevitable outcome of the apparent near universal adoption of neoliberal economic philosophy.

Neoliberal thinking has done the exact opposite to Keynesian thinking: it has told politicians that they can only do harm. We now have a generation of politicians brought up on this ethos, and they still believe it. The result is a cowardly state.

Given that the consequences of this situation are so significant, including a threat to the democratic process itself, they need to be explored further before modern alternatives to neoliberalism can be considered that might restore faith in government, democracy and the possibility of politics that seeks to deliver the well-being of everyone in society. Therefore the next chapter looks at the myth of markets in more depth.

1   Skidelsky, R. (2009) *Keynes: The Return of the Master*, Penguin, London
2   Taleb, N.N. (2007) *The Black Swan: The Impact of the Highly Improbable*, Penguin
3   http://www.nytimes.com/2008/10/24/business/economy/24panel.html
4   *The Turner Review: A regulatory response to the global banking crisis*, FSA, London, March 2009 http://www.fsa.gov.uk/pubs/other/turner_review.pdf

CHAPTER 4

THE MYTH OF THE MARKET

Neoliberal economics says that if markets are given free reign in an economy then we are all better off as a result. Such a belief would obviously be acceptable if it was clear that in an era when neoliberal economic policies had been adopted economic performance was clearly better than during an era when they were not in use. Since we have had neoliberal economic policies in the UK since 1980 and not before then, this hypothesis can be tested. And since neoliberalism's criteria for success is economic growth we can look at HM Treasury data[1] for UK growth in GDP from 1956 to 2010 and assess the evidence. The relevant data is shown in the figure below.

The average rate of growth from 1956 to 1979 was, based upon this data, 2.62% per annum. This generously understates the average for the Keynesian period that more accurately ended in 1973 by including data up to the late 1970s. The same average for 1980 to 2010 was 2.12% p.a. If growth is the objective of economics, then neoliberalism did not supply it as well as Keynesianism did. The fact the period 1946 to 1973 was almost entirely free of recession while since then we have lived through economic crisis after crisis might be another indicator. The track record is not good. And yet we remain wedded to neoliberalism that denies government a role in the economy that it enjoyed during the previous, pervasive period of stable growth, which was also the goal of Keynesian policy.

Annual growth in UK GDP, 1956–2010 (%)

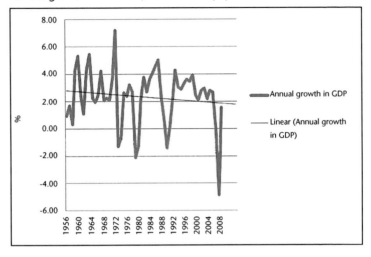

Source: HM Treasury

What is clear is that as both the UK and much of the world looks likely to enter another recession as 2011 draws to a close, the trend of continuing crisis associated with the neoliberal era is continuing. My suggestion is that in this case neoliberal thought is quite simply wrong when it suggests that government intervention has a harmful impact on economic activity and well-being. The truth, as the evidence shows, is the opposite. Strong, confident, democratic and accountable government is in fact the foundation of a population's well-being because it can deliver growth (although in a new era of environmental awareness we need to be careful to define what this means) and its intervention is key to providing stability, which is at least as important.

There is ample evidence to support this idea – much of it documented in books already referred to in earlier chapters that are at least in part dedicated to assessing this evidence in much more detail than I can devote space to here – but which also makes clear why it is important to understand what the state must do if an economy is to work, and what markets can and, as importantly, can't do within the context of the economy that only the state can create.

The role of the state

Of course it is possible to live without a state and without the rule of law. Somalia and some other places have done so. The outcomes are extreme poverty and rule by the gun. It is hard to imagine anyone endorsing such outcomes, but it is equally important to note that while most neoliberals accept that government has a role to play in any country there is now a strong tendency among many to seriously qualify this belief. They might argue it is the duty of a government to defend the state, to uphold law and order and in the process to maintain property rights. Beyond that, increasing numbers of neoliberals – including quite a number now in parliament – argue that there is little further legitimate function for government.

Indeed, some more extreme neoliberals with strong libertarian leanings (many of whom seem to populate the comment column of the *Guardian* newspaper and, if only I let them, my blog) seem inclined to the view that even this might go beyond what is desirable. It is now argued by some – including by members of the UK academic community and by right-wing think-tanks of supposedly reputable status – that governments have no legitimate right to create law as democracies oppress those with wealth. They argue this is because voting is a mechanism for indicating choice vastly inferior to that supplied by the market where, they say, the expenditure of cash indicates real preferences in society. In the process they openly acknowledge that this gives those with wealth a preference. Indeed, Lancaster University academic G.R. Steele recently said in an academic paper:[2] "The sanction of tyranny is the democratic flaw: that of the majority over minorities." In so doing he only reflects a steadily developing train of thought in the UK of which few seem aware but which is taking strong hold among right-wing parties that rejects any role for government.

This situation should be of profound concern to all who have faith in democracy and who consider the struggle to deliver a universal adult mandate was at the core of creating the modern state. I do believe that and like, I suspect, the vast majority of people think that the state has a much bigger role to play in society. It is my argument that the state is, in fact, the foundation of our prosperity. The crash in 2008 proved that: without state intervention it is very likely that social chaos would have broken out in the UK as bank after bank would have failed and our whole system of electronic bank payment – which is fundamental to the operation of the economy, and with it such basic things as ensuring we all have access to food – would have collapsed with them.

However, important as the government's role is in being the guarantor of last resort – the institution on which we all (even our banks) fall back in the event of a crisis – that is still a somewhat negative view of government, so let's move to the positive, without wishing to spend too long on this issue.

State regulation

The role of the Courageous State is to do those things not possible but for its involvement. That is why it has to defend a territory. Without freedom from fear of the overthrow of any society no one can prosper. Without a state people cannot flourish.

That's why government has also to define property rights, because markets exchange property rights: that's their purpose. As a result (as I will explore in more depth later) effective markets cannot exist without the active support of government. Markets are not what support government: it is governments that provide the environment in which markets exist.

But as I have already shown, and will do so again in much of what follows, if left to their own devices markets fail. That's not because there is anything inherently wrong with markets: far from it, they are fundamental to our well-being and they are an absolutely essential part of the modern economy. Nothing I say here is intended to contradict that statement. But the fact is that the conditions which neoliberal economists say provide optimal outcomes for well-being do not exist. Markets do not have perfect information on which to base their decisions. There are massive externalities created by markets that mean their pricing of the goods and services they supply is frequently fundamentally wrong. And, of course, markets do not supply capital to all who need it so all can operate within markets on the basis of a level playing field. Indeed, markets go out of their way to make sure the exact opposite is true, by denying access to capital to many (just ask any small business person how easy they find it to borrow from their bank for confirmation of this point) while businesses, with the connivance of far too many governments (and especially those of tax havens) go out of their way to make sure there is imperfect information available about what they do to assist them make monopoly profits by exploiting others a result.

This problem – known as that of asymmetrical information – lets the seller exploit the purchaser by not telling them all they need to know about the risks they face from buying. Tax haven and commercial secrecy are both designed to ensure that this asymmetry is deliberately increased, with the inevitable result being exploitation. That is its purpose and that is why a Courageous State has to ensure there is transparency and accountability within commercial contracts.

As a result, in varying ways since at least Babylonian times it has been the role of government to make sure that the parameters within which markets work are properly set. For those who aren't sure about the point, a study of the role of the Temple in Jerusalem in the Old Testament might be illuminating. Of course it was a place of worship but it doubled up as a weights and measures department and much more besides. Market regulation is not a new issue: the need for it has existed since people began to trade, and most especially since cash crept into our dealings.

So what are those tasks that government must undertake if an economy and society are to function properly? It begins, of course, with regulating money – the medium for exchange. As noted later, governments no longer create most money but they do legitimise currencies and have the power to regulate it, and so they should. It's an issue to which I will, inevitably return.

The role of government continues be defining what property is, who may own it, how and when its ownership may be transferred and on what terms. This is the whole law of property and contract. Without such law trade would very rapidly fail. The relationship of trust on which we assume trade is based is underpinned by the willingness of all participants to be bound by these rules established by government.

There will, however, always be those who are willing to undermine that relationship of trust. Fraud is now and has always been commonplace. It takes an enormous variety of forms but it's wise to remember that it need not be complex. Passing rotten food off as fresh is fraud. So is selling a car as safe when it is in fact a death-trap. Health and safety law in all its forms is not, as far too often represented, mindless regulation (although there is no doubt that on occasion errors in application occur). They are actually exercises in protecting people from abuse that can happen in markets. But they are not anti-market measures; they are absolutely fundamental to making markets work. Those who oppose them, as a result, also oppose fair markets. Government, by creating and imposing these regulations has liberated economies. Without the confidence they provide we would not be willing to take the risk in buying goods and services from people we do not know.

The state as market overseer

Helping consumers is not the sole role of government in the market. Government also creates the structures for organising markets – things like limited companies, partnerships and more besides. This also means that when privileges such as limited liability are granted government rightly demands that responsibility is accepted in exchange – through measures that, for example, require that the accounts of such companies are on public record so that the use people make of the privilege others have been granted is made known. That does, however, also require that government regulates those who abuse the privilege, and that it should do so robustly.

Even with such structures in place things go wrong: businesses fail. So government has also to ensure that when that happens, people and other business are protected, while ensuring the debtor gets a second chance. A life of enslavement by debt is just not acceptable any more. That is why we have bankruptcy laws. Remarkably, the fact that we have developed mechanisms to allow people to fail in organised fashion is fundamental to markets: the raw claw of the market that would (if many neoliberals had their way) demand payment of the last penny of debt with the alternative of a life of servitude is the foundation of effective markets. Who would take risk if the downside was the debtors' prison that

Charles Dickens so rightly campaigned against and which the neoliberals, with their belief in the supremacy of property rights would support? It is the state that supports innovation where the market would only deliver chaos.

And while the state therefore plays an essential role when there is market failure, it should also be remembered it has an equal role to play in ensuring markets grow through innovation. The role of the government as customer is incredibly important: in many sectors it is the largest customer for many goods and services and in that role its demands function as a massive inspiration for innovation. It plays the same function when, for example, it demands reform for the sake of protection. Almost all modern equipment has had its design and development fundamentally (and almost invariably beneficially) influenced by the demand of government that minimum performance standards be met.

In the direct relationship between the government and markets, there is no doubt in which the direction of benefit flows. In principle, government can exist without markets (although I would argue very strongly against trying it) but what is obvious is that there could be no effective markets without government.

However, this review of the role of government with regard to markets seriously underestimates the importance of the state. Because markets are so imperfect, and so unable to assess external costs and benefits, they are, for example, also entirely unable to undertake some of the most important functions in the economy. This is an issue I will explore in much greater depth later, but it is not chance that the era of prosperity we have enjoyed since the Second World War has been associated with state provision of education, healthcare, pensions, much infrastructure and more besides.

The state as service provider

While my focus later on will be on why the market cannot supply these services universally, my point now is as important: because all the services have universal benefit, much of which extends way beyond the reaches of the market price mechanism (as is shown, for example, by the fact that care for the elderly who have no further economic contribution to make to production is clearly illogical within that price mechanism) the market cannot also procure these services. Only the state can. And the fact it does should be a cause for celebration for us all, and yet you would think otherwise if you were to listen to neoliberals.

I well remember in this context an interview I undertook a number of years ago with Alvin Rabushka, one of the co-inventors of the flat tax idea so beloved of neoliberal thinkers (because it automatically diminishes the role of the state). He said this to me in 2006:[3]

> "I think we should go back to first principles and causes and ask what government should be doing and the answer is 'not a whole lot'. It certainly does way too much and we could certainly get rid of a lot of it. We shouldn't give people free money. You know, we should get rid of welfare programmes; we need to have purely private pensions and get rid of state sponsored pensions. We need private schools and private hospitals and private roads and private mail delivery and private transportation and private everything else. You know government shouldn't be doing any of that stuff. And if it didn't do any of that stuff it wouldn't need all of that tax money so that's the fundamental position and as long as you're going to have government do all that stuff you're going to have all those high taxes."

This is a philosophy I fundamentally reject.

Those who accept it (and they are now more numerous in positions of authority than many think) believe markets work. But they do more than that. They think that those who do not generate wealth within markets are undeserving of sympathy. They do not believe that welfare or benefits should be offered to those who have suffered misfortune, whether from natural causes such as arise as a consequence of illness and disability, or as a result of the failings of the market.

The people who have suffered such misfortune are of course legion, and most especially at times like the present when due to market failure we are in recession and millions of people are unemployed or underemployed through no fault of their own. It's important to note though that neoliberals do not agree with this last proposition: it is their contention that the unemployed and underemployed are only so because first, government has interfered in markets by, for example, imposing minimum wages that mean they cannot price themselves into work (even though it is, of course, already obvious that it is near impossible for anyone, let alone a family to live on the minimum wage in the UK) or second, that people have voluntarily decided not to work (for which there is no evidence, but which is a convenient myth that supports demands that people be forced back to work against their will or lose benefits even if there are no jobs to be found).

Those of more compassionate and empathic disposition do not agree. Thankfully, the majority of people are in this category: in fact as psychologist and social scientist Dacher Keltner says, the rich really are different, and not in a good way. He has found that their life experience makes them less empathetic, less altruistic, and generally more selfish.[4] That means that the wealthy, who tend to be neoliberal precisely because of its predisposition to treat their needs as paramount, as noted by Alvin Rabushka above, are much more inclined to lack empathy in general and concern for those in poverty in particular than the population overall. No wonder they describe democracy as a tyranny, for it is that process of democracy which the empathic majority have used to ensure that the vulnerable and the unfortunate have been protected from their misfortune by the state.

This support for the poor is, of course, a policy any Courageous State should strongly endorse but across the political divide we now see it challenged. The claim is made that we cannot afford to pay benefits, or that people must work for what they get when the market is so clearly failing to deliver jobs, and neoliberal politicians are refusing to use the power of the state to create work that markets will not supply. Nothing is surer indication of the cowardice of politicians in the face of neoliberalism than this, yet it is happening. The Courageous State would have a duty to reverse this trend, while ensuring that work is available to all who want it so that they might flourish, because there is no doubt that meaningful work is, for those able to do it, a condition for achieving a state of well-being.

Accounting for externalities

What this suggests is that the state's job is very, very much more than that role ascribed to it by neoliberal politicians in whatever political hue they present their arguments. The job of the state is to support markets and at the same time to correct the externalities that arise as a result of their operation. Because neoliberals assume that everyone in the marketplace knows everything, they assume that the costs of externalities arising from a transaction are all accounted for in the price at which goods and services are exchanged. In practice, externalities arise when a business process imposes costs on someone who is not a party to the subsequent sale or purchase transaction, which means that the price paid for goods and services does not represent the true cost of that supply.

The perfect example of an externality is, of course, pollution. Many business processes are substantial polluters but the price for that pollution is not paid for by business but by those who live around the contaminating production unit. Those people's well-being is harmed as a consequence, as is the broader environment both at the present time and in the future. Unless the government intervenes the market does not price for this externality.

Pollution is an extreme example of an externality. But as extreme is the power of banks to control money for their own benefit, which imposed cost on us all in 2008. And equally important is the ability of business to capture excess profit because a few can capture control of vital resources, as some companies in the extractive industries do, or as happens when land is in the possession of a small minority in society who can exploit that situation to their advantage. Externalities also arise when business does not pay the full cost of the services it consumes, such as when it is supplied with well-educated people at no cost to itself, or a healthy workforce for which it does not bear the cost, and never would. The implicit insurance the state supplies to the workforce of any business – that they will also be cared for if the business fails – is another externality that business likes to ignore, yet but for it those employees would have to demand much more in wages to insure that risk for themselves.

As noted before: business and markets make an enormous contribution to well-being, but only because they are supported by the state. Without that support business and markets would fail, our prosperity would collapse and millions would head for destitution for reasons that I will explain in Part 2 of this book. For now let me conclude: the state is fundamental to well-being and we cannot do without it. That's why we need a Courageous State.

And I would stress, that's not just for economic reasons. Neoliberalism might seem to be an economic idea but its impact is much bigger than that. Life is about more than markets. As will be examined later, to live well we need to do much more than meet our material needs. We need to have strong relationships, we need to live in communities, we need to relate to another, to have a sense of our worth and our achievement, and ultimately, however we choose to express it, to have a sense of meaning or purpose. It is my contention that neoliberalism has undermined all these things.

The Courageous State and society

Neoliberalism has defined our purpose as being consumers. It has defined community as watching a television programme together rather than in isolation. It has reduced learning to being the acquisition of saleable skills. It has dumbed us down as to the possibility of purpose. In very many ways it has muted our passions to the point where excitement about our next purchase is as far as they go.

I resent that: I will be unambiguous about that. I value my family and friends. I treasure shared meals. I like cooking them. Occasionally (and too rarely at present) I grow what I eat. I have a deep affection for the place where I live and the people who also live there and the county of which we are a part.

I learn for the fun of it. I live in a house happily overburdened by books and I admit I find those that aren't hard to understand. There are two televisions in our house, I admit. But none upstairs. There are places where it should not go, boundaries it should not cross. And I do really think each and every person has a unique contribution they can make to others. Finding what that is could well be what life is all about.

Neoliberalism sets out to destroy all this. It assumes we are to consume, uniformly. One of the things I find depressing about travelling (as I have done, too much for my liking, in recent years) is arriving in places far from home to realise people all look the same: 'fashion' is the same, music sounds familiar, and far too many oppressive brands are to be found that I recognise. Thankfully, that's not always true of food, but the burger, pizza and fried chicken are to be found everywhere. It's as if the thought police had been sent out on patrol.

The Courageous State has to protect community, learning, society and our purpose from such threats. Sometimes this will be in mundane, but highly practical ways. For example, the market does not consider the value of communities when closing businesses. In addition, business is not required to consider the cost of unemployment once it has settled its obligation to make redundancy payments. Also, a large company might use its economic power to temporarily distort prices within the market to eliminate smaller competitors and be considered successful if it does so, but the loss to society of that competition and of the abilities contained within the teams of people who make up the smaller organisations that disappear as a result of this exploitative behaviour is not taken into account when assessing this behaviour by the larger company. That is because the market does not price all the consequences of the transactions that are undertaken within it yet these transactions have real consequences for us all and the societies in which we live. There are good reasons to demand that companies must protect those they make redundant: people without work cannot function well within their communities, whether that be the family or the broader community. And we do need to very proactively protect the local, diversity, and the small from the large. We cannot flourish unless we do.

That is why a Courageous State needs a comprehensive policy to ensure that as far as is possible the adverse external consequences of markets are corrected, either by imposing a charge on those participants that would not otherwise bear the cost of

THE MYTH OF THE MARKET

their activities, or by collectively correcting for the market failures that it witnesses through a comprehensive social, environmental, trade, agricultural, food and welfare policy, all of which must be financed by taxation.

These policies do not hinder the well-being created by markets; they are necessary corrections for the harm created by some market activity (and I stress, some, but not all market activity) that neoliberal economics simply ignores when reaching the simplistic conclusions that markets always provide optimal solutions and which influence the popular mantras of those politicians who have adopted its thinking.

In saying this is I am of course aware that many economists have sought to address many of the issues raised here in their more advanced work. That, however, does not alter my point: this advanced work is ignored by those politicians and neoliberal populists who maintain that the basic model of neoliberal economics, which says that markets always provide the best solutions for human well-being with government intervention invariably acting to their detriment, is the one that actually influences political behaviour. The nuances of the more advanced economic studies which try to overcome these defects in the basic model, without ever remedying them, do not change this. Since those models are built on the basis of assumptions designed to ensure market solutions are considered the best (since this is an article of faith not based on fact but on assumptions for neoliberals) the market-based model survives because that is the inevitable consequence of the conclusions made at the outset, which invariably foretell this outcome.

The advanced modelling may allow for chaos theory, externalities and much more besides, but they are adornments to the basis model. It is as if these advanced models provide the emperor with a crown and other jewellery, but none of this hides the fact that he remains naked, because he still is. The fundamental failings of neoliberal economics and its political consequences are what matter; the nuances do not.

1   http://www.hm-treasury.gov.uk/data_gdp_fig.htm adjusted for inflation using indices in data downloaded

2   Steele, G.R, 2011, Progressive Taxation: Applying Hayek's Constraint, *The Political Quarterly*, Vol. 82, No. 2, April–June 2011

3   Quoted at http://www.taxresearch.org.uk/Blog/2006/06/12/what-is-flat-tax-all-about/ where other interesting comments by Rabushka on his view of society are also to be found.

4   Reported by Brian Alexander on 10 August 2011 athttp://www.msnbc.msn.com/ id/44084236/ns/health-behavior/#.TpWjgxXw_np based on research by Dacher Kelter published under the title Social Class as Culture in Current Directions in Psychological Science, August 2011

CHAPTER 5

THE CAPPUCCINO ECONOMY

I have explained what I think the Courageous State is. It is a state in which markets are encouraged and supported by the government but where at the same time the weaknesses in markets are recognised and corrected for, as far as possible, and where (as I will explore in due course) those things that markets just can't do are undertaken by the state instead. More than that, it's a state that believes in families of all sorts, communities, the importance of society and which, absolutely fundamentally, wants all people to achieve their potential if at all possible.

To me it seems obvious that government should be like this and that this is the sort of government we should want, but for a great many that does not seem to be the case. We have been told for so long that government does not work that even our politicians seem to believe it, and many governments, including the UK, are now openly dismantling the mechanisms that ensure our mutual well-being is the priority of government and are instead passing the structures that sought to guarantee this over to private companies where just a few will enjoy the benefits of the resulting well-being. What we seem to have lost is a way of describing just what the virtues of a Courageous State should be and as a result we have also lost the ability to defend it from attack.

I sometimes explain my understanding of the Courageous State by using a metaphor with which many will be familiar: a cappuccino. This narrative may work for you, and it may not.

In case it does I offer it here; if it does not, just skip to the next chapter.

The ingredients

A good cappuccino works on the basis of a number of critical ingredients. Most obviously they are water, coffee, milk, heat, the ability to froth the coffee and (maybe) add nutmeg or grated chocolate on top, plus sugar to taste. There's slightly more to it than that though. There's also a need for a recipe, someone to teach it and the necessary equipment (whether a cappuccino machine or not). On top of that there must be a barista, whether professional or of the more common domestic variety, to put the whole thing together. But even those conditions are not enough to enjoy the cappuccino: a cup is also needed, so is a consumer, and somewhere to drink it. All those things are clear indication that this is a complex product, but then so is the modern economy.

Underpinning the cappuccino is something quite fundamental. Of course it is good coffee on the bottom, frothed steamed milk on top, the latter decorated and sweetened to taste but what is really important is that the components of a cappuccino are distinct, separate and identifiable while only existing in relationship one with another. That relationship of one with another is what is vital – it's synergistic: the whole is undoubtedly more than the parts. Indeed, for a great many enthusiasts of cappuccino the individual components – be they black coffee or hot frothy milk – hold remarkably little appeal.

On the other hand, cappuccino is without doubt a coffee. Without the coffee it's not a coffee-based drink. It's hot frothed milk, and that's something very different. But in that case, with which ingredient is cappuccino in closest relationship? The hot milk or the black coffee? After all, black coffee is also coffee, albeit in a cruder, rawer form that by no means all can stomach. But while cappuccino and black coffee are both coffees, frothy milk is something else. So, like it or not, cappuccino is identified more by the coffee within it than by the milk.

What's all this got to do with the Courageous State? Simply this: I believe that a democratically elected government capable of collecting taxation to fulfil its electoral mandate and which delivers clear social, economic and environmental policies is the bedrock on which any economy and society is built. That sort of government is the coffee in the cappuccino metaphor. That is important – in my view it is the state that underpins a vibrant private sector, and not the other way round.

The correct mix

Back to the cappuccino: make the coffee too weak and the milk dominates. Make it too strong and it can crowd out the froth. Getting the role of the coffee in cappuccino right is a delicate art. So too is the art of getting the role of government in society right. It too has to reflect taste and yet be strong enough, robust enough, of sufficient quality, and be sufficiently assertive in its role to make its presence felt to ensure that the economy and society as a whole works. Overdo it and there's risk of the whole thing falling apart. The same is true of underdoing it. That is the paradox of the Courageous State.

If in this metaphor the coffee in the cappuccino is the state sector then quite clearly the frothy milk is the private sector. It is as important to the cappuccino as the coffee: just as the private sector is as important in the economy as is the state. But whether we're talking the economy or coffee, the froth on the top needs the coffee or government underneath it to support it and give it its identity.

Remember, the private sector needs the rule of law to operate. Without property rights there is no private sector. Only the state can provide those laws.

And the private sector needs educated people to deliver its goods and services: it cannot, and never will train young people for up to seventeen years before they earn any return on that effort in the workplace. The state must do that.

Private business also needs a state-underwritten healthcare system to keep its people at work and to contain its costs: private healthcare in the US costs twice state-provided healthcare in the UK, much of it paid for by private companies. UK business cannot afford that cost.

As importantly, business often needs the stimulus of legislation to spur it to innovate. And it needs to state to create the market for many of its new products and services

Perhaps most important of all, private sector employees need the state to provide them with a safety net if their employer fails: if it did not they'd have to demand higher wages to cover that risk. The state directly subsidises business in this case by providing that security to its employees.

And, with all that being said, on occasion business undoubtedly needs the state to leave it alone so it can get on with delivering the results of its endeavours.

When these things happen, the froth is strong and refreshing. When they don't, the froth collapses and a poor apology for a latte results.

The final component

But what is it that lets the two parts of the cappuccino relate to each other? It is, of course, water that the milk and coffee have in common. In the cappuccino metaphor water represents money. It is money that provides the means of exchange between the private and state sectors.

As I will explore in more depth later, money is a mysterious beast. 97% of it is now electronic and that cash is created almost entirely in the private sector. And yet the credibility of money is based wholly upon the state. And it is the state that has the responsibility for it, and the regulation of the credit that gives rise to it. It is the state that can also demand that taxes be paid using that currency and nothing else – so effectively demanding its use in the economy. Unless as a result that essential means of exchange has credibility, is properly regulated, and is used appropriately – subject to the requirements of society as a whole, in other words – then that membrane on which the whole private edifice of wealth, business and prosperity rests is at risk of collapse, as the events of 2008 only too clearly demonstrated. The froth came as near as it could to collapsing on that occasion. It was only because the state stepped in that the private sector survived on that occasion.

This is why the proper regulation of finance is essential, as is a requirement that banks act in the public interest. This means that the essential role of real banks – the sort most of us recognise – which manage transactions and provide conventional deposit holding and lending activities are entirely different from casino-style investment banking, from which they must be separated as a result. That proper banking role underpins the whole economy just as water does the cappuccino. If investment banking puts it at risk, the whole economy can fail just as the cappuccino would without water.

But what the metaphor now says is that the two parts of the cappuccino are quite different and yet they clearly relate one to another. That has to be the case: no one can drink a cappuccino without mixing the coffee and the milk together. It's just not possible. Ultimately the two parts relate one the other. When the coffee and milk are in harmony things work best. I happen to think that is true of the relationship between the state and private sector as well. What determines the appropriate mix between the two? The spoon does that. And in the cappuccino metaphor the spoon represents democracy – which is the only appropriate mechanism for deciding upon the boundaries between the state and private sectors.

So what of the other ingredients of the cappuccino, not yet noted? Water and heat are essential to the making of a cappuccino. If water represents money in the metaphor, then the heat needed to create the cappuccino represents the other basics of life without which people are in poverty. These are those fundamental elements of well-being that all must have. As I will explore as this book develops, these needs are complex and yet the market all too often fails to provide them. As such they are something the state must guarantee to all. If they're not available to any person, real poverty results and as we're empathic beings the suffering is not individual, it is collective because we suffer as a society as a whole.

This can be translated to the cappuccino metaphor: the cup in which the cappuccino is made is of a particular type. It is designed to suit the product made in it. So too is the type of government we enjoy a reflection of the society we live in: the cup in this metaphor therefore reflects society.

And in that case the saucer has a role too: it reflects the welfare state that is a feature of our compassionate society that seeks to ensure all have a right to participate and a chance to achieve their potential. Those who might otherwise fall out of society are kept within it by government action – just as the saucer catches cappuccino that might otherwise slip out of the cup.

Assembling the mix

This, however, is not the limit to what the state does: no one could make a cappuccino without equipment. It's just not possible. That equipment is equivalent to the infrastructure we all depend on as we go about daily life. What we consume today is dependent upon the past investment made in the infrastructure that supports our economy – whether a cappuccino machine, school or hospital.

Infrastructure is a complex issue – even in the case of cappuccino machines. The same equipment that can make the cappuccino can also make Americano, latte, hot milk, hot chocolate, and even hot water for tea. And they don't do it once. By definition they endure for some time and are used time and time again.

That's part of the complexity of infrastructure: no one can be sure quite how much it will cost to supply. When it's first built no one knows for sure how long it will last, how often it will be used, what mix of product it will be used to make.

In some cases that does not matter. The cost of the cappuccino machine is remarkably small in comparison to the price of the final product it makes – at least if bought in a bar, café or restaurant. The margin for error in charging for the cappuccino machine is wide compared to all the other costs involved in the supply, and the margin earned on it.

That doesn't mean most of the world can have their own cappuccino machine – that's clearly not desirable or possible for a wide range of reasons, one being cost (it definitely pushes the price of cappuccino way out of reach for most if the machine is used very infrequently). It's also just not environmentally desirable to duplicate resources. So good cappuccino machines are clearly best seen as communal resources – but ones that the market can more than adequately price into the economy. Indeed, there seems to be clear benefit from private sector competition in the supply of cappuccino – more and better coffee outlets seem to arise as a result. So cappuccino is, when all is said and done, part of the froth in the economy!

However, that is not true for all infrastructure. Most infrastructure costs much more than a cappuccino machine to supply. In many cases – such as schools, roads, transport systems, hospitals, power and water distribution systems and the like – it's also true that the cost of the infrastructure is a major cost of the supply of the service. Indeed, this is so much the case that even the prospect of duplicating these resources is, as is noted in the next chapter, impossible to contemplate. Worse than that, while competing cappuccino machines clearly seems to produce benefit, competing hospitals would simply produce duplication and waste to a degree society cannot afford.

So, while happily for coffee lovers the market manages to smooth out the rough edges in pricing when it comes to cappuccino machines, that does not imply there's just one right answer on infrastructure supply. As a rule of thumb, the more invaluable and essential a resource is to a community if all are to share in it, the more likely it is that the resource in question must be provided by the state. That's why our roads, schools and hospitals and energy and water infrastructure should be state owned, and why cappuccino machines need not be. And that is why the state has also to supply the services using these resources: having ensured that these resources are available to society the state cannot take the chance that they are not properly used for its benefit.

Responsibilities of production

None of this infrastructure would, however, be of any use without a barista. The skills the barista needs are complex. They range far beyond the few weeks' training it probably takes to make pretty near excellent cappuccino (at least in the eyes of all but the absolute expert) but that is far from the complete range of skills they need. They also need to communicate, be literate, be numerate, be courteous, and much, much more besides. The state has to provide much of this generic training – not least because it can be reused by the barista in other occupations and in their broader life as well. As a result, no business could bear that external burden of the full training of a barista all by itself, at least not without shackling the barista to its employment, maybe for life. Few would want that. Most education has, therefore, to be provided by the state – and that education should be the best that's possibly available.

The same long-term view that the state must take on much of the infrastructure needed by society and with regard to education is reflected in the role it must adopt with regard to the environment. Can cappuccino be green? Isn't that obvious? Of course it can if it's delivered using the minimum of resources and as much recycling as possible of the products used in its manufacture. Composting the coffee grinds is one way to do that. But being green is more than recycling. It's about ensuring that the benefits of the multiplicity of trades that bring the coffee bean to the machine, the milk to the frother (and further back, the cow to the milking machine) take place in a sustainable and fair fashion so that the cappuccino we'll drink today need not be our last. There would be little to savour about it if it was.

There's even a role for the nutmeg, chocolate and sugar in this cappuccino theory. Of course we all need some frivolities in life. The Courageous State does not promote a puritan manifesto. There is room for fun in sustainable living. That said though, it's vital that we appreciate that the extras in life – such as the nutmeg or grated chocolate on the top of the cappuccino – are not essential. They add excitement, but only when we realise that they're an extra to be appreciated, and not an integral part of being. That is why it is wrong that so much of consumption is portrayed as essential when in fact it is, like the nutmeg, a frivolous (but enjoyable) extra in life.

It's a big mistake, too often made by those who support neoliberalism, to think that because markets can provide some things that are exciting then the choice that they offer on such peripheral issues can somehow be extended to the supply of life's essentials. That, of course, is impossible. The private sector does a great deal that is essential – but it would be wrong to confuse the hot milk that represents much of the private sector in the metaphor with the hot chocolate or nutmeg: they are very different. The amount of our income dedicated to buying products where we have real choice is very often quite limited. That's not to deny the importance of choice when it is available, but it's as important to realise that all too often even the private sector presents us with limited options, and that is because of the inevitability of our constrained nature. And this is also precisely why a great deal of what the private sector does has to be regulated. When choice is limited the state has to ensure that the consumer is protected by regulation. That's not nearly so likely to be the case when considering the supply of those goods which can be bought out of what is usually called 'disposable income' – most of which, by definition will be among those that are represented by the nutmeg in the cappuccino metaphor.

Getting the most out of the final product

In that case, the nutmeg or chocolate pose their own questions. Are they worth having, if we have to work so hard to get them that we forget that the very purpose for them is to add a moment of pleasure – a pleasure we need time to savour, to reflect upon and to just enjoy? When having the nutmeg is more important than enjoying it, there may be something very wrong with our value systems and yet that seems to be what has happened over the last few decades. We toil for luxury and yet have forgotten just what enjoying that luxury feels like. The toil is then just toil.

That appreciation only comes from accumulated wisdom. And yes, there's a cappuccino metaphor for that too. Where does the recipe for cappuccino come from? More widely, what gave rise to the culture of 'going for a coffee'? Who created the idea of 'café society'? These are all metaphors for our culture. This is, of course, a big issue because that culture is about our relationships, our having time to explore our intellect, the time to ponder slowly over a coffee just why we're here.

None of this culture can belong to anyone in isolation and yet we all need to participate in these things if we are to achieve our potential as human beings. The cappuccino is not just a drink. It may be about material nourishment, but that is only a small part of the story. It's also about being a friend, about sharing ideas, about pondering the bigger issues in life and on occasions it is just about being and enjoying ourselves. And we should remember that too. These things are about what life is really all about. They're about purpose. They're about sustaining us, our lives, other people's lives, now and in the future while working in creative harmony (and constructive tension) to build relationships that deliver well-being.

That's what the Courageous State seeks to deliver. It's what the cappuccino metaphor seeks to explain: that the state and private sectors need to co-exist in constructive tension within democratic societies to deliver sustainable well-being for all, in communities that recognise the importance of individual and communal ownership of property and the consequent private and mutual supply of goods and services as each of us contribute to well-being – well-being that is also dependent upon our right relationships with work and the bigger meaning of life.

And democracy should not be ignored either – represented by the spoon in this metaphor, which determines the right mix for the cappuccino – but which also adds the sugar that is sometimes needed in the form of a sweetener to make the resulting combination palatable to some who might otherwise reject it.

It may be pushing a metaphor a long way to reach such conclusions. So what? Understanding is key – and this is what this book is about.

CHAPTER 6

WHERE ONLY THE STATE MAY
VENTURE

The Courageous State necessarily involves a mixed economy. Neoliberal thinking would have it that the market can supply any goods or services better than the state. That is just not true. There are numerous tasks that, as I will argue, only the state can properly undertake if we are to have the society and the goods and services we desire and deserve. The tasks in question are big. They include things like providing education, health, housing social care, pensions and transport infrastructure.

Before anyone says it, I do of course know that all of these services can be provided by the market. That is obviously true, even in the UK. We have private airports, private housing, private schools and private hospitals. But that is not my point. The point is that while the private sector is capable of providing these resources to some in society, that same private sector model is quite unsuited to supplying them to all in society. Just because each of these activities can and does exist within the private sector does not mean that the private sector can change the scale of its activities and provide them universally. That common extrapolation that underpins the logic of those who argue that the state must withdraw from these activities is simply not true.

Where the private sector does not always work best

There is a logical explanation for this. As is very obvious in any marketplace, the private sector undertakes the most profitable activities first. And, unless prevented by regulation, the theory of markets suggests that they will continue to supply services until such time as those supplies are not profitable. Now, I do not think this is the science that economists suggest: I have too much experience of running real companies to think that could be true, but the evidence appears unambiguously clear, and that is that while in countries like the UK there is a potentially profitable market in the supply of education, health, housing, social care, pension provision and transport infrastructure in which private sector companies can participate there is also not just a demand but also a social need for these services which exceeds the ability and willingness of the private sector to supply them. This is not just because doing so might not be profitable, although that may be true. It is actually because the conditions required for the private sector to operate cannot exist if these services are to be supplied by private sector businesses to everyone who needs them at a cost that the economy as a whole can afford.

Again, this claim is relatively easy to explain. There are, without doubt, certain conditions that must exist before any market can operate, even imperfectly. The first condition is that there have to be willing buyers for the products. Without such buyers there is no chance of selling products, let alone at a profit. Second, if abuse is to be avoided as a result of monopoly profits being made there has to be competition in the marketplace. If there were, for example, to be only one commercial supplier of an essential service, such as healthcare, then the opportunity for price abuse would be enormous. This is especially true when purchases of healthcare frequently arise in situations of high stress when the opportunity for finding an alternative supplier is limited (or to put it another way, the purchaser is almost invariably at a disadvantage to the supplier at the point when they must buy because they are in pain and far from being able to make an objective decision). Only competition and informed decision-making can, to some extent, limit that opportunity for abuse of the consumer and even then only if what is called oligopolistic behaviour can be avoided.

Oligopolistic behaviour happens when there are just a limited number of suppliers in the market and they can, whether explicitly or otherwise, cooperate to ensure that they can collectively earn monopoly profits that are exploitative. Precisely because informed decision-making on issues such as healthcare or pensions (for example) is very hard to achieve the private supply of these services will always be open to considerable abuse, as the failings of pension privatisation have already proved.

But even if competition could help when informed decision-making was possible it is also true that competition also has a downside. This downside is that, by definition, competition requires that there is excess capacity in a market. There can be no such thing as effective competition if every single supplier in a market is operating at full capacity: in that case, there is no opportunity for choice (whether informed or otherwise) on the part of the consumer. That consumer is left, if all suppliers are operating at full capacity, having to take whatever opportunity might be available to them at the supplier's convenience, and at the supplier's price. However, this means that to be effective competition is dependent upon all market participants always working at less than full capacity, which means that competitive markets must always (whatever the theoreticians may say) be inherently inefficient in practice because all participants in the market must be underutilising the resources that are available to them if the consumer is to get the choice that they desire.

Why markets are inefficient in practice

This realisation explains a curious phenomenon. This phenomenon is, for example, found in one of the most inefficient markets in the world, that of car manufacturing. It is notoriously difficult to make a profit in this market, even though the economies of the world are based on the use of the car. The problem with making money is not so much that people do not want cars: they clearly do. It is that there is enormous excess capacity in this market.

Estimates made by the OECD[1] vary between about 20% excess capacity in Europe and up to 35% excess capacity in the US: a commonly quoted average of at least 30% excess capacity seems to be widely understood to exist.

Unsurprisingly, US car manufacturers have faced a torrid time as a result, with many suffering bankruptcy during the recent financial crisis. Europe has not been quite so badly affected, but making money in this industry is very hard. This is not helped by the fact that almost all cars are fundamentally similar, since they fall into a quite small number of categories of fairly homogenous type (a few cars at the luxury end of the market perhaps being excepted) while there are sufficient companies in the market to prevent oligopolistic behaviour and so price competition can prevail. This has the result that consumers, for once, face real choice that the excess capacity of the industry permits, and yet that excess capacity at the same time threatens the profitability of the entire sector.

Indeed, the only way in which profit can be generated in this market is because those remarkably homogenous products are differentiated one from the other by the industry spending an enormous amount on marketing, advertising, promotion and product placement, whether paid for or not, in the media. They do this to seek a return above that justified by the true cost of manufacture of the product.

The reference to cost here is relevant: market theory says that products should be sold at their marginal cost of manufacture. That marginal cost is, however, when large numbers of cars are made in a capital-intensive process, remarkably low. Car manufacturers could never make a profit if they followed this rule of economics, so they don't. Instead, they try to make money by selling attributes of their product that it quite probably does not really possess. The reality is that, like it or not, while possession of a car may well have significant impact on a person's life, the choice of one car over another is unlikely, despite the money spent on promotion, to have any really significant impact on the quality of the person's relationships, family life, job prospects or anything else, despite which fact the motor industry spends a fortune trying to persuade us otherwise, and presumably thinks it makes a return on that investment even if the claim is only marginally true at best.

The significance of this advertising spend is, however, that it compounds the inefficiency that already exists within this marketplace as a consequence of the excess capacity that is necessary to ensure that all demand can be met in reasonable timescale by then ensuring that the product supplied is incorrectly priced. If we're sold attributes of the product that do not really exist, and are persuaded for sufficient duration that they might be of benefit to us, the inevitable consequence is a price distortion that we only suffer when the true value is appreciated. The evidence of that appreciation occurring is clearly available: cars that are only a few months old are apparently worth substantially less than the equivalent new models of the same type still sitting on the garage forecourt. The price differential does not reflect the value of the product in use: a car with a few thousand miles on the clock is inherently worth almost exactly as much in use over its remaining life as the identical new model still sitting on the garage forecourt, but it does not have attached to it the marketing hype surrounding the new car. What the fall in the price over the first few months of a car's life therefore indicates is that the marketing hype delivers value over a remarkably short period. This is a sure indication of the price distortion that advertising creates in the market, which is the price paid for the inefficiency that arises because choice must be inherent in competition.

This fact about advertising is in turn one of the clearest indications that we have that markets do not work in the way that economists suggest. Economists, as I have previously noted, assume that there is perfect information available in markets to inform decisions which are then made optimally. In other words, they assume that we all know everything we need to know about quite literally everything, and that we do so without there being any cost to knowing this. Advertising proves that is not true. Even in its most basic form (such as the newspaper small ad) there is a cost to advertising. So that assumption does not hold. Worse, advertising in many ways reinforces all the problems of asymmetric information that mean that markets do not allocate resources efficiently because one side to any transaction (the advertiser) always knows more about what they are describing than the other side to the transaction (the purchaser).

But there is more to it than that: the object of great deal of advertising is not to inform, but to persuade. If markets were to work properly as economists imagine this should not happen. Economists assume that markets work by each individual expressing their own personal preferences with regard to the choice of products and services that they consume. And yet the very purpose of advertising is to impact on that choice and to change it. As a result, and especially because the information inherent in advertising is not perfect, those choices that a consumer makes in an economy where there is advertising are always going to be suboptimal: they may well not reflect the individual's own preferences if only they were free to make them without interference from advertising.

There is no point pretending that people could make a free choice if they so chose: the reality is that we know that advertising does influence our behaviour, whether we like it or not. Its all-pervasive nature guarantees that. This in turn has another consequence, which is that we might choose to consume more in an economy where there is advertising than we would do otherwise. Thorstein Veblen,[2] one of the great economists of the late nineteenth and early twentieth century, had a theory he called 'conspicuous consumption', which stated that advertising and marketing and a great deal of supposed product innovation have just one purpose, which is to persuade us that the product that we just bought is very soon afterwards one with which we should be dissatisfied, so that we wish to replace it with yet another new product even though if, truth be told, they are actually remarkably similar. This is, of course, why the specification of so many products is changed so often and it is also the premise on which the entire fashion industry operates. Perfectly good products are, as a consequence, dispensed with to be replaced by others of which the sole potential gratification is based upon the perception of value that advertising and marketing have created for them, rather than their inherent worth. If that is the case then not only do advertising and marketing increase prices to cover the inherent inefficiency in markets required because of the excess capacity that competition requires, they create market inefficiency in their own right.

Why we can't afford markets in essential services

What has all this got to do with government and the supply of essential services? It is a simple fact that when a service such as healthcare has to be provided to everyone, the costs of competition just explored cannot be afforded by society as a whole.

So, for example, we already know that it is incredibly expensive to maintain a network of hospitals within reasonable distance of most people in the UK, particularly outside the major conurbations. If, however, genuine competition were to now be part of the supply mechanism for healthcare, it would be necessary to have alternative suppliers of medical services available for all to choose from. But that would, by necessity, require duplication of resources since there is no competition to prevent market abuse when a person cannot choose between two hospitals within reasonable distance of where they live. If, however, two (at least) reasonable alternative hospitals are to be made available, each hospital must first have excess capacity so that this choice can be exercised, and second each must maintain that excess capacity indefinitely. As a result, they must always run at less than full capacity and doctors and nurses will have to wait around in them in the hope that patients might arrive even if they do not, but must be paid nonetheless.

Perhaps worse still, those competing hospitals would very soon be spending a great deal of the cash previously directed at healthcare in promoting their services through advertising. Any supposed efficiency benefits arising from the pressures of competition (none of which have materialised as yet after more than twenty years of pension privatisation) would be more than eroded by that spending. In the meantime any prospect of informed decision-making by many patients would disappear entirely if general practitioners, who make most referrals to hospitals, began touting for business, undoubtedly backed by advertising suggesting the supposed perception of added value that they might supply ("we promise you'll never leave without a prescription" is a horrible marketing scenario that comes to mind that would, however, please many patients). This process would in turn in all likelihood be backed by a pharmaceutical industry that has the capacity to make monopolistic profits because of the patents system on its products which guarantees them above-average returns on a successful product for a considerable period after its introduction to the market, and which they could then use to drive up demand for their products by manipulating this system of private medical supply to their advantage.

The cost we would incur if we created such competition is obvious: the outcome of all that excess capacity would be a considerable increase in the cost of supplying healthcare in the UK, or any other country where such choice might be made available. The evidence of this can already be seen when the cost of healthcare in the UK is compared to that of the US. The cost of healthcare in the US is approximately US$7,290 a year, according to a recent report by the Commonwealth Foundation, a US-based research body. The comparative cost in the UK is $2,992 a year, with the US being considered by this organisation to supply much worse healthcare despite the price differential.[3] In terms of total costs as a proportion of GDP, the UK spends approximately 8% of its national income on healthcare, which is lower than any of the other seven major countries to which the Commonwealth Foundation compared it, whereas the US spent 16% of its GDP on healthcare. Also, because of the substantial variation in the quality of healthcare provision in the US, where about a quarter of the population are dependent upon very basic services from the state, with the remainder being covered by an insurance-based system that is extremely expensive to operate with between 30% and 50% of all spending (the estimate depending upon the report noted) being absorbed by administration costs, outcomes are no better and may be worse despite the greater spend. This is clear indication of the inefficiency of the market when choice is provided.

Where the markets don't meet needs

What is clear from this is that if it is desired that everyone in the UK has fair access to healthcare and similar universal services such as education, pensions, housing, social care and transport, so that everyone can in turn have fair access to employment and other social opportunities, we cannot afford to let the private sector supply these services. I reiterate because of the importance of this issue that this is in the first instance because we cannot afford, for resources cannot be duplicated. This is true in the healthcare example but is also largely true of education. In that case a pupil can only attend one school or college at a time if a balanced curriculum is to be provided. The option of picking and choosing is not realistic, and in very many areas is not possible: the geography would simply not permit it. As a result in education, as in healthcare, if the object is to provide services of the highest possible standard in an environment where for practical purposes only one supplier can meet the needs of each consumer then it is only the state that can efficiently undertake this task.

It takes only a moment to realise this is also true for a great deal of transport infrastructure: we do not need two major roads between places, or duplicated railway lines. We need one integrated system that works really well, but that necessarily requires that the state provide it.

It is, in fact this feature of integration that also demands this outcome. Returning to the example of healthcare, it is not competition between providers that is needed in an effective healthcare system. Such a system is dependent upon relationships of trust and cooperation between providers and competition will always undermine these relationships making it the last thing that is needed if effective healthcare outcomes are to be delivered. Only the state can ensure effective supply of services in this case. We must, therefore, have a National Health Service that makes no pretence to be a private service; schools that have public service at the core of their ethos and other services where the duty to provide is paramount. We cannot afford any alternative.

Housing is a slightly more complex situation. In an economy where well over half the population live in property that they own it is clear that the market has a much greater role to play in this sector than it has in education, healthcare and transport infrastructure. And yet if a significant minority of the population will not ever enjoy the chance of owning their own property then it is very clear that an alternative model of housing is needed. What is apparent at present is that the private sector is not meeting that demand for a number of reasons.

The first reason is that suitable accommodation is not available at appropriate prices. That is why so much rent subsidy has to be paid by the state (a cash subsidy to landlords required in large part because of the excessive cost of housing resulting from the tax exemption granted to owners of private homes when they make a capital gain).

The second reason is that in far too many cases the private sector supplies substandard property because costs are avoided as a result of the profit motive driving supply. This, however, is in conflict with the social objective of ensuring people have the opportunity to live a good life wherever they might live.

The third reason is that because land is an economic resource that behaves in very many ways unlike any other, not least because it is automatically constrained in supply with regulation only exacerbating this trend, the market for land has ensured that a great many people would, without state intervention, be denied access to any suitable property of any sort. If that were allowed the consequence would be wholly unacceptable poverty for some and resulting inequality that would threaten the entire structure of our society. This is unacceptable and the result is that despite the significant engagement of the private sector in housing, the state still has a fundamental role to play in ensuring that the basic human necessity of decent accommodation is available to everyone.

That is also true of social care. Many of the elderly, the sick, the young and the disabled in society need assistance from others to enjoy the most basic standard of living. However, precisely because they are elderly, sick, young or disabled many of these people will not have the resources to buy the services that they require. This is precisely why the state must again intervene to ensure that they can do so, or all these groups are at risk of facing very real poverty. Gross inequality and desperate lives would be the result if the state did not intervene, which is precisely why we need a Courageous State that will do just that.

The pensions dilemma

There is a clear basis for intervention by the state in all these cases, as there is also in the case of pensions. Pensions are an example of a situation sometimes found where a model that appears to work for a limited number of people who use it in the private sector is not capable of extrapolation for use in the population as a whole and where the state must therefore take action instead.

This issue needs to be viewed from a very broad perspective to understand it. Pension provision has not been an issue of concern throughout most of history. People either died before they got too old to work or they would be cared for by their extended families or, in limited cases, they enjoyed the wealth to ensure that working was not a necessity, quite often throughout their entire lives. Pensions did not, therefore, exist as such. This changed with the substantial advances in healthcare that arose during the Victorian period and the state old-age pension has been a feature of British life for a century since its introduction in 1908. However, it is important to note that at that time it was paid to those over the age of 70, and most people did not expect to live to that age. This was a decided 'back stop' provision for the exceptional people who lived long enough to need it.

In the aftermath of the Second World War retirement ages were reduced and life expectancy increased. The cost of state provision of the old-age pension inevitably rose as a result, but that was a price that society thought worth paying as part of the post-war cross-party political consensus commonly called Butskellism. Popular as this pension was, and as dependent upon it as many people were and still are, rising prosperity among many in the middle classes in Britain which took place during the 1950s and 1960s encouraged the development of private pension provision in addition to this basic state provision. As a result, increasing numbers of people were members of pension schemes, while tax relief for personal pension contributions for the self-employed and those outside formal schemes was introduced in 1956.

These new top-up pension funds were of two broad types. The first, operated almost exclusively by the state on behalf of its employees, was similar in many ways to the arrangements for the state old-age pension. Current revenues raised by taxation were used to pay the current pension obligations arising for those in old age who had previously been in state employment. No savings mechanism was involved and as such this arrangement was and is called a 'pay-as-you-go' pension scheme.

The alternative arrangement, commonplace among nationalised industries, large companies, and also available for the self-employed and those outside other pension arrangements, ensured that contributions made by either an employer or employee, or both, were paid to a pension fund, organised as a trust, which invested those funds in the hope that a pension could be paid using the sum accumulated in due course to the person on whose behalf the contribution had been made, or who had made it themselves.

These arrangements were again of two types. The first, usually associated with nationalised industries and large companies, was described as a final salary scheme, where the benefit paid was a proportion of a person's earnings at the time they retired, the proportion being dependent upon the length of service in most cases, with the resulting pension being expected to increase over time in line with inflation. These were called defined benefit schemes.

The second arrangement is called a defined contribution scheme, because in this arrangement a fixed sum of money is paid into a fund and the amount of pension to be paid as a result was not and is not determined until such time as the person for whom the contribution had been made retired, when in most circumstances an annuity is purchased to be paid throughout the remainder of the pensioner's anticipated life, which then guarantees them an income which may or may not increase over time depending upon the arrangement made. As is obvious as a consequence, defined benefit schemes are much more attractive to employees and offer greater certainty to them than do defined contribution pension schemes, which, however, are preferred by employers as they reduce their risk.

Until the 1970s (by which time almost 50% of the working population were members of an occupational pension scheme) there appeared little awareness on the part of the state of two things. The first was the potential liability it might have to make pension payments as life expectancy steadily increased but anticipated pension ages, if anything, reduced. The second was the relative lack of awareness of the poor provision being made by many for their retirement, particularly if they were not a member of an employer-run pension scheme as was commonplace, for example, among many employees of smaller companies. When this was appreciated, state earnings-related top-up pensions were made available to those in employment who were not members of formal pension schemes, with different rates of National Insurance been paid by those who wished to participate in these arrangements. As with the state old-age pension this arrangement was not savings based: it was a pay-as-you-go scheme enjoying the popular name of SERPS – the State Earnings-Related Pension Scheme.

This in turn, however, gave rise to an increased perception of risk on the part of the state. In the late 1980s the Labour-created SERPS scheme appeared to impose too much potential obligation on the state to make future pension contributions when compared to the likely future income receipts. The result was that the then Conservative government sought to find a private sector alternative, and encouraged people to leave the SERPS scheme by offering to make direct contributions of part of their National Insurance payments into their own private pension plan. The intention was to ensure that the state was only liable for the basic state old-age pensions for these people, and that they assumed the risk on the amount of eventual pension they would receive on top of that, dependent upon the return that their chosen pension provider might generate for them during their working life.

Where the market failed

It was from this moment onwards that a great deal began to go wrong in the UK's pension system. The idea that pensions might not pay an appropriate sum to ensure a person's well-being in old age did not seem to have occurred to pension providers or potential pensioners before this point. Indeed, that awareness continued to a very large degree to be deferred throughout the 1990s. While it was well known during the course of this period that endowment insurance policies sold by the same companies that were operating pension funds on behalf of individuals and companies in the private sector were delivering an investment shortfall compared to anticipated returns, an awareness that the same problem might arise in pension funds was deferred for two reasons. The first was a failure to appropriately account for the additional liabilities that these funds were incurring as a consequence of the increase in life expectancy. The second was the consequence of the steady growth in the value of the stock exchange throughout that decade which, in combination with the noted failure to account properly, disguised the true nature of the potential and problematic liabilities that private pension funds were facing.

This situation has changed rapidly in the last decade. After the crash in the value of the stock exchange following the dot.com bubble bursting, coupled with developments in pensions accounting, there were sudden and dramatic reappraisals of the health of many large corporate entities' private pension funds, including those of the previously nationalised utility companies. Despite these funds' accounts having suggested that they were in surplus for many years during the 1990s, meaning that they claimed to have assets in excess of any that might reasonably be required to pay the pensions they believed they were contractually obliged to deliver to their members (leading to many such surpluses being used to pay pensions on the early retirement of employees made redundant during a period of rapid reorganisation of many such companies) they suddenly found themselves in a position where they faced significant pension deficits that they were obliged to reflect in many cases on the accounts of the company that sponsored the scheme. To put it another way: the private sector had massively underfunded their potential liabilities to pay, and that in turn meant that the obligations of the state to pay pensions were reappraised and were claimed by many to be bigger than previously realised.

Without exploring this issue in detail, the rapid reaction to this situation by many of these companies was remarkably similar: they sought to close defined benefit pension schemes and transfer their members to defined contribution schemes so that the risk of a potential pension shortfall fell on their employees, and not on the company itself. It is now quite difficult to find a company in the private sector that operates a defined benefit scheme that accepts any new employees, and many have closed for existing employees as well. The last bastion of defined benefit pensions has, therefore, become the state, where the failure to account on the basis of the potential accrued liability based upon actuarial expectation of the life of members compared to contributions made has, some would argue, assisted the perpetuation of such arrangements.

This diversion into pension history does, however, have a serious point to make. It is obvious that as a result of the failure to account for all potential costs, to invest appropriately and to ensure appropriate advice has been given, the market has seriously failed many current and potential pensioners. Too many have argued that it is the state that is now supplying inappropriate pensions to its employees, but that is not true: the reality is that after more than twenty years of private sector domination of the pension debate private sector pension funds have failed to deliver on their promise. They are delivering poor pensions to those who trusted them, many of which will be much worse than people were led to expect, and the risk of the future supply of these pensions has now been transferred to pensioners and away from the employers who undertook to deliver them.

If demonstration of the failure of the market to meet a universal need were ever demanded this is it: the pensions industry demanded and got access to large quantities of public funds (the state subsidy to the pensions industry was £38bn in 2008) and yet it cannot deliver on its most basic promise, not least because much of that subsidy has over many years been used to profit the financial services sector. The same pattern will undoubtedly be followed if other sectors move in the same direction.

This not only means that the state will, once again, have to fulfil its role as guarantor of last resort, but it will also, somewhat more proactively, have to recognise that this is a situation where, yet again, the market is unable to meet a demand for a service that is going to exist long into the future.

Market constraints

The reason for this problem not being appreciated is that it was ignored that any market yet invented has limited capacity. So, for example, some markets are limited by physical constraints, so if there is no more wheat supply available in the world then at a point in time the market cannot create it: there is a lead-time to growing wheat and there is nothing the market can do to get round that fact if the existing crop has already been sold. The reaction to excess demand in this situation is price inflation in the secondary market for wheat.

In other markets there may appear to be no physical constraint – such as that for credit derivatives where the sums traded have surpassed most imaginations. And yet there is a capacity constraint: that is the need for capital to back up the promise of payment in the event of a default in this case, as we are only now appreciating.

In pensions the matter is more complex still: both these constraints apply and that is why the market has not as yet proved itself able to deliver a pensions solution for the UK. When all the hype is cut away from the pension debate, unless there is some major change in the demographic of the UK (probably resulting from major immigration, which creates its own risks with regard to the stability of society because human beings have a limited capacity to accept a great degree of change in their communities over a relatively short period of time) the fact is that population of the UK will, on average get older for some time to come, with more people who are relatively old, infirm, and unable to work having to be supported by a reduced population of younger people who will be in employment. This is inescapable, and because the

UK, thankfully, no longer has an empire which it can exploit this is a problem that it will have to manage within the constraints of our own society, especially as countries such as China, Brazil and India are now all claiming a greater share of world resources for their own populations, and rightly so.

This means, however, that there is a straightforward limitation upon the capacity of the savings market to provide suitable mechanisms in which people currently at work can save to provide for their retirement. That is because, while in a fairly limited (by which I mean small in absolute size in relationship to the economy as a whole) savings market it will almost certainly be true that a purchaser for any asset in which a person invests will be found in the future, presuming a reasonably prudent choice was made, this simply cannot be guaranteed to be true in the case of a very large savings market in which a significant part of the population is engaged and on which they are dependent in the long term. We move into an entirely different dynamic at that point.

For the next fifteen years or so at least, some of the baby boomer generation will still be buying up assets in which they can save for their pensions. If the conventional logic of pension investment currently in use is followed, many of those savings will be used to buy the shares of companies that are already in issue, existing property and bonds issued by companies that also issue shares. A limited part (if annuity investment is ignored) will be invested in UK government bonds and the bonds of other countries. As the Office for National Statistics has noted, 39% by value of the UK stock exchange is held by UK-based pension companies and life assurance funds.[4] However, according to research in the *Financial Times*[5] just £1.3bn worth of new shares were issued on the London Stock Exchange in 2010. That Exchange was, however, in May 2011 worth approximately £2 trillion.[6] It becomes immediately apparent as a result that if approximately £80bn of contributions are made to pension funds a year[7] and a significant part of that sum is invested in shares, the vast majority of shares purchased with new pension contributions are shares that are already in issue.

This brings me to the key point, which is that, as is clear from this ratio of new shares issued to new pension contributions being made, the market simply does not have the capacity to shift wealth of the order required between generations using the savings mechanisms available to it. There aren't enough shares in issue to invest in to do that without massive price distortions and without the demand for shares exceeding their supply for considerable periods, resulting in speculative behaviour that leads to bubbles and crashes and the dashing of hope, until the process has (to date) been forlornly recommenced. Similarly, the demand for property as a savings medium has moved the price of housing beyond the reach of those who actually need to access it for the purposes of living.

And despite this the mechanisms for savings used also fail to deliver the one thing that those who are seeking to save for their old age really need to create – which is new capital. The fundamental inter-generational pension contract that should exist within any society is that one generation, the older one, will through their own efforts create capital assets and infrastructure in both the state and private sectors which the following younger generation can use in the course of their work. In exchange for the subsequent use of these assets for their own benefit that succeeding younger generation will, in effect, meet the income needs of the older generation when they are in retirement. Unless this fundamental compact that underpins all pensions is honoured, any pension system will fail.

The need for real capital investment

This contract is ignored in the existing pension system that does not even recognise that it exists. Our state-subsidised saving for pensions makes no link between that activity and the necessary investment in new capital goods, infrastructure, job creation and skills that we need as a country. As a result, state subsidy is being given with no return to the state appearing to arise as a consequence, precisely because this is a subsidy for saving which does not generate any new wealth. This is the fundamental economic problem and malaise in our current pension arrangement.

That is because the funds now saved in pensions are very largely not invested; they are used for speculation. That means they do not create real value in our economy, but as the next section of this book will show, float outside it. That is of massive importance. It is why our pension arrangements as currently structured cannot work.

Put simply, the money put aside right now for old age is just that: money put aside for old age. But when the time comes that the very many people now putting that cash aside reach old age they will find that (for the first time) a smaller successor generation will not be persuaded that the cash the old have to offer is a sufficient inducement to make that younger generation keep them. This is because the old will at that time have cash, but cash is not king. The old will want the young to keep them but they will not have ownership of the assets that they must transfer to the young as compensation for the income that the young will have to forego in exchange to maintain the old. The young will, as all generations have done before, maintain the old including their parents, but only if the old have more than cash to offer in exchange: they will have to offer real capital in exchange for the income that the young will forego as a consequence.

Real capital is schools, hospitals, infrastructure, productive capacity, technology, communications systems and so much more. If those who reach the age of retirement have invested in such things in sufficient quantity, they have their ownership of those assets to trade with the next generation. If the retiring generation have instead simply speculated – in buildings that they value at more than their cost of replacement and in shares where the price they pay for them is way in excess of the underlying worth of the companies in question – and worse, if they have not invested in public infrastructure that the over-burdened next generation will need to have ready and waiting for them if they are to divert their efforts into keeping more old people, an activity which will necessarily mean that they will not have the resources to replenish and invest in infrastructure – then the fundamental pension contract will fall apart.

As a result the old may find they have cash-based assets but the next generation will rapidly assert who has priority in the claim upon the wealth that they will by then be generating. They will do that by refusing to trade in over-priced shares, as a result of which their price will collapse. And they will assert their authority by refusing to buy over-priced property, as a result of which its price will also collapse. And they'll even refuse the pensioners piles of cash if need be by simply eliminating its value by allowing inflation to erode. And that's how existing pension arrangements will fail.

This failure will be the consequence of thinking that pension arrangements that a few can enjoy without seriously distorting values in the underlying economy can be extended to a significant part of society without a similar distortion of values in the underlying economy occurring. That extension is not possible: the market cannot deliver this transfer of value between generations on the scale required. It can do it for a few million people maybe, but it cannot do it for us all. It could improve, without doubt, on its current abysmal pension performance. The Dutch model of pension investment clearly proves this,[8] but even that cannot be sure to deliver on the promise that is being made by the market to too many people about a future of which far too little is known.

The reality is that the state is the only agent that can ensure that more elderly people can have the right to live in dignity, by guaranteeing that the necessary transfer of value between generations takes place. The state has to do this by guaranteeing that appropriate investment in capital by the current generation takes place, and by guaranteeing that the value in question is transferred when necessary to the next generation so that they will keep their forebears when the time comes. Nothing else and no one else can solve this problem. Only a Courageous State can anticipate that need by requiring a massive change in the approach that we take to this issue. This is a matter to which I will return in Part 3 of this book. For now, the point is that the state has to meet many of the basic needs of people in modern societies for the two fundamental reasons noted. The first is that markets are inevitably and hopelessly inefficient when it comes to supplying universal services to a high standard. The second is that there are some transactions that must take place to meet society's needs and yet the market does not have the capacity to fulfil them. The result is that not only does the state have a fundamental role in creating the environment in which the market can function, it has also a role of its own to play in addition to its task as acting as guarantor of last resort, corrector of market externalities, inspirer of innovation, redistributor of income and wealth, and guarantor of access for all.

1   OECD, 2009, *The Automobile Industry In And Beyond The Crisis*, page 2, http://www.oecd.org/dataoecd/57/61/44089863.pdf

2   Those looking for some insight into Veblen's work could do worse than to look here http://en.wikipedia.org/wiki/Thorstein_Veblen

3   *Mirror Mirror on the Wall: How the performance of the US healthcare system compares internationally*, 2010, Commonwealth Foundation http://www.commonwealthfund.org/~/media/Files/Publications/Fund%20Report/2010/Jun/1400_Davis_Mirror_Mirror_on_the_wall_2010.pdf

4   See *Pension Trends: Chapter 14: Pensions and the National Accounts 2011*, National Statistics, available at http://www.statistics.gov.uk/downloads/theme_compendia/pensiontrends/PTChapter14final.pdf

5   http://www.ft.com/cms/s/0/fde2f874-a0f2-11e0-adae-00144feabdc0.html#ixzz1QYZBVIfV from June 27 2011,

6   London Stock Exchange Main Market Statistics May 2011 http://www.londonstockexchange.com/statistics/historic/main-market/may2011.pdf

7   Calculation of this sum is explained in Murphy, R. (2011) *Making Pensions Work*, Finance for the Future LLP available at http://www.financeforthefuture.com/MakingPensionsWork.pdf

8   See http://www.telegraph.co.uk/finance/personalfinance/pensions/7921778/Why-British-pensions-should-go-Dutch.html

CHAPTER 7

FINANCING GOVERNMENT ACTIVITY

Based on what I have argued to this point it is clear that the Courageous State has a significant role to play in its economy: the coffee in the cappuccino is double espresso.

However, this leads to the inevitable question of how the government is to finance these activities.

The government's primary source of revenue is obviously taxation, whether on income, gains or other transactions. It does, of course, have secondary sources such as charging for services and investment income, but I will ignore these for the moment because when neoliberalism considers the role of government the subject of tax is often at the forefront of its concern.

The right to tax

It is important to be upfront on the issue of tax and make clear straight away what might be assumed by many to be obvious: states have a legal right to tax. Although most will assume this is true the idea has been challenged from the right wing of politics in recent years, where it has become commonplace to say that all tax is theft and to add that the fact that the state endorses that theft does not legitimise it.

This commonplace claim by many neoliberal thinkers is wrong. In fact it is not just wrong – it is blatantly untrue and

95

those who believe in the importance of the state have a duty to say so. They have an equal obligation to challenge those who also argue that tax avoidance and even tax evasion are acceptable because all tax is institutionalised theft and those undertaking these activities are merely claiming what is rightfully their own. There are a number of reasons for challenging these pernicious claims, and it is important that they be made clear:

- First, no modern society has survived without a government. There have been states without an effective government, such as Somalia at this point in time. But that society is failing, and at the end of the barrel of a gun. Assuming that this is not the wish of those saying tax is theft then government is a fact of life that they must accept.

- Second, no modern society can survive without property rights that can be protected without resorting to physical violence. Failed states are characterised by property rights enforced by violence. Successful states are associated by property rights enforced by laws passed by governments that can be upheld in courts, set up and maintained by those governments. So, again, unless those saying tax is theft are suggesting that property rights should be enforced through physical violence they must support the right of government to establish, maintain and defend those property rights.

- Third, if those arguing tax is theft do accept that governments establish property rights then they have to concede that this is a monopoly right: there cannot be two competing systems of property rights in a jurisdiction. If there were to be so there would be no such thing as rights; there would simply be competing claims and that is something quite different. But that in turn means that those who argue tax is theft must concede the right of the state to make law.

- Fourth, once that right has been conceded then it has also to be agreed that the state also has the right to make other law: including the right to levy tax to ensure that the

96

system of property rights it has established can be maintained by law. But this means that tax laws are created by the same process that creates a right to property: the two are indistinguishable. The right to property is the same as the right to tax: both are simple applications of law.

- Of course the legitimacy of both laws is dependent upon the legitimacy of the government: it is accepted here that for all practical purposes a government elected on a universal mandate without interference in the electoral process is legitimate. In that case then the fifth reason follows, that property rights and taxes are equally legitimate. More than that though, they are in fact one and the same because a property right might grant a person the right to hold a particular asset, but so do taxing rights. A tax is, after all, no more than a claim on property by government.

A taxing right says that if an event happens, such as receipt of income, then tax is due (albeit in some cases the right amount of tax might be nothing). And, again, it says that if an asset is acquired then in a great many cases value added tax is payable, and so on. In other words, the right to acquire, hold, use, transfer, sell and even discard many types of property is conditional on the taxes due as a result of those actions having been paid.

Two things follow from this observation. The first is that almost without exception in a modern economy property rights are conditional: the claim to an asset is conditional on tax due being paid with the right of remedy on the part of the government if it is not paid.

The second consequence is that the commonly held view, oft quoted by politicians, that governments spend other people's money is, quite straightforwardly, wrong. Governments spend their own money, legally theirs, properly collected, and not subject to a claim by any other person. Of course governments are accountable through the ballot box for the amount of tax that they wish to collect, and for the use of the tax collected, but that does not mean that they are agents for those who make payment of tax. The government is the sole agent making decisions on the use of tax, which is precisely why it needs to have confidence in its own actions, both on tax and macroeconomic policy more generally. For it to willingly incapacitate itself by believing that it is agent for those who make payment of tax, and in particular (in a neoliberal environment) that it might consider itself especially accountable to those who might make some of the largest tax payments, is simply wrong. Tax paid arises because tax is due: no single pound of tax paid gives rise to any greater obligation to account for its use than does any other. That is not to say that the government is not accountable; far from it, but it does say that is a universal, and not a particular obligation.

In that case the neoliberals' argument that tax distorts behaviour is wrong. Their argument is based upon their belief that individuals know best how to spend their own money on their own behalf, and so maximise their own well-being if allowed to do so. But that argument assumes that the individual's gross (pre-tax) income is theirs to enjoy, and as I have shown that is not true. As such the claims made by neoliberals about tax are also wrong.

The power of taxation

Given that this is the case it is quite remarkable how timid UK politicians are on the subject of tax. Their language is the first indication of this. It is quite common for them to refer to the funds they manage as "taxpayers' money". As noted, that is not true. The language used by politicians is misleading and inappropriate in other ways as well. For example, it has been commonplace for the UK government-owned National Savings organisation to market UK Premium Bonds on the basis that they are tax-free, as if that is a virtue. This reveals an extraordinary ambiguity on the part of a government agency tasked with increasing government net revenues with regard to the virtues of taxation. The message being delivered, no doubt with political approval, is that not paying tax is somehow a good thing, when it is clearly not the case if the government is to fulfil its responsibility to supply services.

These examples of political ambiguity towards the virtues of taxation on the part of politicians are, however, seemingly indicative of those politicians' real sentiments. It is obvious that they have a paranoia about raising tax, and income tax in particular.

They can excuse increases in national insurance as if this were a charge for services supplied, when it is not, and while both Labour and the Conservatives have increased VAT rates since they were cut during 2009 to provide an economic stimulus in the aftermath of the financial crash in 2008, these increases are the exceptions that prove the general rule that UK politicians are very reluctant to increase taxation charges.

The result of this reluctance is that, as the OECD noted in a recent report[1] on growing inequality in its member states, the impact of taxation in tackling inequality is diminishing. The consequence of this failure to act in raising taxation has been, as the UK's Office for National Statistics has noted,[2] a complete failure of direct taxes in particular to impact on overall income distribution in the UK for more than two decades. This is despite the fact that, as a recent IMF report on inequality and the financial crisis noted,[3] the financial crisis was itself very much the consequence of that inequality. This, they argued, was because growing wealth disparities meant that a wealthy elite resorted to excessive lending to those of more humble means before the crash, leading to excess leverage of many households on average incomes in the UK and elsewhere, and a resulting incapacity to pay back accrued debts on those households' part. This would not, the IMF noted, have occurred if only the inequality gap had not been as big as it was in 2008. Quite clearly, as the OECD has noted, the failure to tax appropriately contributed to this inequality.

Raising tax is not then just a duty imposed on government to pay for the necessary activities it must undertake. Government also has a duty to tax to reduce inequality in the interests, as it turns out, of preventing financial instability, let alone as a meritorious act in its own right for the benefit to those whose poverty is alleviated as a result.

The evidence for the existence of increasing income inequalities is not hard to find. As the *Financial Times* noted in June 2011:[4]

> "Fork-lift truck drivers in Britain could expect to earn £19,068 in 2010, about 5 per cent lower than in 1978, after adjusting for inflation. Median male real US earnings have not risen since 1975. Average real Japanese household incomes after taxation

fell in the decade to mid-2000s. And those in Germany have been falling in the past 10 years."

As the same article noted, this was despite considerable real increases in national income. This trend is found in the UK, as the May 2011 report of the independent High Pay Commission noted.[5] The table below, reproduced from that report, shows the increase in the growth of real incomes for people in different parts of the income distribution, over a decade during which the overall growth in UK GDP[6] amounted to 37.4% at an annualised average rate of 3.2%.

Growth in real incomes at different points in the income distribution, 1996/97–2007/08 (%)

Percentile	Overall growth	Per year growth
10	3.7%	0.3%
25	5.2%	0.5%
50	7.2%	0.6%
75	9.3%	0.8%
90	13.1%	1.1%
95	16.1%	1.4%
96	18.2%	1.5%
97	20.9%	1.7%
98	26.6%	2.2%
99.0	34.3%	2.7%
99.1	34.5%	2.7%
99.2	35.8%	2.8%
99.3	36.7%	2.9%
99.4	38.5%	3.0%
99.5	40.4%	3.1%
99.6	41.9%	3.2%
99.7	46.1%	3.5%
99.8	53.5%	4.0%
99.9	64.2%	4.6%

Source: High Pay Commission

99.3% of people enjoyed overall growth in their incomes less than that of the economy as a whole. For 95% of the population their growth in income was less than half that of the economy as a whole, and the increase in income falls rapidly as earnings drop.

In contrast, the top 0.5% of the population enjoyed growth in their incomes substantially greater than that in the population as a whole, and much greater than that in the economy as a whole. It should be noted that this data also fails to take into account the fact that the share of overall returns to labour fell in this period, with a greater return accruing to profit and the benefit of that profit goes to highest paid overall, as they own the most capital and so get the greatest share of all returns from investment. The result is that the above data on earned incomes is bound to under-state the increase in overall income disparities in this period.

Just in case this evidence is not sufficient it should be noted that in terms of cash, expressed entirely at 2007/08 prices, the income of the lowest 10% in the UK as ranked by earnings was £6,900 a year in 1996/97 and £7,200 in 2007/08, whereas the income of the top 0.1% was £328,000 in 1996/97 but £538,600 in 2007/08. The differences in income growth are starkly obvious. Tax has the power to correct these growing disparities. Therefore it is clear that tax has a role to play in addressing income inequality in the UK as well as simply raising revenue to pay for government activity.

Redistribution of wealth

Income inequality is not the only issue needing to be addressed – wealth is as seriously distorted as income in its distribution. Between 1976 and 2003 (which is the last year for which HM Revenue & Customs publish data[7]) the proportion of UK wealth, excluding housing, owned by the top 1% of the UK wealth distribution increased from 29% to 34% of the total, and the proportion owned by the top 10% increased from 57% to 71%, with both changes likely to be seriously understated as a result of the considerable shift of wealth offshore, which is beyond HMRC's ability to record it during this period. The share of assets owned by the bottom 50% of the wealth-owning population fell, astonishingly, from 12% to just 1% during the same period. To restate, the wealth of half the population has been almost wiped out by neoliberal economics to the point where they might now be called 'wealthless'.

All of which leaves my hypothesis intact: it is the role of government to ensure that they tax not just to pay for the goods and services that government supplies, but also to ensure that income and wealth are redistributed to ensure that all have the access to the market that only sufficient income can deliver; that all have access to capital; and that all have the security that both these situations can supply so that a more equal, fair and economically stable society is created; all of which the IMF predicts should follow from greater equality.

In so saying I make a prediction that might appear odd to those not familiar with the work of Thorstein Veblen, whose work was noted in the previous chapter and which has been largely side-lined by neoclassical economists. That sidelining is, no doubt, because he suggested that once basic needs are met much, if not most, consumption is undertaken for the purposes of ostentation. Veblen's 'conspicuous consumption' describes this phenomenon that is attested to in the current economy by, for example, the *Financial Times*' weekend magazine entitled 'How to Spend It'.[8]

The issue that Veblen so clearly understood and described is that what is important in these situations of having income in excess of basic need is not the absolute level of consumption, but the comparable level of consumption that an individual who participates in conspicuous consumption can display. The significance of this is that, so long as taxes are imposed impartially and without opportunity for abuse through avoidance or evasion, the outcome for the perception of well-being by those who can afford to conspicuously consume (who by definition are in the upper echelons of the income distribution noted above) might be marginal: their relative perception of well-being can be maintained despite a taxation charge if it is applied consistently. So long as there is limited opportunity to avoid or evade tax, anyone's relative position in the hierarchy of consumption will not be affected by a change in the tax charge, and that relative position is what matters to them much more than the actual consumption itself. This suggests, therefore, that it is not tax rates that matter so much to those who oppose taxation charges but the impact that they have on distorting relative well-being.

This brings us to the final of these broad purposes for the state that I have sought to outline, and that is that it acts as the guardian for society and as such as the repository of hope for those who would otherwise fall by the wayside. By that I mean that while the state does have a role in driving the economy, in delivering effective markets and in precipitating change, and is also responsible for ensuring that all can participate in these processes, that is not enough: these are in most cases actions that facilitate or correct the behaviour of the market. Yet it can do more than that:

- The state can support the family.
- The state can support society.
- It can promote education for its own sake.
- The state can support our identity, individually, as groups and collectively.
- The state can support the maintenance of wisdom – especially through the arts.
- The state can and should ensure our freedom to agree, and differ.

All those things it can and should do. I have known that instinctively – as I suspect have millions of others – for years. But why should the state do these things? I have argued that it should do so, but in Part 2 of this book I seek to explain why as well. And that requires us to get back to economics, and to start thinking again from scratch, before in Part 3 I look at what can be done with the understanding that new theory creates.

1   *Growing income inequality in OECD countries: What drives it and how can policy tackle it?* 2011, OECD, Paris http://www.oecd.org/dataoecd/32/20/47723414.pdf

2   See http://www.statistics.gov.uk/cci/nugget.asp?id=332

3   Kumhof, M. and Rancière, R. (2010) *Inequality, Leverage and Crises*, International Monetary Fundhttp://www.imf.org/external/pubs/ft/wp/2010/wp10268.pdf

4   Giles, C. 27 June 2011, 'Spectre of stagnating incomes stalks globe', *Financial Times*, http://www.ft.com/cms/s/0/0e0f51e0-a0e2-11e0-adae-00144feabdc0.html#ixzz1QXtq3mGU

5   *More for Less: what has happened to pay at the top and does it matter?*, Interim report of the High Pay Commission May 2011http://highpaycommission.co.uk/wp-content/uploads/2011/05/HPC_interim_report2011.pdf

6   Based on HM Treasury data at http://www.hm-treasury.gov.uk/data_gdp_fig.htm

7   See http://www.statistics.gov.uk/cci/nugget.asp?id=2

8   http://www.howtospendit.com/

PART 2

THINKING THE COURAGEOUS STATE

CHAPTER 8

A NEW WAY OF ECONOMIC
THINKING

In Part 1 I argued that there is no hope of economic revival, political revival and the survival of democracy itself if we continue to
believe government is a bad thing when it isn't. In fact, as I hope
I showed, government is something that is fundamental to our
well-being in a great many ways.

Arguing the case is one thing; providing a more thorough
explanation is something else altogether, and something not
readily available in economics at present. The absence of that
logical explanation for what many know to be intuitively correct
is, I think, one of the biggest reasons why we have a cowardly
state: a state dominated by the thinking of neoliberalism that
says anything and everything government does makes people
worse off than if it left well alone – however intuitively wrong we
all know that to be. We need a theory of the Courageous State.

I have lived in forlorn hope of someone offering that alternative explanation for more than thirty years now. That is why
I offer my attempt at that explanation in the pages that follow. I
am well aware of the enormity of the task. I am also well aware
that within the space available in this book I can only scratch the
surface of this alternative thinking, but to abuse a Chinese prov-
erb, unless the first step is taken a 1,000 mile journey cannot
begin. What follows are those first steps.

The existing model

I will spend very little time in what follows repeating what is wrong with the existing widely taught model of economics. To again slightly simplify my reasoning, it is fair to say that there is only one thing wrong with that model and that is everything. A moment of explanation will be enough.

As just about anyone who has ever been taught that model of economics knows, the introductory course on the subject focuses heavily upon a series of graphs. I am not, of course, pretending that such introductory materials are a fair reflection of the enormous amount of academic study that underpins the whole of economics: that would be a gross simplification. But it is equally true to say that the vast majority of those who have any recall of the study of economics, including I suspect most politicians, will only remember something very basic about those introductory graphs and little else. That is my fundamental point here: the caricature that they offer of human behaviour and the way in which it is manifested in our economy is the point of significance in existing economics teaching, and the truth is that those graphs very accurately reflect the underlying assumptions of neoliberal economics.

All those graphs are ultimately built around a graph that looks something like this:

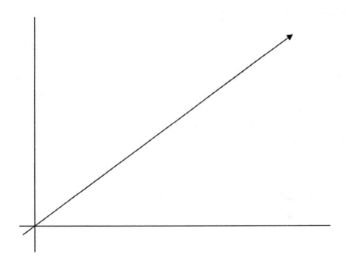

There are three fundamental elements to this graph that create problems that we now see reflected throughout our economy. The first is that it has two axes. That means it suggests that at any time we are only capable of comparing two variables. That is, of course, absurd: life is just not like that, but existing economics is. The result is that economists assume that somehow we can compare one decision at a time with the entirety of the rest of our decisions.

They also assume, critically but incorrectly, that when making these comparisons we make them consistently. Their entire logic and world view falls apart if we prefer product A to product B and also prefer product B to product C but then when given the choice prefer product C to product A. That logic may appear utterly irrational to an economist but they only have to witness behaviour in any high street store to realise just how bizarre their assumption of rationality is. We just aren't like that. We are perfectly capable of making entirely inconsistent judgements, and are more than happy with the result. Two axes just aren't enough to explain the complexities and irrationalities of life.

The second problem is that if the decision an economist wants to consider is not contained within the axes of this graph, it falls out of the economist's consideration. Of course, economists can claim that everything is within the axes of this graph, but this is not the case. Although economists like to argue when presenting their very simple graphs that human beings seek to maximise their utility (something which they find hard to define) the reality is that economists quickly resort to questions of cash when offering explanation of how the world works. As a result non-cash transactions have, for economists to make their models work, to be translated into cash values, however illogical that might be. So we end up with the bizarre logic of what is called cost-benefit analysis, for example. This process of ascribing a cash value to every form of human interchange offends human sensibility, and rightly so. It is the type of logic that led, ultimately, to News International no doubt justifying to itself that it was appropriate to hack into the telephone of a murdered girl to secure a story that increased the circulation of their newspaper. Cash was generated but morality disappeared in the process. The fact is that there are issues to be considered in economics that do not conform to the economist's cash-based ethos. The example used may be considered extreme, but they occur daily throughout our lives: for much that is really important to us there is quite simply no cash alternative. Economics has to recognise this, but right now those decisions are basically beyond its ability to deal with: they're outside the area of the graph.

The third problem, and perhaps most important, is the line on the graph heading north-eastward. The economist's simple and entirely false assumption implicit in this simple arrow is that more always equates to better, and that furthermore, there is nothing to which this belief cannot relate. This, however, is not true. Not only can we tire of things, we are constrained as individual human beings and, on a broader level, as human beings living on a finite planet. Even though I recognise that economists have built such constraints into their more sophisticated work, and much as I also recognise that they argue that the whole purpose of studying economics is to learn how people decide how to allocate limited resource, the implicit notion that more is always better which this graph communicates is inherent within the whole logic of the neoclassical (and therefore neoliberal) economics. And it is this simple arrow that in turn drives the notion that growth is always good.

Therefore this simple assumption that more is better drives politicians' desire for increasing GDP, whatever its composition. The same assumption is the foundation of economics' endorsement of conspicuous consumption. It is the basis of the threat to our ability to sustain life on Earth. And all that arises from the weakness implicit in this graph that communicates so powerfully the core idea of this false economics, that our only goal as human beings is to increase our consumption and that nothing else matters.

What is more, the economists who use these graphs believe they can through them show how human beings can maximise that consumption. Even more bizarrely, they believe that once they have shown how to achieve that, the nirvana they predict is then maintained at the point they call 'equilibrium'. In other words, Utopia exists in the world of these economists and once we have found it we can have it forever, as if we lived in those fairy stories where once the Princess gets her man she lives happily ever after. The world of the economist really is that absurd, precisely because this concept of equilibrium – an optimal world where nothing changes – is the focus of a great deal of what they do. No wonder we're in a mess!

I reiterate, because I know that the challenge will be made, that this is a caricature of neoliberal and neoclassical economics (which are essentially the same thing – a point I again stress). But that is why I reiterate as well that this caricature is precisely what is important: every nuance, every development and every supposed reworking of the models of neoclassical, neoliberal economics to overcome these fundamental failings in the basic model simply disguise the truth, that at its core this model of the world is fundamentally flawed. That is why a new model of economics is needed, because the message of this old one has resulted in the mess we are in.

111

The basis for some alternative economic thinking

That new economics has to be based on something much more logical and readily comprehensible, which has to appear to reflect the realities we face in our lives and the situations we see in the world. It is that logic that is, I hope, apparent in the way of thinking about this issue that I suggest appropriate in the next few chapters of this book.

What I stress in offering this alternative is that it is something very different from the model I propose it should replace. It's so different I won't even use the term 'model' for it, because that's a term tainted by association with all that I am criticising. In particular, the neoliberal model has that term applied to it because it is intended that it be subject to mathematical manipulation. There's not a single formula in what follows, and that is for good reason. I have no intention that my thinking be limited by the constraints of maths, and most especially (and critically) the limitations of available data to which it can be applied.

That demand for mathematical modelling in neoliberal economics has necessarily restricted the thinking of the subject and the areas of human activity to which it can be appropriately applied. The result has been all too obvious. The areas of economic concern have become narrower and narrower. What is economic has increasingly become restricted to that which is exchanged in cash. And much, if not most, of what is important in life has fallen by the wayside in the process. The cost to us all has, literally, been immeasurable, but we can be equally sure, quite enormous.

The result of rejecting this whole methodology is that what follows is not a model as such – and so cannot be criticised using the criteria of existing economic models, which is good news, as they are so flawed. It is instead an exercise in thinking about economics in a new way. It is intended, of course, to be logical, but in saying that I am not suggesting it is intended to be provable in the way so many economists would like to suggest their models offer proofs that they would like to think equivalent to the natural sciences (which is, obviously, absurd). It is simply an explanation of how I view the economy and an explanation of the thinking that has underpinned my work. I make no more claim for it than that.

First, I suggest that economics has to recognise that we are not just economic beings: we are whole human beings. This is easily represented by the following diagram:

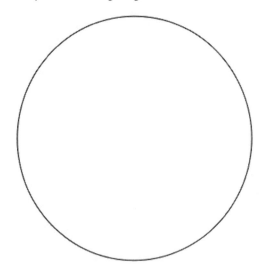

Yes, that's a circle. Here it represents a whole human being. What it shows is that while we are all rounded beings, with a wide range of interests, concerns and objectives, we are at the same time constrained in what we can do, hence the use of the circle to represent our finite limits. You can move in any direction in this diagram and you will find that action beyond a certain point is constrained: that's the reality of life. That is why a circle is the basis of the diagrams that follow.

The economic dilemma

It is important to recognise immediately that the world is made up of a wide range of economic entities: it is not just individuals that are important but families, friendships, businesses, clubs, compa-nies, government, international organisations and the world itself that matter and all are economic entities. Of course each differs from the others – just as all individuals are different – but what all the economic entities have in common is the potential to achieve the expectations of those who participate in them. Of course, they can also fail to do that. That is the economic dilemma.

Recognising potential

The achievement of potential is, I suggest, the goal of economic entities: the reasons why we fail to achieve our potential is the issue that requires explanation.

In what follows the core economic objective people is this achievement of potential: the reason for government involvement in the economy, which underpins the whole logic of this book, is that nothing guarantees that the widespread achievement of potential will happen but government intervention definitely helps it do so.

Some have said, and many have subscribed to the view that all people are born equal. The UN Declaration of Human Rights says in its first sentence: "All human beings are born free and equal in dignity and rights". The unfortunate reality is that the world does not live up to this promise. Whether by accident of geography or as a consequence of race, caste, gender, sexual orientation, disability, poverty and a range of other factors, equality is denied to people at the time of their birth, and forever thereafter. None of that is true, though, of a person's potential. None of these things that might discriminate against a person alters the inherent potential a person has to achieve. The outcomes resulting from that potential may be thwarted because of discrimination and for all the other reasons that this book explores, and the potential one person has to offer may be very different another, but nonetheless each person has this unique capacity to fulfil their potential. In that sense we are really born equal.

Each of us has the capacity to achieve that of which we are capable; distinct and unique as it might be. It is precisely because potential is unique in possessing these qualities that I use it as the basis for exploring here what we as individuals have in common. However, this use of a person's potential liberates the analysis that follows in other, quite fundamental ways. For example, whatever neoliberal economists say, their models have prescribed a view of the world where consumption is the uniform objective imposed upon human beings. Such a uniformity does not, however, exist. Potential has no such assumption within it: from the outset I recognise that people's potentials are fundamentally different. Some of the policy consequences that arise from this simple recognition of a basic truth will be explored in Part 3 of this book.

Next, potential is real. It is not some metaphysical objective like utility, which is the supposed goal of neoclassical economics, although no one knows what it is. Nor is it ephemeral like happiness, which is beyond our ability to compare or equate. The achievement of potential is about action. It only by doing things that potential is achieved. So, for example, everyone has the potential to learn. But achieving potential requires that people do learn. If they could learn more they have not achieved their full potential, but what they have done can be recognised. And we can do that not just for ourselves but for others: this is a tangible aspiration. Intangible benefits such as happiness may arise as a result of achieving potential: indeed, I am convinced they do. But something so ephemeral is no basis for assessing what takes a lifetime to achieve, only the achievement of potential allows that comparison to be made.

In addition, choosing the achievement of potential as the goal of an economy lets me overturn another of the perverse assumptions of neoliberal economists. They ascribe all their economic objectives to the individual: it appears to be their belief that we live a peculiarly solitary existence focused solely upon our own gratification, indifferent to the needs of others. The policies and attitudes resulting from their work certainly suggest this is a fair reflection of their thinking. But yet again, this is not true. Human beings can only function and even exist in community.

Of course, the nature of those communities differs for different people, different societies, at different times. The family is a fundamental unit in which many people coexist, but equally many build alternative and successful social arrangements that do not involve those who have a blood relationship with them. And just because the family and other social arrangements work well for the meeting of human emotional needs, the raising of children, the sharing of culture and much else besides, that does not mean that they are necessarily an appropriate basis on which many would wish to build viable working relationships aimed at producing goods and services for exchange with others by monetary means. For those objectives different communities are usually needed, which implies that we are capable of working in a wide variety of collective organisations, each of which can be adapted to many purposes. Any economic thinking has to recognise this and the compromises that these relationships demand of us, just as it must recognise why collectively we can hinder as well as encourage the achievement of potential. How and why this happens is of enormous consequence to us all.

My argument is quite straightforward: the Courageous State sets itself an ambitious goal and that is to help each and every person to achieve as much of their potential as they desire and want in the circumstances and communities in which they live and work. More than that, a Courageous State recognises that there are limits to its ability to achieve this outcome and that there are activities much better left to others. It takes courage to know this, to intervene when necessary and to back off when required, and to only intervene when it is appropriate to do so. This is the definition of courage that I use.

Defining potential

In saying this, it is vital that what I mean by 'potential' is appreciated. Potential is defined by the New Oxford American Dictionary as "having or showing the capacity to become or develop into something in the future". This is appropriate: of course economics is about hope. And of course economic objectives are about things getting better. More than that, those objectives should be about what is possible. Potential recognises possibility, not impossibility. But potential shows something else as well: that the achievement of potential is a matter of choice. No one obliges another person to achieve his or her potential: indeed, most of the time most of us will not do so. There is no utopia like 'equilibrium' in a realistic economics; there is only a reality that recognises

that all too often, and quite appropriately, we are entirely falli-
ble human beings who are more than happy to satisfice (in other
words, they simply say they've had enough rather than say they're
full!) and not maximise. That reality might make the maths of
neoclassical and neoliberal economics downright hard, if not
impossible. An alternative economics must not be constrained
by that fact: as Keynes noted eighty years ago, the maths of those
economists is wrong in any event because they ignore fundamental uncertainty. We need to move on from maths that constrains
our economic thinking.

The achievement of potential lets us do that. Potential is invariably described in relation to a specified objective. So, people
describe their potential earnings as a metaphor for the material standard of living they desire, or they relate potential to the
jobs to which they aspire, the vacation they want or the hopes
they have for their family. These ambitions are no doubt real. But
they are rooted in material issues: they relate to what we might
consume. Even when parents discuss their children it is all too
often in terms of the lifestyle they would wish for them.

Potential is, however, much broader in terms of its scope, and it
is time to recognise that as well. Potential is the limit of a person's
possibility. It is the best they can do. And people's aspirations in
this sense are not constrained to the material aspects of their lives,
important as that aspect is. Their wishes will also be for the well-
being of their family and its emotional health. They will also have
aspirations for their communities. To fulfil that communal wish,
people have a desire for the wide range of intellectual skills they
need to participate fully in society. Most of all, behind all this,
people desire a sense of purpose that gives them meaning in their
lives.

Economics has always concerned itself with the material aspects of life, and this book inevitably and appropriately
embraces that theme, in part. The other three themes mentioned
(emotion, intellect and purpose) are, however, alien to modern
economics. And yet they are core to a person's perception of their
well-being. It might be a little simplistic to say a person cannot
live by bread alone but it also happens to be true. To restrict

the subject of economics to the material dimension of life alone neuters its capacity to make useful input into some of the most important debates in the societies in which we live. In discussing potential in all these dimensions as a core economic concept this book seeks to liberate economics from that constraint.

In doing so, I consider the achievement of a person's potential in four key areas of their life:

1   Material well-being – the ability of a person and a community to live to capacity within the limits of the resources available to them.

2   Emotional well-being – their ability to relate to others meaningfully in the communities in which they live.

3   Intellectual well-being – the opportunity a person has to develop the skills and resources they need to fulfil their potential. At a broader level it represents the capacity of a society to develop coherent models for living that allow those who live within it to identify with that society while respecting the differences that will exist between the people living within it.

4   Purpose – I stress, this is not the same as religious faith, although some will explore this part of the life through that medium. Nor is it what Maslow called 'self-actualisation' – although it is related to it. Maslow said of self-actualisation: "A musician must make music, an artist must paint, a poet must write, if he is to be ultimately at peace with himself. What a man can be, he must be. This need we may call self-actualisation. It refers to the desire for self-fulfilment." But that requires two things: an understanding of what a person wants to be or even must be to achieve their potential, and the opportunity to do it.

Purpose embodies the idea that we have something to offer in life – that each of us, uniquely, has something to contribute and that if we don't do so then the world is a poorer place for it, as are we. This is about having a narrative that makes sense of what is to some extent inevitably unknowable within a lifetime and yet which must be resolved if life is to be lived to the full. Purpose can be readily differentiated from the intellectual. Intellectual pursuits are rational. Purpose is about what may be irrational but which is nonetheless the wholly real passion that drives a person to achieve. It is at the end of the day what gives a person's life meaning.

These four areas can be explained by examples, summarised in the following box that uses single words that might be associated with each of these aspects of life.

Material	Emotional	Intellectual	Purpose
Food	Family	Law	Wisdom
Heat	Friends	Tradition	Meaning
Shelter	Spouse	Custom	Belief
Transport	Children	Learning	Purpose
Entertainment	Company	Language	Drive
Possessions	Networks	Skills	Motivation
Holidays	Relationships	Teaching	Culture
Accumulation	Love	Qualification	Achievement

A person has to enjoy many of these things, and more, if they are to fulfil their potential.

Making sense of these ideas

Making sense of these issues is a challenge. I have chosen to do so diagrammatically. As noted already, I do not think maths is the ideal medium for doing this because it almost invariably restricts the scope of practical analysis and thinking to those areas where data is available, as has happened in the case of neoliberal economics. That would be a mistake. The alternative of using narrative alone would, I think, be cumbersome. And anyway, one of my objectives is to replace the awful graphs used, almost universally, to introduce people to the miserable subject of neoliberal economics. That is why I have adopted the approach that follows.

Putting potential on the map

If the achievement of potential is the objective of human beings – and therefore of economics – then it is explained diagrammatically in the simplest way possible. A person's potential can be shown as the circumference of the circle that represents that individual, as already noted above (see Diagram 8.1).

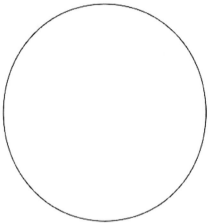

Diagram 8.1

As also noted, this diagram could in addition to representing an individual also represent a family, community, company, country, or the world itself. Each has the potential to achieve. It may represent a point in time: what could be done right now. More likely, it will represent possibility over a period of time. The point of the diagram is the same whichever circumstance is represented. Potential is always achievable. It is also always constrained. And it is always reached on the circumference of the circle.

The limit to potential

The lifetime of an individual is limited. There is only so much that can be achieved in that time.

Similarly, few dispute the world began and that it will end – it is finite. Ultimately there is an inevitable limit to all possibility.

120

This is what the boundary of the circle represents. It suggests that we do not have unlimited choice. We have to choose between the options available to us. Within those limits we have multiple goals. Each of us has real needs, and each of us has at the same time the potential to meet these needs in others as well as ourselves.

Our different needs

I have already suggested there are four groups of needs. They split the circle as shown in Diagram 8.2.

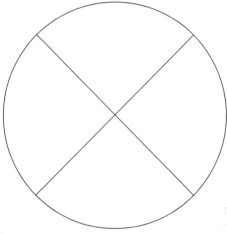

Diagram 8.2

The axes are deliberately diagonal: I cannot accept the idea that we might be back on the conventional economist's graph already. We're not. Each of these quadrants has equal positive value, but by using horizontal and vertical axes this might not be obvious.

Each quadrant represents a type of human need. One is for material well-being. We all need air, water, food, shelter, clothing, warmth, and more besides to survive. In our modern world we believe we need much more than that.

Another is for emotion. Just start with the needs inherent in a person's relationship with their mother and move on from there: there is no one who can survive as a healthy human being without effective emotional relationships.

Next there is a need for intellectual development. We all need language. We must learn to interact within the society in which we live. We are curious.

And, perhaps most contentiously, a person has a need for meaning. I call that their purpose.

You can lay them on the diagram as shown in Diagram 8.3 (using M = Material, E = Emotion, I = Intellectual and P = Purpose).

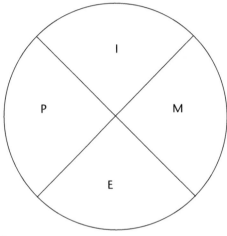

Diagram 8.3

The allocation of the quadrants is arbitrary. It's just the one I use. Another would do just as well.

Absolute poverty

Having created the quadrant methodology it needs more depth before it can become meaningful. First, there are two critical additional circles to draw. The first of these is tightly defined and will, for most people, appear insignificant because of its remoteness to their lives. This is an inner circle that indicates absolute life-threatening poverty. This might be caused by hunger, emotional isolation, an inability to communicate or the failure of your purpose: all can be life threatening (sometimes making people take their own lives). If a person's level of experience is reduced to this level of achievement then they are at imminent risk, even of death. Urgent action is needed.

This state of being is indicated by this inner circle, marked A (for 'absolute' poverty) in Diagram 8.4.

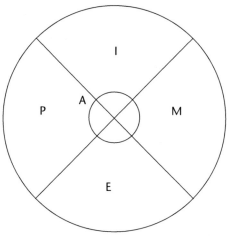

Diagram 8.4

Thankfully, for most people most of the time this is not an issue: they are surviving at a higher level than this. But we should never be in doubt that absolute poverty exists, and in the way defined here it is also prevalent within those countries and communities where there is material plenty. There are also, of course, far too many places in the world where absolute material poverty occurs and recurs all too often.

Relative poverty

That said, many will go through life without experiencing absolute poverty. But they can still be in what society would define as relative poverty; their well-being is below that which it is generally considered to be necessary to achieve a reasonable standard of living within their society.

The point on consideration is important: there is no doubt that this issue is in a sense subjective. Obviously, if only a few people had a mobile phone in a society then not having a mobile phone would not be a matter that could put a person in relative poverty. If, however, having a mobile phone was not only commonplace but a virtual prerequisite for accessing many of the activities in society then clearly not having a mobile phone would not just be an inconvenience, or the loss of a status symbol; this lack would reduce a person's potential to engage with others and to play a full role in their communities and broader society beyond them.

Subjectivity must therefore apply to relative poverty since there is no consistent standard around the world as to what it might be and yet at the same there is no doubt that within any society at any point in time it is clear that relative poverty is an absolute that can be appreciated by all who live and work there. What is more, relative poverty is intimately related to the definition of well-being used in this book: it is being denied the opportunity to participate as others can and do to achieve your potential.

People instinctively know when this denial of opportunity is happening to them. Having, or not having, a mobile phone is now an issue of relative poverty, especially for the young when so much of youth communication now revolves around social media. No less importantly, being denied access to decent education, to appropriate work, to reliable and timely healthcare, to suitable housing, to hope for your children and to leisure facilities and so much more when it is obvious others enjoy them are all measures of relative poverty.

These measures are, thankfully, understood by many who are not presently suffering from such problems. A Courageous State is led and is supported by empathic people with concern for others. As a result a Courageous State will always tackle relative poverty and the ways and means in which it can do this are addressed as this book develops.

It is equally true to say that cowardly states do not address relative poverty. Cowardly states realise that people can physically survive in conditions of relative poverty: that this is true is something I do not deny. They therefore choose not to address these issues and do not take action to ensure as many people as possible are taken out of relative poverty. This is an issue with consequences, however. When there is sustained relative poverty it means, by definition, that there is sustained relative prosperity: the two are corollaries one of the other. Either the relative abundance of some can be used to reduce the gap between the two in these relative positions, or it need not be.

Whether to tackle relative poverty or not is a matter of choice for any government. But it is not a choice without consequence, as will be noted in more detail later. The gap between the two groups (one relatively prosperous, the other not) and the relative difference between the two is likely to be a very accurate measure of the relative stability of a society. When too many are in relative poverty but many more enjoy relative well-being and the opportunity to achieve their potential social instability results. The evidence has been apparent in the UK in the summer of 2011. When relative prosperity is enjoyed by the vast majority, or even all in society – i.e. relative prosperity is eliminated – then stability results. All can enjoy their prosperity in peace. Inequality matters, in other words.

In that case, economic theory that ignores perceptions of well-being is not worthy of the name, as relative poverty is a crippling blow to a person's capacity to achieve their potential, which is why it is important. This justifies the addition of a second circle, between that which represents absolute poverty and that which represents a person's potential achievement. It is shown in Diagram 8.5 marked R (for 'relative' poverty).

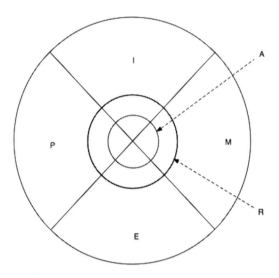

Diagram 8.5

There are now three concentric circles. The innermost circle, marked A represents absolute deprivation. The area that surrounds it, marked R represents relative poverty. The area between poverty and a person's potential represents, for now, relative abundance.

Achievement

All of which then begs the question, where am I on this diagram? Am I achieving, or not? After all, having some indication of achievement is a key part of economics: if it can't be done then there's little point in discussing the subject.

I suggest that achievement can be plotted on this diagram, but I would add straight away that this plotting is subjective. Individuals themselves might do it. Someone else could do it. In either case the result is subjective because the criteria for assessment will always be subjectively chosen in the first place. This, however, is not a criticism: it is a realistic assessment of all measurement tools in economics. Those who argue that there are objective measures available anywhere within economics are mistaken: all involve judgements, and all are to some degree relative, even if cash is involved. After all, cash itself has a relative and therefore subjective value.

This plotting process is helped by a desirable characteristic of a circle, which is that it offers an infinite number of radii that can be drawn within it. The reality is that out of the enormous range of choices available we will choose a very limited range of options to try. That is one of the characteristics of being constrained, if only by time, which this approach explicitly recognises. For each option that we try a radius could be drawn from the centre of the circle indicating the range of achievement we had reached. Analysis could be done on those choices. I am not pursuing that line of thought now, though. Instead, I want to draw a line joining a person's achievements together. This becomes their area of achievement. It might look like the area in Diagram 8.6 (and is described as C, the 'consequence' of actions).

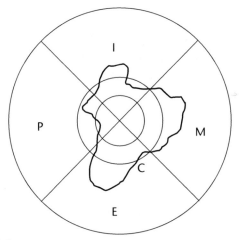

Diagram 8.6

This is a person who is materially sufficient: they have enough to live on. They are largely emotionally satisfied. They have only two areas of relatively limited emotional concern. Their intellectual life is constrained, but only partly. They are, however, suffering a substantial lack of purpose and this is creating a serious threat to their well-being because they have moved into an area of absolute deprivation.

This situation is easy to translate to the reality of life as we see it. There are very many people who are materially well-off and emotionally supported and who can apparently interact with society perfectly well who are nonetheless in crisis. The indication of this malaise in a person's spiritual well-being is relayed through anxiety, stress, mental ill-health and ultimately the threat of or actual practice of suicide.

The importance of the methodology presented here is immediately easy to see. Conventional economic models only relate to material well-being. My approach defines well-being in a very different fashion while (as I will show) being able to handle the issues that a conventional economic model addresses. The implications will be explored later. The importance should be noted now.

What the appraoch lets us do is assess relative well-being with comparative ease. For example, this person's life is obviously unbalanced, as shown in Diagram 8.7.

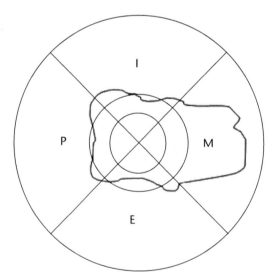

Diagram 8.7

They are clearly materially well-off, but despite that have very poor relationships. It may well be that their sense of meaning is diminished as a result. In popular jargon, it's likely they have a poor 'work / life balance'.

The reality is that once a person has escaped relative poverty they are almost certainly going to be better off when their activities result in reasonably balanced achievements. This could be explored mathematically but it can also be explored diagrammatically. The following diagrams suffice. The person whose areas of achievement are shown in Diagram 8.8 (which are now smoothed for ease of presentation and with area C, the consequence of action, being highlighted in bold) is better of than the person in Diagram 8.9.

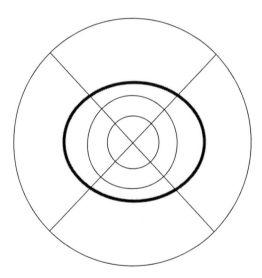

Diagram 8.8

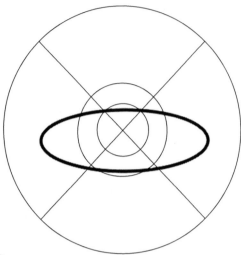

Diagram 8.9

The first person may not have the peak experiences that the second one does with regard to both purpose and material well-being but nor are they in relative poverty, or even life-threatening destitution in any area of their life, whereas the second person is in that situation.

In fact, it is also possible to say that the person in Diagram 8.8 is better off than the person whose position is shown in Diagram 8.10.

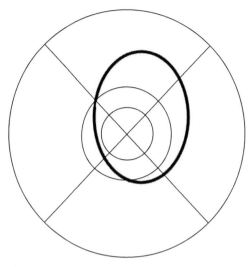

Diagram 8.10

Balance is best even when absolute poverty is avoided.

There is another important point to note before progressing. The way this diagram is drawn might imply that issues are only assessed with regard to their impact on a person's material well-being, emotional achievement, and so on, with each a matter of concern in isolation. That, of course, is not true. It is almost certain that all activities interact on all four levels of achievement at any time, if only on occasion to limited degree. The diagram might show attainment in each area as if each distinct activity was a radius from the centre in its own right but in fact any radius will be made up of an element of each activity, so looking something like this:

M	E		I	P

Representing this on a two-dimensional diagram would be decidedly difficult. The diagram used is an approximation to the truth that works, but it is always worth remembering that it is no more than that. The approach I am suggesting is a representation of a system, it is not the system itself.

It is therefore also important to note that an alternative representation of these ideas is also possible. A cross-section through the most basic diagram before any level of achievement is plotted offers a quite different perspective on this issue, shown in Diagram 8.11.

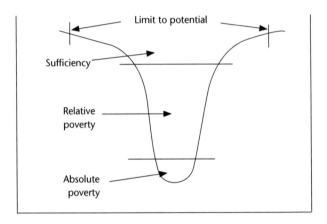

Diagram 8.11

The area of achievement can then be placed on this diagram, for example as in Diagram 8.12.

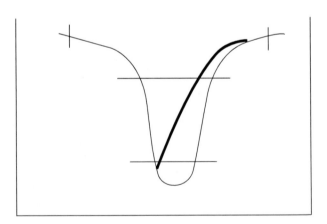

Diagram 8.12

The thick line represents the person's achievement, drawn from their purpose quadrant through to their material quadrant. It shows that in this case they move from deprivation with regard to purpose through to relative abundance in some parts of their material well-being.

It is obvious that a person with the situation shown in Diagram 8.13 would be better off than the person in Diagram 8.12.

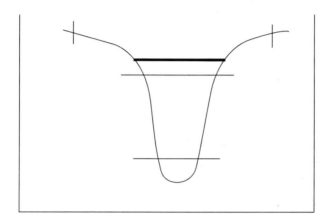

Diagram 8.13

They have, as the diagram makes clear, reduced their area of material achievement. But they have eliminated their area of deprivation and have improved those aspects of their life where they were in poverty. The trade-off is clear. The reason is obvious. The resources dedicated to their additional material well-being in Diagram 8.12 produce relatively little overall benefit (as shown by the small additional progress it makes on the vertical scale) whereas the benefit from foregoing some of that material well-being is substantial, yielding a very large increase in achievement on the vertical scale. As noted previously, balance is always better in these diagrams, as it also very often seems in real life.

Understanding the area of achievement

It is important to note that the area of achievement (C) is more complex than these diagrams imply. What we achieve is in fact a composite of interaction.

The number of interactions in which an individual can engage are, of course, enormous. An explanation like this is, however, like a map – it is not the terrain itself so it must abstract from reality to represent those issues of greatest importance. In this context there are a number of critical issues to consider which make up the area of eventual achievement, although I can only scratch the surface of this issue here.

To start with, it has to be appreciated that there is an area of achievement that represents the contribution a person would like to make to their well-being. This indicates what they want to produce, what they give they give to their communities, what they share with others and how they contribute to the achievement of purpose. This might look like Diagram 8.14.

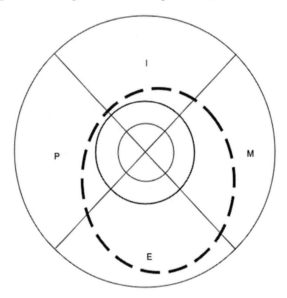

Diagram 8.14

This person has clear ambition to meet their needs in all areas, but with strong interest in providing material comfort and in fulfilling their emotional relationships. They might well be considered a person who takes their family responsibilities seriously.

That, however, is their ambition. There will be constraints on their ability to achieve. So, while it might be presumed the individual is themselves pushing outwards to achieve their potential (or as much of it as they desire once relative poverty has been avoided – because there is choice in this matter, and people are not by nature driven to maximise) then it is almost certain that this is not all that determines their achievement. What they achieve depends upon a range of further factors.

The first of these further factors is the help they get to achieve. Take as an example a child, who will have little chance to know themselves how to achieve their potential and will therefore be heavily dependent upon the interaction they have with others to help them do so. It is now widely recognised that a supportive family makes a massive difference to a person's well-being and that this benefit starts right in infancy. Similarly, whether or not parents can provide appropriate material support has a massive impact on development, as does what the state provides for the benefit of children. So there are choices to be made here. Children naturally want to learn, to communicate, to play, and most certainly want to be fed! They want to bond too: there is an obvious desire on their part to be loved. So while a young child may have relatively little idea as to what their purpose is (and the goal of education is to help them find that out, in my opinion) there is no doubt they have emotional and intellectual objectives that provide them with security – the closest thing to purpose they know when young. That means they do have drives that might well result in Diagram 8.14, with those drives being shown in Diagram 8.15.

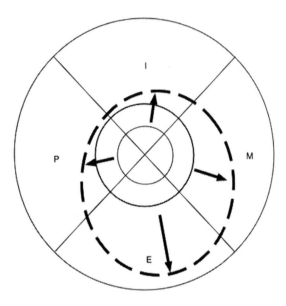

Diagram 8.15

But this result need not happen. The child may have the misfortune of having parents who do not care. Or the parents may not have jobs and the state may not provide sufficient support to ensure that the child lives in a situation where relative poverty is avoided. And the educational needs of the child – which we now know start at a very young age with need for play and social interaction – may not be met by the state supplying appropriate resources for the child to learn if their parents cannot afford to provide them.

So there could be real pressures from external sources that frustrate the ability of this child to achieve its potential, those pressures being shown in Diagram 8.16 as inward-facing arrows seeking to reduce the area of potential achieved, which of course they succeed in doing.

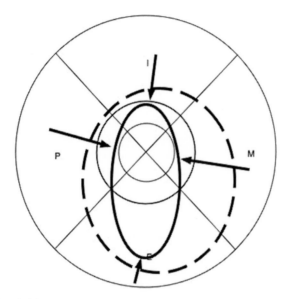

Diagram 8.16

The diagram suggests the parents here have done as well as they can but pressure from too few material resources, too little input from society in the form of education and even (and I think this possible at a young age) the sense of not being wanted that society can convey which can crush a person's purpose have all had their impact on well-being. The desire to achieve has been overwhelmed by external pressure.

Of course, external pressure need not be like that: it is entirely possible that it can be positive. Parents can push a child to believe what they did not believe themselves capable of, society can support those in relative poverty and make provision to ensure that there need be no such thing as child poverty and the state can supply all the educational support a child can need to ensure it can fully integrate in society and so find its purpose. The arrows of external pressure need not therefore all be negative; far from it, in fact.

The point, however, is immensely important: no one achieves their potential single-handedly. To do so, we all need the cooperation of others on occasion. To pretend otherwise is absurd; the myth of the self-made person is just that: a myth. And like it or not, Frank Sinatra did not do it all 'My Way'.

However, this also gives clear indication for policies that have to follow from this awareness. The relief of relative poverty is essential. The provision of opportunity for a person to use their own drive to succeed to their full ability is as vital. And at the end is the goal to build communities that are positive: the arrows all flow outwards, instead of ones with any, some or too many negative arrows that oppress. Of course there is no panacea: some people will not try to help themselves whatever happens, but I would suggest that is very rare. And we have to accept that human beings simply make mistakes – sometimes with telling consequences for others that take massive effort to correct. Both those are statements of reality, but they excuse nothing. The role of the Courageous State is to build environments in which the state and society at large helps beat poverty in all its forms and goes on to help people fulfil as much of their potential as possible.

In saying that it's also important to remember that balance is always better once poverty in all its forms is avoided. If those surrounding an individual can enhance what the individual has to offer and encourage them to flourish, they will clearly all be better off. This is not a process of give and take, this is a win:win. There is no zero sum game here. The diagrams, which could of course apply in many different situations in life and are not just applicable to a child make that clear, I hope, but if in doubt Diagram 8.17 shows a situation where the external influence of others is additional to what the individual might achieve themselves.

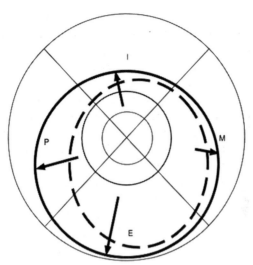

Diagram 8.17

The same dashed area of achievement that the individual might have secured for themselves is still shown, as it has been throughout this series of diagrams, but now it is clear that because of their positive interaction with others they achieve more than they might have considered possible. This is what happens in a Courageous State: it is the result of the synergy of working together rather than in oppressive ways.

What the diagrams also, I hope, make clear is that if my belief that the goal of human life is to achieve one's potential is right then you seek to explore the possibilities available to you to the full within the constraints placed upon you. That means that logically, you would want your area of achievement to approach the outer circle of your limit of possibility, whether you do that alone or with the assistance of others.

The clear implication of the approach being proposed here is that in Diagram 8.18 the solid bold area is better for the person who enjoys it than the dashed area: it is not just that they appear to have more, they have come closer to fulfilling their potential for achievement, and that is their aim.

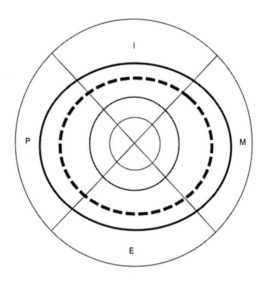

Diagram 8.18

But both are better than any area involving poverty. Both these areas represent limited stress: poverty involves stress. Such stress both motivates the Courageous State to intervene, but it can also cause festering harm if left to continue.

The limits to potential

This begs the question, what is the real limit to potential? Saying that anyone is limited in what they can achieve is one thing, but what is the practical implication of that?

Obviously, to some degree we are constrained by our finite nature. It is important to recognise that fact, just as it is also important to realise that the constraint on our achievement is also externally imposed upon us. Unconstrained possibility is simply not on the economic agenda because the simple reality is that we cannot consume without limit. The world is finite. It began, and it will end, and that means that at any point of time there are limited renewable resources available for use. They are determined by the ability of the world to convert the sun's energy into usable resources without constraint being imposed upon the ability to do this sustainably in the future.

People are part of the resource available for this task of energy conversion into life-sustaining activity. We are not alone though. The whole biostructure plays a part in this goal. As such it is part of the economic equation.

Importantly, that equation of conversion is not fixed in a number of ways, and most especially by the second law of thermodynamics that relates to entropy. Entropy represents the amount of energy in a system that is no longer available for doing mechanical work. As energy changes from one state to another some is lost in the exchange. That energy is then no longer available for further useful purpose. Entropy is as a result the enemy of sustainability.

If entropy increases in a period then sustainability reduces. This limits the capacity to repeat this process. If people are concerned for the long term, and there are signs that some at least are, then a reduction in sustainability has an impact on their intellectual and emotional well-being, and their sense of purpose. It may also have an impact on material well-being if action to counter the effects of the increased chaos resulting from the reduction of order in natural systems (for example, the need for flood defence mechanisms) has to be taken.

The limit to our capacity is, therefore, reduced if entropy rises. Entropy rises if excessive energy is released in a form that cannot be used again. That process of entropy can, however, be slowed. Recycling can slow it. So can more efficient conversion of energy. Both are of benefit because they reduce the rate of decline in the world's systems since entropy is irreversible.

Before this all sounds too depressing it is also important to note that capacity can also be increased. That is possible if understanding is created which allows for a permanent improvement in the methods used to convert energy into use. Advances in understanding, fuelled by increases in learning and the willingness of society to embrace the necessary changes to use the resulting processes, can have this effect. Sustainability might then be defined as a position where the improvement in knowledge in a period was enough to counter the entropy caused by the consumption of physical resources that release energy in the course of that process during the same period. This is shown in Diagram 8.19.

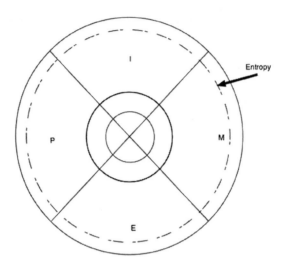

Diagram 8.19

Entropy has reduced capacity from the previous outer circle of a previous period (which is the outer solid line) to the new inner circle, which is dashed. At the same time increases in knowledge can have the effect given in Diagram 8.20.

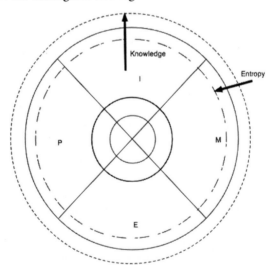

Diagram 8.20

Knowledge (shown, of course, within the area of intellectual activity, just as material entropy is shown within the area of material activity) has pushed capacity above levels previously known because increased efficiency is now being created within energy systems that reduce waste both now and for the foreseeable future. If the effect of entropy is matched by the effect of increased knowledge then the result is sustainable, assuming only the resources of the period are considered.

None of this alters the fact that the calculation of the limit to the world's capacity at a point of time would be complex. Variables in the equation would include some things to which we simply do not know the answers (which adds somewhat to the complexity of the calculation!). Perhaps most significantly, we do not know the relative age of the world at this point in time. If it is now 99.9% through its period of human habitation we need not worry too much about human exploitation of resources: there will be enough to go round for all of us who remain so long as we are (and I have a suspicion that this is true) largely indifferent to the sustainability of other life forms after humans have ceased to be.

If on the other hand, the timespan for humans on earth is somewhat longer than that, then we might well take a very different view. The state of biodiversity, the number of people on earth, the amount of energy we might receive from the sun and our ability to convert it for use, the state of our knowledge, both technical and in the form of wisdom (which I think is much undervalued) have impact, and so on. I'll not seek to develop formulas to link all these issues (and doubt my expertise to do so or their value if it were possible, since any conclusion may be spuriously accurate): suffice to say that, however they work out, it is very clear that at any point in time we will only have claim upon a very limited proportion of the material resources of the world if we are to leave the world intact for those future generations we hope will follow us.

In that case it is obvious that if we define our limit to achievement as being what is possible when making the best use of the resources available to us subject to the external constraints that are imposed upon us by our own finite nature and the finite nature of the world, if we are to leave future generations with the same opportunity to achieve that we ourselves enjoy then seeking to fulfil our potential within that constraint is not something that puts us in conflict with the finite world but instead requires that we work with that finite world to realise the best that is possible in life. Seeking more within the constraints of the circle drawn here is not therefore a negative exercise – it is a positive one of achieving personal potential in a way that does not cause harm.

Two further points should be made. First, if this is the case the available resources of the world should be allocated equally subject to the impact of geography, which is a necessary component factor in distribution of the benefit of those resources.

The second point informs the first, and is that no one has an a priori claim to well-being over another person, which is a way of saying that equality of opportunity is vital, even if equality of outcome cannot be achieved. If this assumption is extended to the future, as well as the present, then the duty to act sustainably is obvious.

Given these assumptions it follows that there is a fixed material amount of resource we may each enjoy at a point in time. That in turn defines a practical limit to material achievement for each and every one of us, without exception, at that point in time.

Working within our limits

So what, you might ask? Does the fact there are limits to the material consumption that we might enjoy constrain our emotional and intellectual achievements or impact upon our purpose? In theory it does not. But there is a much more practical constraint on these: our own predispositions and abilities define the constraints of our own achievement in these areas. We can approach, and might even occasionally reach our potential in all three areas but we can do no more than that, for if we suggested otherwise we would simply have incorrectly defined our limits. In fact, therefore, in all three of these quadrants our individual achievement will always be within the constraints of the outer circle that indicates the limits of our potential, even though as I noted above, collectively the development of new knowledge can expand capacity over time.

That collective observation does not change the fact that individually we cannot over-consume emotionally or intellectually, nor with regard to our purpose. This is not, however, true of our potential to consume material goods. Here we do not know the limit of our own ability. We can waste that which should reasonably belong to others. We can consume that which should belong to generations that should follow us, knowingly or unknowingly. But however we look at it, we can actually do what is shown in Diagram 8.21.

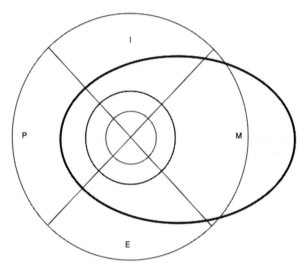

Diagram 8.21

This is important, and is a recurring theme of what follows. First, the fact that we can consume more than we should if we are to act either equitably or sustainably has consequences. We remain finite, even if we consume more than we should. That excess consumption does not create 26 hours in a day. It does not mean we can either receive more from or give more to our emotional relationships. In fact, the reverse is likely. The time spent consuming material goods does not just create waste in the sense that others are deprived of what is rightfully theirs: it denies us the chance to do all we might to achieve a balanced lifestyle. I propose something quite simple: to the extent that we over-consume materially we constrain our ability to achieve in other aspects of our lives. Diagram 8.22 shows this.

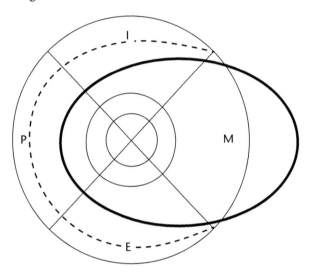

Diagram 8.22

The dashed line shows that the area of intellectual, purposeful and emotional achievement has been constrained by having sought to consume to over-capacity in the material area. And, the more we over-consume the more the relative impact of that constraint is, I suggest. That is because of a simple rule well known to conventional economists, called the law of diminishing marginal returns. This is not a perfect rule: it is a way of thinking and like all abstractions from reality it has flaws, but within reasonable limits it holds true. It says that as one has more of something (anything, it does not matter what) the value you attribute to each additional unit you have of that thing falls.

Basic instinct says that this is usually true. Diagram 8.23 clearly demonstrates the impact, drawn as a cross-section.

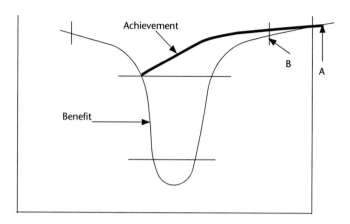

Diagram 8.23

This person is consuming at a point where they still perceive a gain from doing so since their benefit curve is still rising at the point where their achievement line reaches it on the righ-hand side (which in this case is in their material quadrant). However, at some other points they are not achieving much over a level of relative poverty, as this diagram also shows. They are not in balance. This result means that they could always achieve an over-all gain for their well-being if they were to forego some of their excess material achievement in exchange for benefit elsewhere because as the diagram makes clear, they suffer steadily diminishing returns from increased consumption in any area. So if point A is what they consume and point B is their limit to sustainable achievement, then because the gradient of their benefit line above point B is always shallower than that below it they will always benefit by substituting achievement above point B in the material area for achievement below it in another.

The result is that over-consumption gives rise to an increase in material well-being and yet a loss in the overall sense of well-being. It is a phenomenon well known among those now observing developed economies. And what is most important is that we are worse off as a result.

Which leads to the final conclusion of this section, that the optimal position for a person must be as in Diagram 8.24.

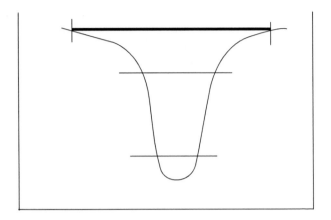

Diagram 8.24

At this optimal point they have reached the limit of their potential in all areas, they have abundance to the limit of their capacity
to enjoy it and the spread of that fulfilment is equidistant in all
directions. Drawn another way, this optimal position occurs as in
Diagram 8.25.

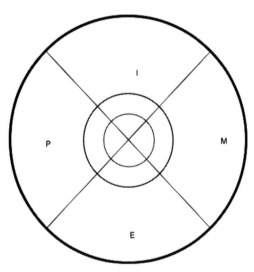

Diagram 8.25

The limit of achievement is the same as the potential for achievement. The person has achieved their capacity for fulfilment. This can only happen if the diagram is circular.

If that is so, an optimal position for a person has been defined. The obvious question to ask is, why isn't this achieved?

CHAPTER 9

THE PROBLEMS CAUSED BY OTHER PEOPLE

How to achieve our potential

I showed in Chapter 8 that we have the potential to achieve and a capacity limit on what we can actually achieve. We can exceed that capacity for material consumption. We cannot do so in the rest of our activities. But how do we determine what we achieve? Why is that it we do not all exist in an optimal position? Why, when we have potential to do better do some live in poverty, or worse still, in situations of absolute deprivation? And why is it possible that someone, who appears to have it all in the material sense that society so readily notices, can be so unhappy? When that happens why do those people appear unable to correct the situation? These are key questions for economics. In due course they are also the questions that lead to the justification for government involvement in the economy by a Courageous State.

The answer is, of course, that most people left to their own devices would seek to achieve their potential. But we are not left to our own devices, as noted in Chapter 8. This of course can be of benefit. It would be hard to achieve our goals otherwise. For example, emotional well-being is difficult to achieve in isolation. That is the positive aspect of living in a community. The

151

negative aspect is that while people can provide opportunities for well-being they also provide threats.

The threat from other people is real. There are scarce resources. Other people want them. People vie for our affection, and withdraw as well as extend their own. Societies can define who can and cannot participate in activities on the basis of criteria that are not always rational or fair. As a result they can deny us the opportunity to achieve our intellectual potential. And we may simply fail to identify with the world in which we live, as defined by the mutual beliefs, understandings and goals that identify the social groups through which we might achieve our purpose.

There are two ways to look at this. First, we need to redraw the basic diagram from Chapter 8 to recognise that people do not live in isolation, but in communities. This is a straightforward exercise, the result shown in Diagram 9.1.

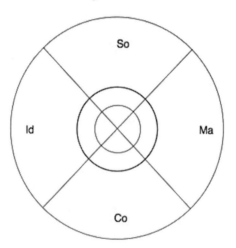

Diagram 9.1

The previously identified areas have been renamed. *Ma* is the material economy and relates to the *material well-being* of the individual. It, of course, is consistent with the area M which represented the individual's well-being.

Co stands for 'community' and represents the body of relationships in which individuals look for their *emotional well-being*.

So represents society, and is the formal structure that defines the broader rules of engagement between an individual and the wider world at large, whether it be language, or law, or education and the standards set for them. To participate in all these relationships the individual does of course have to engage in *intellectual activity*.

Id represents identity. If P represents purpose in the representation of an individual then identity represents those roles to which they relate and of which they are a part, be they obvious ones such as their nationality or their country of origin, or which are personal to them such as gender or sexual orientation, or those that are chosen, such as faith. However defined, this identity will help them formulate the standards which allow them to establish their meaning or purpose beyond themselves and so place them in the broader narrative of life which can never be wholly comprehended, but to which we must relate if we are to enjoy well-being. This is obviously closely related to issues such as culture and wisdom.

This diagram looks like that of an individual but it is not the same. It is that of a collective: a group of people. Of course, any collective is porous. People will belong to overlapping collectives. So, a work organisation will have employees in common, but many of those employees will have unconnected family lives. That is inevitable. But if the diagram is used for an identifiable community, that is acceptable. And if it is used for an aggregated community, for example a village, town, region, country or other grouping of size, that too is acceptable. The aggregate simply requires that the degree of overlap between groups is sufficient for any representation to be valid. This is a way of thinking, after all, and not a literal representation.

This suggests it is possible to have a model for a community of which a person is a member. In that case, it is also possible to link the two, which takes forward some of the ideas explored in Chapter 8 in a slightly more formal way. In effect, the diagrams of the individual and community can be layered, one on the other, to show the synergistic impact of one on the other. That is not to suggest the individual and the organisation are synonymous; it suggests that, very obviously, they relate to each other. The result is, however, a combination of three factors. The first is the desire of the individual to achieve. They will wish to push their area of achievement out as far as possible, as shown in Diagram 9.2.

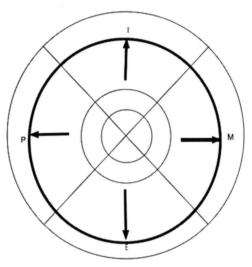

Diagram 9.2

This individual is seeking to achieve more of their potential by interaction, as the arrows represent.

The world with which they interact can help them to do that. By sharing work, dividing labour, exchanging what each person does best, material, intellectual and emotional well-being can be increased, with purpose being realised as a consequence. This has been understood since time immemorial and in economic theory (at least with regard to material activity) since Adam Smith wrote about it more than two hundred years ago.

A family or other social group can support a person, provide them with the confidence they need to face the world, make them feel good about themselves, and be cherished. Or it can simply entertain them. In combination, their emotional well-being can rise.

A society can provide opportunity for a person. Teach them, provide them with security, encourage their intellectual development, provide the means to communicate effectively and protect the right to do so, and more. This lets them explore the society they live in to its potential.

A confident community identifies the purpose it is seeking to fulfil. If a person can share those goals, openly and with doubt if necessary, then they can relate to that purpose and let it inspire their own life. That nourishes their intangible purpose.

That is the positive aspect of community. It creates Diagram 9.3, which looks like that for the individual but which represents the goal of the community for that person.

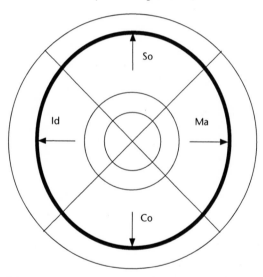

Diagram 9.3

Society in this case is seeking to empower the person. Both the individual and society are working in harmony to enhance well-being.

But society need not do that. Markets do not distribute well-being equally. People do not come to markets with equal resources, be they accumulated wealth, or goods or the services they have to offer in exchange. Some locations suffer special problems caused by geography, meaning that access costs deny much of the opportunity to benefit from the material resources of the world, oppressing those who live there. Markets do not work on the basis purely of price information. Power has influence on the process of exchange. It can distort the distribution of the benefit of exchange so that some get less than their share, and others more. The result is that the process of exchange can be blatantly unfair, and oppress as a result.

Communities, whether of families, friends or wider networks, can support and uphold people. But they can also oppress them, deliberately or inadvertently. They can even place barriers on a person extending their range of emotional support. The cost to the person who suffers the restraint can be considerable.

Societies can empower people. They can also use law to oppress people. They can deny them the right to do things. They can create obstacles to a person's achievement. They can prevent learning happening. They can deny access to power or any form of participation in it.

Communities of which a person is a member, whether a national grouping or faith, can uplift. But they too can lose their way. When they do, they can confuse or alienate the individual. Worse, they can mislead them and persuade them to act contrary to the best interest.

When these things happens society acts against the individual, as shown in Diagram 9.4.

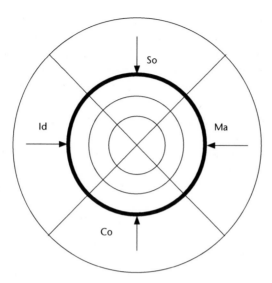

Diagram 9.4

The individual is now being denied opportunity by the world in which they live.

The reality is that all these things can happen at once, and usually will. There will be supportive and oppressive aspects of societal behaviour affecting the individual at all times, and the net impact upon the individual's ability to achieve their own goals can be either positive, or negative in total. The Courageous State will obviously seek to make those impacts positive. The two opposing forces that the individual and the Courageous State must address as they are in conflict are shown in Diagram 9.5.

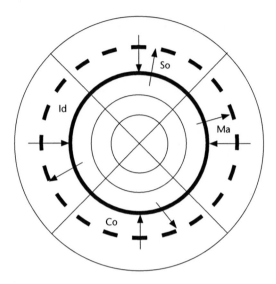

Diagram 9.5

The dashed, outer line shows what society and the person are trying to achieve. The inner line shows the pressure which might stop them doing so.

Of course, the reality is that both lines will be decidedly uneven in shape. Each radius represents a distinct and unique activity. The lines of achievement as drawn here represent the joining together of the extremities of those radii the individual chooses to pursue and the radii that are curtailed by the action of society. On occasion these will directly conflict. The individual wants a material possession they cannot have, or they wish to pursue a course of action which society deems unacceptable for them. In this case there will be a head-on collision of wills:

Quite often, they will be different radii. The individual might successfully pursue an objective, but the benefit they achieve from it might be curtailed by an obligation imposed upon them by others. Then the radii will overlap in opposite directions:

The net result may be the same in terms of well-being in each case: when these forces oppose the individual cannot achieve what they wished.

Of course, that may be desirable: what the individual wants to do may be simply antisocial. It might have been deemed illegal. It may just be something that social taboo deems unacceptable. In many ways constraint in such cases, while seeming to harm the individual, will result in an overall net gain for the community and society at large. One person's constraint is quite often many people's source of support when seeking to achieve their potential. It is the role of a Courageous State to exercise judgment on such issues. The important point is that the interactions of an individual with society are a combination of positive and negative factors. The net outcome of those factors will be our achievement; where we get to with the help of some and despite the hindrance of others, having taken into account the force of those relative pressures, will in turn also encourage or hinder our own will to expend effort and therefore impact on our desire to achieve our full potential.

Choosing what to achieve

Knowing that we can achieve is one thing. Knowing that there are constraints on us doing so is another. Choosing what to achieve is as important. Choice is essential. The human being is finite. It is not possible to do everything and, thankfully, the human capacity to achieve their potential can easily be achieved without doing everything that is possible, something that is not sufficiently appreciated.

When choosing what to do, a person is seeking to achieve as much of their potential as possible. This is true of all decisions. In this sense there are no 'buy' or 'sell' decisions. That is a wholly artificial divide. So too is the divide between transactions which involve money (of which more later) and those that involve direct exchange, which are the majority for the simple reason that much cannot be supplied any other way. The individual does not rationally seek to worsen their lot. As such, in any transaction they will only seek to expand their area of achievement, as shown before in Diagram 9.2 which represents an optimal transaction that has improved a person's achievement in all areas. Few will have that balanced effect. I suspect most people might think the situation shown in Diagram 9.6 more likely.

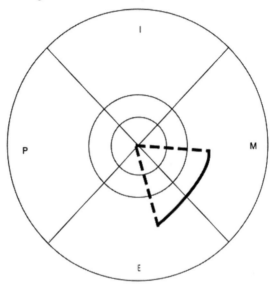

Diagram 9.6

This transaction has improved the achievement of abundance by this person in their emotional and material quadrants. It has apparently had no noticeable effect at all on their purpose or emotional well-being. However, that is, as has previously been noted, unlikely. There are two reasons for this. First, as already argued, most transactions will have some impact on all four quadrants, however small some impacts might be: as such this diagram is exceptionally unlikely to be of much use.

Second, this transaction appears to only have positive outcomes. Again, this is very unlikely. Most transactions involve a degree of trade-off. There may be a gain and a loss. For example, fruitful work will involve advantage in all areas of life, but even the most rewarding of jobs requires sacrifice for many people. For example, a parent has less time with their child then they might wish. A compromise is involved: in the pursuit of material well-being emotional benefit is foregone. This can be shown diagrammatically as being a change on the person's position of achievement as the result of the transaction. They might start in the position shown in Diagram 9.7.

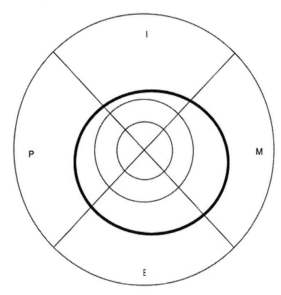

Diagram 9.7

Further to undertaking the transaction, their position improves as a result of the benefits secured to the position shown in Diagram 9.8 (the scale being exaggerated in all likelihood for the sake of demonstration).

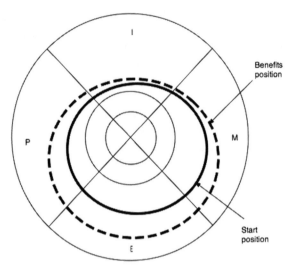

Diagram 9.8

The benefits should always improve a person's position or there will be no reason for doing the transaction.

There may well, however, be negatives from the transaction and these are described in Diagram 9.9.

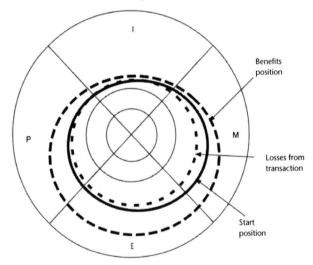

Diagram 9.9

In this case the transaction has not impacted on intellectual well-being or purpose in any significant negative way. Material well-being in a different form from that secured has, however, been foregone to secure the benefits obtained, as has also been the case emotionally.

As the figure makes unambiguously clear in this case, the losses from undertaking this transaction have been far exceeded by the benefits. It was clearly worth doing. But it is only by considering the totality of the human experience of the transaction that this can be determined. In isolation, no quadrant can be a guide to the benefit to be obtained from a transaction. Nor can any transaction be seen solely as a 'buy' or a 'sell' deal. The split personality of conventional economics that considers people on some occasions to be suppliers and on other occasions to be purchasers is simply wrong. All transactions engage the whole person and should benefit that whole person, if they act rationally.

There are, however, reasons why a person may not behave rationally. Outcomes do not match expectations as a result. How these impacts affect people will be considered next. Only when that has been done can the overall impact of decisions be considered.

CHAPTER 10

CASH AIN'T KING

The value of money

Most people will think that economics is about money. So far this subject has been almost completely ignored in this book. That is rightly so. Transactions that involve money are only a part of an economy. They are probably a smaller part than those involving non-cash exchanges. The bigger picture has, therefore, been looked at first. Money, however, cannot be ignored.

It has to be stressed that money does not represent in itself an area of achievement. Money is effectively worthless unless it can be exchanged. It is of course also a measure and a store of value between periods. Ultimately, however, the measure is one of exchange value and the store of value is worthless if it cannot be realised in exchange.

It is therefore worth asking what gives money its value. Once it was scarcity value. That is no longer the case. The vast majority of money is now created at will by banks. They do this by extending credit to a person. In doing so they effectively do two things. They put money into a person's bank current account so that they might spend it. At the same time they create a loan account for that individual to record the sum that they then owe to the bank. The two are equal and opposite sums. They add up to nothing. There was no cash before the person asked for and was given a loan and in net terms immediately after the loan is created there is exactly the same amount of cash in existence as there was beforehand: adding up the loan made and the current account balance comes back to zero once again. This might seem an obscenely simple explanation and yet about 97% of all money is now created in this way and all of it by commercial banks. Only 3% of money is created by the government in the UK in the form of notes and coins and the ratio is probably little different elsewhere, at least in developed countries. The rest is made out of thin air. Which also results in another incredibly important, and to many people quite shocking realisation, which is that what banks lend has at least in theory nothing to do with what is deposited with them. And it is also worth remembering that in almost every case the deposits made with banks were in any event originally created by bank lending. The only reason they have to keep any cash back is to prevent a run on the bank (something we thought long gone until Northern Rock revived the art), but it's only ever a small part of total lending held in this way.

What is extraordinary in that case is that banks charge interest for the use of the cash that they generate in this way that is, effectively, costless to them, but what this does prove is that the value of money is clearly not related to its intrinsic worth. This has to be true because it is created in a process that generates no value. Its value must instead be related to the acceptance of the obligations inherent in that process of creating money: an obligation on the part of the bank to settle the sum owing to the person who is paid from the sum credited to the current account, and the obligation of the borrower to settle the sum due to the bank.

By definition, both of these promises are what might be considered incomplete transactions when the totality of the economy is taken into account. It is the outstanding promise to pay what that money represents that underpins its value. Money (the vast majority of which is, after all, just an entry in a computer ledger) does not by itself provide that value. The expectations pinned to the transactions creating the money do that. The transaction involving the current account is, after all, underpinned by a belief that a future benefit will arise as a result of the spending made out of the sum borrowed which will more than justify having incurred the promise to repay the resulting debt. The value of the loan account is only justified by the belief that the loan will be repaid. If both propositions hold true, this money has value and it's quite fair in fact to generalise this proposition. Money gets its value from being debt and it retains it (in most cases) if debt in general is repaid in the amount anticipated, and loses it if there is the prospect that debt will not be repaid. To put it another way, money in general retains its value so long as transactions are completed. It loses its value when transactions are not completed in the envisaged form, or for the amount anticipated.

Money and the real economy

This gives rise to the obvious question of how money relates to the real economy that has been described so far in this book in which individuals seek to achieve their potential. At the level of the individual the money economy may look something like Diagram 10.1.

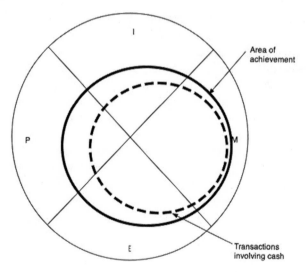

Diagram 10.1

To avoid complication, the areas of deprivation and poverty have not been shown. These are absolute measures in any case, and are only indirectly related to money.

In this diagram money transactions form a subset of the transactions as a whole that the person undertakes. The subset is wholly contained within the area of achievement, although occasions when that might not be the case will be noted later.

The area of cash transactions is biased towards the material quadrant. That is likely to be true. Money can be and is expended in pursuit of the other objectives, but in the developed nations of the world few now grow and many don't even cook their own food; heat and light are purchased as is clothing and shelter and most transport involves cash exchange, walking seemingly being an unknown activity for many. Material activity is therefore the most likely to be dominated by cash transactions. The other three quadrants are not. Money, as in the song, can't buy you love; intellectual achievement requires some home-grown graft and purpose cannot be purchased. The bias in the diagram is deliberate.

This diagram is, however, but a starting point. It is, of course, possible for an individual to spend more than they have. What does that do to the diagram? What this implies is that, as the discussion of the way in which value is attributed to money suggests, the individual has 'incomplete' transactions – i.e. value has been secured but not paid for. There are two implications. The first is that the person has consumed more than they were able to based on the limit of capacity available to them. The alternative is that they have borrowed to acquire an asset that will have lasting benefit. The diagrams look different in each case. If the individual has simply over-consumed then the picture looks like Diagram 10.2 in the first instance.

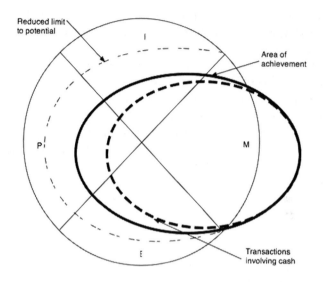

Diagram 10.2

It should be stressed that areas may be exaggerated to make the point clear.

The first point to note here is that the impact of overspending on material consumption is seen in a reduced capacity to fulfil potential in other areas of human activity. The reasons for that were explained in Chapter 8.

Second, when looking at an individual who is over-consuming before the impact of interest is taken into account it is highly likely that the transactions giving rise to that over-consumption will take place using money. That is not necessarily so: material over-consumption without the use of cash is not impossible because in this quadrant the limit to capacity is defined by the ability of the world to sustain itself despite the consumption the individual makes over time. It has to be possible that this capacity could be breached without the use of money. Equally, it has to be said that this is unlikely: we are all physically constrained and finite. As a result, where we observe communities that use little cash we observe vastly lower levels of material consumption than those generally found in money-based economies. I am not saying those levels of consumption are desirable, sustainable, or otherwise. All I am noting is that the more we depend on our own efforts, the lower our likely level of material consumption will be, and therefore if there is over-consumption then that is likely to be associated with cash transactions.

Third, this over-consumption in cash has future consequences. Time is, inevitably, a factor in any equation with regard to money. If all transactions were concluded with a complete exchange of value for everyone involved taking place at the time that they occurred there would be no use for money. That is the definition of a barter economy. Money exists precisely because transactions are not completed immediately, and involve a promise to make settlement in the future that creates debt.

That, as already noted, is how money gets its value. However, that also means that the static analysis of the impact of over-spending in one period is insufficient if the consequences are to be understood. The implication of Diagram 10.2 is that a person can materially over-consume and there are no consequences barring the reduction in their potential to achieve their emotional and intellectual well-being or to realise their purpose during the course of the period in question. That, however, is only true if the over-consumption of material goods arose out of cash already in their possession arising from previous under-consumption, allocated to this activity in the current period, i.e. the overspend was paid for out of savings that arose for that reason. That pattern of behaviour, it must be stressed, can be sustainable.

If, however, and has certainly been the more common case in recent years, the over-consumption arose out of borrowing of bank-created money with no previous under-consumption to compensate for it, then this is a much more serious situation. Unsustainable behaviour may be taking place, and the action giving rise to it will, because it puts the person out of balance with themselves, result in a reduction of their potential well-being assuming that they would otherwise have opted for a more balanced approach to the achievement of their potential. Cash certainly assists and permits this over-consumption, but why it encourages it needs deeper explanation. The reason why people might make this apparently irrational choice to spend in unbalanced fashion has, then, to be considered before the consequences of that action arising out of borrowing, with the many implications that flow from it, can be considered.

Over-consumption relative to capacity

There are a number of quite obvious reasons why anyone might over-consume compared to their capacity. Perhaps most relevantly, they may simply be unaware of the limit to their capacity, and it has to be acknowledged that this risk will, of course, exist because we simply do not know enough to be sure precisely what is and is not sustainable behaviour at this point of time. As previously noted, if we assume the world will only last a few more years, then just about any level of activity is sustainable and any amount of consumption of natural resources can be justified. On the other hand, if we have very long-term concerns for sustainability it is entirely reasonable to think that the preservation of natural resources for use by future generations, given that we do not know likely trends in knowledge or how changes in resource utilisation might progress, is totally rational and as such we should assume that capacity is limited at this point in time. On that basis we would take heed of many environmentalists who suggest we are, at least in developed countries, seriously over-consuming compared to the capacity of the world to sustain our current material demands.

The point is accepted that this is, inevitably, a matter of judgment and that a range of possibilities must exist, but if current evidence of global warming, resource depletion, environmental degradation and other matters are taken into account, many people in developed countries must be over-consuming. That poses the question that if this is the case, why are we doing so and why do we allocate so much cash to the process when it would appear to be rational for us to allocate it to other activities which might actually increase our well-being more than the material consumption in question, based on the analysis already presented here?

There seem to be two answers to this. The first is the tendency, again already noted, that Thorstein Veblen identified for some human beings to over-consume as a result of the apparent innate desire to differentiate themselves from others in their communities.[1] It has to be accepted that for some this appears to be a part of the human condition. This tendency has, however, been massively commercially exploited. The enormous increase in material consumption over the last fifty years, recorded and analysed in some depth by Juliet Schor in her book Plenitude,[2] cannot be explained by more people having accidentally discovered conspicuous consumption during the course of that period. There has to be a reason for this rapid change in behaviour, and that reason, I suggest, is advertising.

The influence of advertising

The nature of advertising has to be understood. Advertising is not the neutral act of informing market participants of the qualities of the products that might be available to them, as economists would like to think it is. Instead, advertising and its related activities of marketing and market research create the opportunity to sell those things for which need (let alone desire) does not exist. As such, advertising is not a response to the market; advertising is instead the force that creates markets.

In this case advertising provides biased information that is in very many cases targeted very specifically at audiences whose vulnerability has been profoundly understood by the advertiser. The whole purpose of advertising (small ads and maybe job recruitment apart) is not to inform, but is to spread dissatisfaction. Its intention is to make the person who is the target of the advertising campaign feel that their current consumption is inadequate and that they must have the item being promoted to achieve a proper sense of well-being. Advertising therefore is not an action designed to promote the benefits of ownership of the product it refers to; advertising is deliberately designed to make a person feel their current position is inadequate but that this current state would be remedied if only they consumed more of a particular item. It therefore has the impact on a person's chart of well-being as shown in Diagram 10.3.

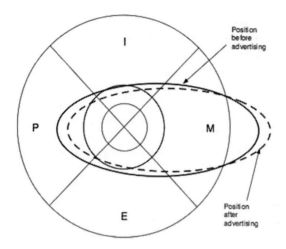

Diagram 10.3

In this diagram, the situation that existed before advertising took place is explained by the solid outline area. The pressure brought to bear by advertising results in a shift in that position so that the dashed area of achievement is desired instead.

The intention of advertising, as noted, is to make the person feel worse off before they buy: if they do not feel worse off they will not buy. This has to be understood: the intention of advertising is to change perception before a purchase takes place. The behavioural consequence of that purchase is the result of that change in perception, which is always negative; it is the sense of a person's current situation being inadequate that drives them to buy what is being promoted. That is why the impact of advertising is negative: its only purpose (bar that very limited part which is informational only, such as newspaper small ads) is to create dissatisfaction. It does this, very successfully. If it did not, the massive expenditure incurred on it (enough to support much of the media in many countries) would be wasted, and it seems very unlikely that those incurring that cost would continue to support it if that were the case.

The consequence of this advertising spending is that individuals are persuaded to change their behaviour. This is shown in the figure by the dashed outline area. Even those who claim that they are not affected by advertising are highly unlikely to be immune in practice. The dashed line results. Increased material consumption takes place – and given the observations noted above, the impact will almost certainly be reduced sustainability. More than that, the individual will, as a result of this new behaviour that they have been persuaded to undertake, be in greater imbalance than they were before. Not only is their area of potential achievement reduced still further by their excess material consumption, they actually have reduced emotional and intellectual well-being and their purpose has been compromised because another agent (the advertiser) has imposed its will on them with the deliberate intention of producing this outcome.

It could be argued that after the event the increased material consumption might increase the individual's emotional and intellectual well-being as well as their sense of purpose, but that is very unlikely to be true for one very good reason. Advertisers are not intent on their purchasers feeling satisfied with their purchases. They deliberately design the products they sell so that they are outdated as quickly as possible. In the fashion industry product cycles can now be counted in weeks. Cars are rapidly updated. Computers and other electronic goods have extraordinarily short lives – models being changed long before the economic lives of the products can in any reasonable way have come to an end. And of course those who have succumbed to advertising once are then targeted as purchasers of these upgrades with the deliberate intent that the new owners of these products will as soon as possible feel dissatisfied with them. The likely chance that they do, as a result of that purchase, feel an increase in their emotional or intellectual well-being, let alone their purpose, is very low. A vicious cycle of assault on their well-being is being undertaken to encourage them to consume more, regularly. But, precisely because we human beings are not rational, we successively succumb to that assault.

The consequence is that we are highly likely to materially over-consume, spending more cash in the process than we might desire on goods and services that we almost certainly would not choose to acquire if we enjoyed higher quality, less biased, more informed detail on the options available that might help us to optimise our well-being within the resources available to us, given the amount of effort that we wish to expand on doing so.

Corporate motivation

So, the overall consequence of this behaviour has to be considered alongside the motivation of those who ensure that this outcome is achieved. That motivation is quite easily explained. The companies that undertake advertising activity do so to maximise their cash generation. Cash is, in these organisations, promoted as king. In a very real sense it is. As is all too obvious from changed management techniques that have developed over the last thirty years or so, as mass consumption has advanced enormously, the consideration of many of the world's largest companies, or indeed of commercial organisations in far too many cases in general, has been focused solely on securing growth measured in terms of cash generation, at lowest possible cost, measured in terms of increased productivity extracted from those that these organisations engage with, whether they be employees, suppliers or the community at large. The result is that a diagram of the changes in emphasis in corporate behaviour over, say, the period of thirty years, might look something like Diagram 10.4.

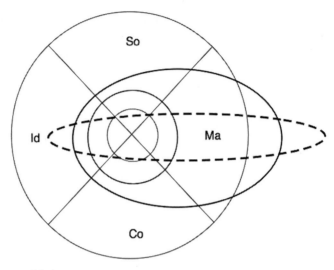

Diagram 10.4

The solid outline in the diagram is the original or start position of these entities, the dashed line the likely current state of play.

Companies have always focused on their ability to generate cash: to some extent that is necessary to guarantee their survival, which is why the objective has always been over-emphasised. But, that said, commercial organisations do realise that they have broader objectives, while still recognising the importance of cash generation. Those companies know that they have responsibilities in society. They provide good working environments, reasonable hours of work, social facilities, works canteens, flexible working and places where social interaction can take place within the work-place are encouraged. This is reflected in the area of achievement marked *Co* for community in the above diagram. This may still be true in some cases, but once it was more commonplace than now. Many such arrangements and facilities have unfortunately now gone: the pressure for productivity has eliminated them. That is clear from the resulting reduction in the community area of achievement shown in Diagram 10.4: there is no doubt that very many people feel that their workplaces are much less supportive, or communal, now than they were.

Changes can be seen in other areas as well. For example, companies once invested in training. Apprenticeships were common; staff with a variety of skills were recruited, and very often provided with significant on-the-job experience over a number of years before they were recognised as making a full contribution to the economic well-being of the company. That is how those leaving school at sixteen (or younger) only thirty years or so ago were integrated into the workplace. The assumption was that staff would stay with the company for a long period and as a result a return on the investment made was likely. Companies made a serious contribution to their employees' educational development as a consequence: they did not assume that this was somebody else's responsibility.

In these, and other ways, companies had material objectives, of course, but coupled with social objectives which indicated the broad sense of purpose for the organisation, including a strong ethical foundation in very many cases. The idea that banks, firms of accountants or lawyers would engage in marketing tax abuse of the sort which many have been convicted of in recent years, especially but not solely in the US, was unthinkable. The idea that many companies would abandon their obligation to their work-forces by closing pension schemes was again simply unthinkable. The concept of corporate social responsibility may not have existed as such much before the 1990s, yet it existed in practice. The terminology has been required to fill the void left as a result of its abeyance. Companies, simply, had identity and purpose; identity and purpose which their employees could relate to and which in many cases they shared.

The pursuit of profit, exemplified in growing cash balances which few companies now seem to know what to do with,[3] has replaced these cultures. Employee welfare has been cut. Real pay for a great many has stagnated. Pensions have been cut or removed. Social activities and staff support functions have for most employees disappeared. Training is rare. Apprenticeships are rarer still. Short-term contracts and flexible working are commonplace, as is outsourcing and contract labour. The relationship between the company and its staff has been reduced to one where profits grow and reward for all other participants has been reduced, including wherever possible for those in supply chains, where many small companies are now squeezed on price to the point where they go bankrupt: the assumption of mutual responsibility in such contracting has disappeared. The company knows what it wants – which is profit – and may achieve more of it in that narrow field, but it does so at considerable cost to its community, social contribution and identity, with which far fewer will identify.

Having set out on this path, however, the company must continue with it. It has set up an expectation of cash reward that its now more limited sphere of interested parties benefit from significantly. Those interested parties are, of course, primarily its shareholders, a group who by definition will already have wealth because that was the necessary precondition of their acquisition of their shareholding in the first place. That expectation is fulfilled by undertaking more advertising, putting more pressure on people to consume.

The difficulty is that this gives rise to a pattern where companies remove reward from most participants in their activities, and in particular employees, while exaggerating rewards to a limited number who are engaged in the management of the enterprise and in its ownership. This explains the trend already noted by the UK's High Pay Commission,[4] where the vast majority of the UK population have seen growth in earnings of well below that enjoyed by the economy as a whole, and a very few at the top echelon of the employment and earnings scale have enjoyed earnings growth considerably above that of the UK economy as a whole, the difference being explained by an increasing share of profits within UK gross domestic product. So, for example, in the relatively limited period from 2000 to 2008 the UK's national accounts[5] show that the share of profits as a part of GDP increased from 26% to 29.4% before, admittedly, falling in 2009 as a result of the economic crisis, while the share of GDP attributable to wages during the same period fell from 55.2% to 53.2%. A clear and unambiguous shift from wages to profit took place.

The question is, how did this happen if the income of most people was growing at a lower rate than that of the economy as a whole? The answer, to bring this back to the question of cash, is a simple one: people borrowed. The rise of total borrowing in the UK has been staggering. As the *Financial Times* noted: "In the eight-and-a-half years from the start of the 2000s to the middle of 2008, UK households increased their total debt burdens by 133%. As a percentage of gross household disposable income, total borrowing rose from 99% to 161%."[6] That is the result of a falling share in national income combined with increased pressure to consume.

How does borrowing impact on the diagram of personal well-being? It does so in two ways. The first is when borrowing is undertaken to fund immediate consumption and the second is when it is undertaken to fund the purchase of an asset expected to realise benefit over the life of the loan. I will consider the situations in turn.

Borrowing to fund current consumption

It is first worth returning to Diagram 10.3, a version of which is repeated here. This (Diagram 10.5) shows the impact of advertising on consumption.

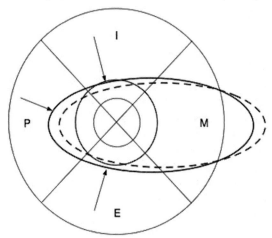

Diagram 10.5

179

The situation that existed before advertising took place is explained by the solid outline area. The pressure brought to bear by advertising is indicated by the three arrows. The consequence of that advertising spending is that individuals are persuaded to change their behaviour. This is shown by the dashed outline area. This consideration assumed, however, that cash was already available to fund this alternative choice, even if it was an imposed choice. But this is not always the case: credit and borrowing are often involved.

In that case the diagram is more complicated. There is a difference between the consumption of material goods that can be afforded and the amount actually consumed. Diagram 10.6 shows how the position before borrowing might look.

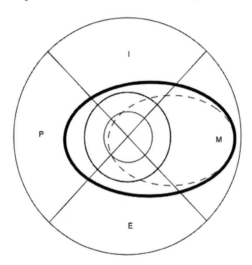

Diagram 10.6

The bold line is the area of achievement, the dashed inner line the part of the transactions involved undertaken in cash.

Now the individual is induced to borrow to consume more, with the result shown in Diagram 10.7.

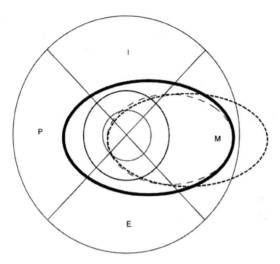

Diagram 10.7

The bold solid and long-dashed lines remain as before for the sake of comparison: the short-dashed line shows that they have now consumed more, using cash that was not their own. This new area of monetary activity replaces the previous area, and of course indicates that more real consumption has taken place, but it does so in a very important way: this achievement is indicated to be beyond the person's capacity in the period that their own efforts would have suggested appropriate, which remains the area outlined by the bold, solid line. Cash activity has resulted in what can unambiguously be considered over-consumption.

The consequences of borrowing

Of course, this has implications. First, although not shown on the diagram for the sake of clarity, there has been material over-consumption which will have an impact on the possibility of achievement in other areas of this person's life, as already noted. Second, over-consumption in the current period will have an inevitable consequence in future periods, and this is the importance in this case. In over-consuming and now by borrowing, this person has issued a promise to repay that borrowing at a future time. Almost certainly they've also accepted an obligation to pay interest on borrowing that has arisen as well. In other words, the amount they will replay will be greater than the sum they have borrowed. Both have very obvious consequences, with each to be considered in turn.

First, assuming a very simple arrangement where the borrowing in the period shown in Diagram 10.7 was repaid in the subsequent period in full, the following diagram would initially result (Diagram 10.8).

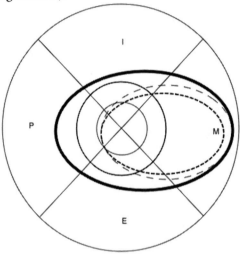

Diagram 10.8

While the solid black line and long-dashed indicative line showing the potential for monetary transactions remain the same, the actual amount of cash available to undertake transactions for material gain has reduced because a loan repayment must take place. This is the short-dashed, inner line. But that, of course, has implications for actual material consumption in this period. Just as that was presumed to increase by the excess of money spending (the short-dashed line) over actual capacity to consume in Diagram 10.7, so will the capacity to consume be reduced in Diagram 10.8 as a result of the repayment. The solid black line might show the capacity to consume if no loan repayment had taken place, but the actual consumption is logically less, as shown in Diagram 10.9.

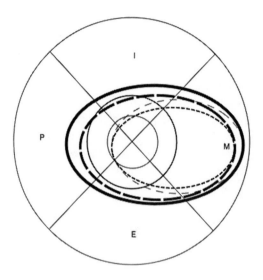

Diagram 10.9

The new inner bold dashed line indicates the new area of consumption resulting from the reduction in the capacity to consume in this period because money is being used to repay the debt arising from over-consumption in an earlier period. Logically, assuming a constant value for money, and no interest being paid (as is the case here) the over-consumption in the previous period should equal the reduction in consumption in the current period, and also equal the fall in monetary consumption in this period compared to that possible but for the loan being repaid: there will, therefore, be an overall consistency, logically, in the areas noted, although not necessarily in well-being since it is obviously possible that repayment could result in relative or even absolute poverty arising, the former being indicated in this case by the inner dashed bold line with regard to intellectual achievement. This suggests that they have as a result of the need to repay debt created a more serious imbalance in their activities than existed before this process began. The message is clear: monetary equivalence is by no means the same as neutrality with regard to actual well-being.

This problem is only exacerbated when interest is taken into account. The initial impact of the borrowing to fund excess consumption is, of course, the same and is as shown in Diagram 10.7. It is also true that the impact of the repayment of the capital will be as shown in Diagram 10.9. But now interest is being repaid too. Obviously the amount of money now available for consumption in the current period reduces still further in that case (the narrow dashed line in Diagram 10.10 is of smaller area than in Diagram 10.9), and as a consequence so too has the overall area of achievement shrunk still further in Diagram 10.10 when compared to Diagram 10.9 (the bold dashed line).

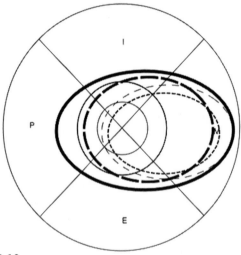

Diagram 10.10

Now the loss both monetary and actual capacity in the current period is greater than the excess consumption shown in Diagram 10.7.

There are, of course, a number of reasons why a person might wish to consider this option, which might compensate for this anticipatable outcome of the transaction. They might, for example, feel they have no alternative. People who have no choice but to borrow because they face absolute poverty will do so without considering future consequences. This is why 'doorstep lenders' can charge such excessive rates of interest.

This situation apart, people can still rationalise the act of borrowing despite this potentially foreseeable outcome of being in the long term worse off as a result if they believe either their income will increase between periods so that in net terms they might remain as well-off in the second period as the first, simply using the increased income to repay the excess consumption of a prior period, or they believe that inflation might reduce the value of money between the time of the borrowing and the time of repayment sufficiently to cover the interest charge and therefore leave them, overall, between the two periods in a similar position. Those could be rational explanations.

What is not accepted as a rational explanation for this phenomenon is that someone has a 'time preference' for current consumption regardless of its consequences. It may be true that this happens, but it is not rational. To be persuaded of the virtue of this requires the suspension of rationality.

Unfortunately for the rational explanations, as previously noted, most people have not enjoyed significant increases in real income over recent years and the noted change in the behaviour of companies, putting downward pressure on incomes and associated benefits from employment including pension rights, has reinforced this, meaning that any rational expectation of a real increase in earnings on the part of most people in the UK cannot be sustained. In addition, it is obvious that government policy is to hold inflation down, meaning that there is every likelihood that real, positive, interest rates will be paid on any borrowing.

The inevitable consequence of these observations is that borrowing to fund consumption must, eventually, in the absence of inflation eroding the debt, result in a net transfer of the ability to consume from the borrower to the lender. Nothing else can happen in that case. But that, also inevitably, means that the wealth gap between those who borrow (who by definition, do not have their own current resources to fund their consumption) and those who can lend (who by definition, have wealth, because the loan represents an asset that they own) will increase. People who live on consumption by borrowing should rationally know this, and maybe they do; they behave irrationally nonetheless, and many continue to consume in this way. There has to be an explanation for their irrationality and that is that they have succumbed to the power of advertising.

Once, however, this cycle of borrowing (however irrational it might be) has been created, and assuming, as is often the case, that the capacity to repay is reduced by the pressure to consume again as a consequence of yet more advertising, the cycle of interest payments, effectively paid for by borrowing, is generated, continually transferring the capacity to sustainably consume from those who are borrowing to those who are lending.

Note, however, what I am saying: what is transferred is a capacity to consume. Those who are lending, by definition, already have wealth. Of course, in saying this I recognise that it is banks that usually lend, but they need the deposits of those who have no immediate use for cash (and who are therefore at least to some degree wealthy) to provide the retained deposits that are an essential part of fractional reserve basis that are a prerequisite in modern regulated banking to making loans in the way previously described. The very fact those people hold cash deposits suggests that they have no intention of completing transactions into which they have entered at any time soon: holding cash is indication of that fact.

In exchange for that holding of cash depositors receive a return on their savings in the form of interest (or a close proxy for it, such as dividends if they save in other ways) but just as it seems that large corporations now earn profits without knowing what to do with them, and as such seem to be simply accumulating cash for its own sake, so it seems that the very wealthy who own most assets in the UK now receive this income without intending to spend it. As a result the supply of money increases. But, since money is almost entirely created by debt this necessarily means that there are more incomplete transactions in the economy with the other side being represented by loans.

Now, I accept that the issue has greater complexity than that, but there space is limited to dedicate to this subject here, and this general case will have to suffice. It so happens that it can suffice for one good reason, which is that the evidence supports the case.

Between 1994 and 2011 personal debt including mortgages in the UK rose from £400bn to £1.45 trillion[7] (approximately 60% of GDP to approximately 100% of GDP using HM Treasury data). Some of that borrowing cycle (more than £200bn of it currently) will be represented by the process already noted, of lending to people to fund excess consumption, a cycle exaggerated by the existence of advertising to ensure that people remain susceptible to this process designed, ultimately, to transfer the income of those who do not have wealth to those who are already wealthy.

This process is not accidental: it happened, I suggest, by design. It is not coincidental that the same companies that advertise also ensure that the capacity to repay the lending that their activity encourages is reduced by lobbying through their trade organisations and directly for policies of low inflation, effective wage control through labour market liberalisation and reduced union rights and reduced taxes for wealth holders (or the owners of its capital as they would justify it). The maintenance of low pay increases for a majority in the population, coupled with low inflation and matched with advertising-induced excess consumption of the products of profit-maximising (and therefore low reward-sharing) companies, guarantees upward wealth transfers – which is exactly what has been seen in the UK since 1980. The congruence of these objectives is, I repeat, not chance: it may be argued by conventional economists that profit maximisation increases well-being, but the truth is it increases the well-being of the tiny minority at the expense of the rest of society, as the diagrams here help show. This is the planned outcome of the availability of consumer credit, such as credit cards, which became common from the 1970s onwards, when mixed with the neoliberal mantra of profit maximisation promoted through advertising expenditure to encourage excess consumption that then transfers wealth, inevitably, to a few.

Borrowing for asset acquisition

There is, however, another type of borrowing that impacts on the diagram of personal well-being, as noted previously. This is borrowing undertaken to finance the acquisition of an asset which the purchaser believes will provide them with benefit over an enduring period of time. Behaviourally, this can be very different from the type of borrowing just discussed. If borrowing occurs for this reason there is a different motive, and a different reaction. In this case, the situation seen in Diagram 10.7 is not replicated. When borrowing takes place to buy an asset, the increase in the area of consumption is only that part of its worth that is believed to arise during the course of the current period. In other words, the excess cash spending is not necessarily immediately reflected by excess consumption: indeed, over the life of the asset there may be no excess consumption at all. All that might happen is that a steady pattern of consumption of the asset (all of which, including buildings, deteriorate over time) happens in the years following debt-financed acquisition with the repayment of the funds borrowed, including interest, in this case either matching the value of perceived consumption in the period when the debt is repaid, or not, depending on perceptions at the time when that repayment occurs.

In this case the cash repayments of borrowing effectively represent the price paid for consumption in future periods, and the interest is not as such a shift in the power to consume, but can be seen as part of the price of consumption.

This, of course, may appear paradoxical when compared to the previous analysis because the suggestion is that the interest can in this circumstance be afforded out of current consumption when that is not true with regard to interest paid on borrowings used to finance consumption in previous periods. There is, however, good reason for this different conclusion when considering the borrower financing an asset purchase. Whereas, as noted previously, the aftermath of advertising-induced excess consumption financed by borrowing is usually a sense of dissatisfaction – because the consumption in question is almost invariably discounted soon after acquisition since advertising suggests the existence of another need that the consumer must satisfy – the purchase of an asset can have a different consequence. The purchase of an asset gives rise to a value in use that is, hopefully, in most cases more than capable of offsetting any impact arising from the outmoding of the assets in question. So, for example, borrowing to acquire a home provides opportunity to maintain a family: that opportunity gives rise to an increase in the emotional well-being of the borrower and their family community. This increase in well-being can be used to more than compensate for the loss of potential material consumption that the settlement of a cash obligation to pay interest would produce in this situation. Diagramatically, the situation in Diagram 10.11 might arise.

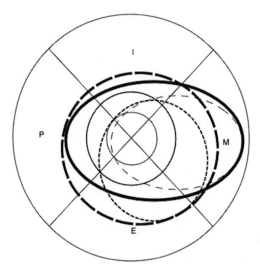

Diagram 10.11

The opening position is that of Diagram 10.6 and is shown by the solid bold line for the area of achievement and the longer-dashed fainter line for the area of monetary activity. After borrowing to acquire an asset such as a property has taken place the area of achievement sees a reduction in material consumption. This is, incidentally, entirely appropriate as the vast majority of properties bought in the UK are 'second-hand', i.e. there is no actual production involved in their acquisition: this is a transfer of property rights. As a result of taking on the borrowing obligation the acquirer inevitably has a reduced capacity to consume for immediate benefit, but the consequence shown here is that they are better able to provide for their family and as a result other potential benefits may arise, including an increase in the realisation of their purpose. The new cash activity area, marked by the short-dashed line, is incidentally equivalent to the previous area, but it has now been skewed heavily towards different objectives. The message is clear: borrowing in this situation can be positive.

The same can also be true in the very different situation where a depreciating asset is acquired for the purpose of undertaking an economic activity with the use of borrowed funds. If the depreciating asset does not result in the excess consumption of material resources (which it could, because the depreciation is in itself a form of consumption) but instead provides the opportunity for the realisation of another opportunity that more than compensates for the cost of borrowing in question, then that borrowing can clearly be justified. The depreciating asset could, of course, be part of a manufacturing process where, for example, enhanced resource efficiency as a result of the process facilitated by the asset results in fewer resources being used overall to achieve a particular material gain, as a result of a yield arising over and above the monetary cost of the asset appreciation plus the interest paid.

However, most assets acquired are not of this sort. To take another example, if the depreciating asset acquired was a school (and governments are just another community or organisation with common interest in this thinking) then the increase in intellectual achievement of the pupils and the enhanced ability that they had to engage in society as a consequence will be more than enough to justify the expenditure on material resources and the interest settled upon the loan used to finance them.

Alternatively, the asset financed may be a consumer durable, such as a car. Here the position in determining the benefits arising is much more ambiguous than in the situations noted above. The situation in this case can be similar to the situation arising when borrowing is acquired for any other consumption: the excess consumption may just be spread over a longer period as may, due to the likely sums involved, be the subsequent period of adjustment. In another case the situation may be akin to that of acquiring a productive asset. The outcome is hard to predict but the degree to which the acquisition was influenced by expectations fuelled by advertising and therefore likely to be of limited sustainable value the more likely it is that the benefit of the borrowing will be of limited duration and that adverse consequences will arise.

It is, therefore, clear that the purpose of borrowing has a significant impact upon the way in which that borrowing needs to be viewed, at least on the part of the borrower. In addition, because the motive for asset borrowing tends to be somewhat different, and probably in most cases more informed, then it is clear that the impact is again, very different.

That, however, is the perception on the part of the borrower. The fact that the borrower can justify the payment of interest that in most circumstances will result in their reduced ability to consume materially, because that is where most cash is expended, must also be considered from the other side of the transaction – i.e. from the perspective of the lender.

The lender's viewpoint

Money, as noted, gets its value from an inherent promise to pay. That promise is necessary because in a cash-based economy transactions occur which do not result in a completed exchange of value between the participants in the transaction. That is the virtue of money as a medium of exchange: to let these incomplete transactions take place with the participants then being able to complete other transactions with other people to conclude the process of exchange. If it did not work in this way we would be restricted to barter, and we know that is a massive constraint. But, the very existence of loans, and the payment of interest, implies something little understood about money, its accumulation, and the consequences of wealth expressed in the form of money.

Increasing cash wealth, which is the goal of most companies that operate in the way shown in Diagram 10.4 – with much of that cash being spent in ways that ultimately increases the monetary wealth of just a few in society – gives rise to a phenomenon to which little attention has been paid. This is the fact these few are not spending what they're accumulating and are therefore not completing the transactions into which they have entered. This means that increasingly, and as a necessary corollary of their wealth, there must be more and more people who have to be making promises to make payments at sometime in the future. This has to be the case: after all, the value of cash simply represents this promise to pay. Increasing asset wealth, denominated in money, on the part of the few means there must be increasing sums owed by a great many to them. That equation must hold true: simple double entry requires it.

However, this means there are an increasing number of promises that might also be broken within the financial system. Unsurprisingly, as a consequence, those with wealth have sought security to back up their asset worth, with the result that they have been increasingly inclined to lend against security that could be backed up by a mortgage on land. There was an additional benefit in this as far as they were concerned. As noted with regard to borrowing to fund consumer spending, one way in which people justify borrowing on security to buy a house is to assume that inflation will help write off the debt over time, so reducing the real cost of interest in future periods. That expectation that may have once been valid with regard to consumer borrowing is not now justified: consumer inflation has been deliberately kept low to ensure that real interest rates remain positive. However, by excluding land prices from measures of inflation and by ensuring the supply of new housing has been restricted – both as a result of planning regulation and, as importantly, because house builders have simply not supplied anything like the number of houses that their land stocks could have permitted, and because the relative security of mortgages charged on land meant that there was an oversupply of cash available to be borrowed in this sector, house price inflation was generated (and virtually guaranteed) over a long period.

This may have appeared to benefit borrowers whose risk of house buying was reduced as a result, but it was also of considerable benefit to those with wealth. They benefited from land price inflation themselves, not least because those with wealth inevitably owned land, but more than that because such inflation meant that borrowers could rationalise increasing amounts of interest payment that then transferred greater and greater shares of wealth to those already wealthy because borrowers also apparently benefited from that process. This apparent dual benefit, even if asymmetrically shared, explains the house price boom. It was not low interest rates that encouraged this: the process was encouraged by security, securitisation, increasing cash-denominated wealth without alternative investment use, a shortage of supply of homes to purchase and banks all too willing to encourage the process by advancing money. Inevitably, and eventually, however, those promises proved difficult to fulfil simply because belief in ever rising property prices cannot be sustained indefinitely, and that eventually undermines the willingness to take on the obligation of interest repayment. That is what is happening in the UK property market now.

This, however, is not the only problem with regard to lending. Most borrowing to purchase houses, which forms a significant part of the UK debt portfolio, funds what might be called 'second-hand assets'. This lending funds transfers of property rights, often at inflated prices, using the mechanisms for cash creation noted earlier in this chapter, where money is made out of nothing but with interest being paid as a consequence, with that interest being ultimately claimed for the benefit of those already with wealth. As a result, much of this value is transferred from income earners to lenders without any real value being created in the economy. That's a major reason for wealth imbalances having arisen.

That situation should, however, be differentiated from lending for asset purchases where the borrower uses the funds to acquire productive assets that are then used to fulfil other objectives, whether that be related to the production process aimed at material consumption within commercial organisations or by lending to government to, for example, build schools. This second type of borrowing is justified if the total cost of capital repayment plus interest is perceived by the borrower to be less than the benefit that they secure from using the asset over time, taking into consideration its depreciation as part of that cost. Depreciation in this sense means the amount by which, measured in terms of cash, the asset diminishes in value as a result of its use during the course of the period.

This equation may work for the purpose of calculating whether it is worth investing on the part of the borrower, but it has almost no relevance whatsoever to the lender. The lender, by definition, either has, or can create, cash for which they have no purpose: that is why they are willing to lend it. Their lending does, however, facilitate an exchange which, while it is understood by the borrower in the way just described as an investment in an asset, is understood by the creator of the asset to be a source of income.

This point is very important: when an asset is created as a result of the expenditure of effort by human beings there is a very real potential imbalance generated in the economy. The acquirer of the asset buys it with borrowed funds because they believe that they will generate value from it over a considerable period of time, but certainly not all in the present. On the other hand, the people who created the asset think they have earned an income and as a result will now be looking to consume most of that income. Excessive investment as a result of too much lending creates, therefore, a situation where inflation is likely. That is not because there is too much investment, but because there is too much income chasing too few resources available for consumption because too much activity has been diverted into the creation of investment assets. The conventional reaction to this has been to increase interest rates to discourage lending, with the result that investment falls, with the eventual consequence that, in effect, there is net disinvestment which then results in an excess supply of resources available for consumption compared to the incomes of those at work (not least because those who would otherwise be engaged making invest-ment goods are now out of employment) so deflation occurs. The consequence of that, however, is, of course, boom and bust.

That is the result of using interest rates to deal with this situa-tion, which is probably the crudest technique available. It is the availability and shortage of credit which really creates this prob-lem and yet this is an issue which is not directly addressed by interest rate policy. The result is that although lending for invest-ment is generally desirable it is far too cyclical, and therefore unreliable, especially when there is an emphasis on lending for the purchase of land and buildings as has occurred in the UK economy, much of which lending is by definition economically unproductive since it just transfers ownership of assets already in existence at inflated prices. The result has been to the detriment of real investment in productive capacity, with the consequences being an over-inflation in property prices, an excessive level of borrowing, an exceptionally high disparity in wealth holding between the majority in the country and a tiny minority, and an excessive interest income flow to a few who are already wealthy. This has led to an imbalance between the number of borrowers and lenders resulting in asymmetric power relationships and a perpetual cycle where those with monetary assets are continually wishing to extend more borrowing to those who have, as a result of the corporate drive for profits that forces wages down, static incomes over time meaning that they must, if they are to fuel their drive for consumption, borrow to fund that consumption, which as has been shown here is a desperately negative economic activity. This is the real cause for our economic crisis.

What happens when cash is king

There are some additional points to note regarding cash, albeit without as much elaboration as might be desirable.

The first relates to the fact that of course cash is, in this example, assumed to be in the form of one single currency whereas in reality currencies are themselves exchanged and are tradable. We live in what are described as open economies because we have floating exchange rates and ready conversion of currencies. The consequence is that not only are there real transactions of exchange to consider within an economy itself, but transactions of real exchange between economies, where goods and services are traded across borders and between currencies, and there are financial flows of cash seeking a return, or being paid as a financial return, across borders and between currencies. Each of these is, of course, a matter of concern to any state but the significance of these flows varies considerably and to treat them all generically as if of one type is a serious error.

Flows with regard to trade for consumption are important because different places have different regional skills, traditions and geographic benefits which mean that some locations have distinct advantages in producing some goods and services over others. Recognition of this is, of course, no different in principle from recognising that different individuals also possess different advantages, to which can be added the difference between people, organisations, societies, and countries that give rise to trade. If everyone could meet their own needs equally, trade would be of no benefit and it would not take place, but that is not true, so it does, which is a good thing.

The pricing of these flows depends critically upon perceptions of the relative worth, overall, of the goods and services traded, as does the value put on trade in any market. Inevitably, and as is also true with regard to transactions, the vast majority of them will relate to material items, or traded services that can be readily exchanged for those items. There is, in this sense, little difference once again from domestic trade, barring two things. First, if there are relative price differentials between the two currencies in which traded exchange takes place, either because domestic demand for goods and services results in differing price offerings, or because of inflation, then it is likely that the quantities of goods or services that flow between the parties will adjust as a consequence. As a result it can, for example, seriously unsettle trade to have significantly different inflation rates between states and any government will be aware of this.

Second, and perhaps more important, other financial flows, such as funds seeking investment, or being repatriated as a consequence of past investment, can have as significant an impact upon relative valuations of currencies as any real underlying value differential based on goods and services actually produced for sale. That is why those flows are of such concern. Any government will, if acting in the best interests of the state, wish to ensure that its economy is producing sufficient valuable goods and services for exchange to, as far as possible, secure the goods and services it wishes to acquire from other countries on an ongoing basis without major price shocks arising; but however effected, that policy can be derailed by financial flows.

Types of financial flow

There are essentially three sorts of financial flow: funds that move across international boundaries to permit real investment to take place; speculative activity across international boundaries; and currency speculation.

Funds that move across international boundaries to permit real investment to take place are funds that move, for example, from wealthy individuals or between banks located in one economy or state to another to fund investment in real tangible assets used in a productive process or to buy land and buildings. These flows relate to actual activity being undertaken in an economy, and have the same consequences as if those activities were funded by banks and wealthy individuals within that economy. In other words, they can give rise to economic imbalances for all the reasons noted above, but not in any particular way that should cause additional concern to a state.

The second flow across international boundaries is speculative activity. This tends to be substantially more volatile than the investment flow used to acquire real assets because speculative flows of this sort are used to acquire financial assets such as shares. For this reason these are usually described as funding portfolio investment. These portfolio investments are traded on stock exchanges and other financial markets including futures exchanges, and also through hedge funds and other such institutions. They can be made and unravelled rapidly. They arise because of the accumulation of financial wealth; a trend that has increased significantly over recent decades. They do not usually seek a return related to any form of underlying economic activity resulting from a real exchange of value between real participants in an economy. Instead they seek to make a return on money itself. It can, of course, be argued that interest takes this form, but the activity referred to here is quite unrelated. Interest on loans of the sort already described does at least relate to activity that takes place in the real economy: portfolio investment does not.

Portfolio investment is speculation in what are always derivative products. So, for example, share capital when first subscribed is similar to a loan: it provides funding to a company to allow it to invest in an activity that is intended to produce a real return. However, subsequent trading in share capital provides the company that issued the shares with no benefit at all: the trade is simply between one owner and another; it is a transfer of title, but not an investment. In that sense it is like the sale of a 'second hand' house. This point is exceptionally important and cannot be understated. Unless it is appreciated, much that really happens in the economy cannot be understood, and often not in much of the economic commentary now offered in the media and elsewhere.

What has to be understood is the fact that saving is not the same as investment. Saving might be defined as a process designed to preserve the value of a claim on wealth expressed in monetary form. Critically, money is key to this, as is the ability to readily transfer any savings back into cash. Investment on the other hand is something quite different: investment is the process of creating assets that have the capacity to deliver benefit in use both in the current and future periods. This means investment requires engagement in the real economy, the creation of new products and it entails the process of managing those products which are then called assets in use over years to come. By definition, that means the realisation of the return on investment is not immediate; time is an essential part of this equation. What is obvious as a result is, however, that there is no necessary relationship between savings and investment.

Despite this, it is often assumed, especially in popular narratives, that the two terms are synonymous, which is entirely wrong and a fundamental cause of misunderstanding in economics. For example, as has already been noted, investment is as likely to be funded by borrowing as by the provision of capital and borrowing from banks usually results from the creation of cash by the banks themselves, unrelated to the deposits that they hold precisely because most of the cash that they lend is created by them out of thin air. Therefore investment activity and its funding need not be related to savings at all, and yet the myth of a relationship persists.

That is not to deny that saving is obviously an issue within any economy. Saving represents the accumulated wealth of those in society who have income in excess of their current needs that they choose not to use for consumption. The total value of savings has increased significantly over recent years because of the pursuit of money profit, as shown in Diagram 10.4, with that money profit being distributed to a very narrow sector of society, and with the rewards of the majority in society having been steadily and systematically reduced in pursuit of the goal of wealth reallocation to those who are already wealthy. In other words, money savings have increased because of the deliberate policy of exaggerating wealth differentials in society which is a fundamental objective of neoliberal economics, which has been in operation since 1980 or thereabouts.

The accumulated cash has, of course, been deposited to earn a return, not least in banks, which action has permitted those banks, because of the rules of fractional reserve banking, to considerably increase the amount of lending that they have made, which in turn has increased the indebtedness of most households in the UK, which is the inevitable corollary of wealth going to a few in society. But that same cash has also given rise to the enormous increase in speculative activity that has occurred over the last thirty years.

House prices have increased because of that speculative activity. Stock exchanges have increased in value beyond their real worth because of the same speculative activity, and have then given rise to occasional spectacular crashes, for example in 1987, at the turn-of-the-century and more recently as a result of the 2008 financial crisis.

Speculation in other, more esoteric derivative products has also increased as a result, whether through hedge funds, investment banking, or simply in cash itself, with as a result the total sums traded on the international foreign exchange markets massively exceeding the world's total income each a year. According to the Bank for International Settlements, in April 2010 average daily turnover in global foreign exchange markets was estimated at $3.98 trillion, a growth of approximately 24% over the $3.21 trillion daily volume in April 2007.[8] World GDP was estimated in 2010 to be about $63 trillion,[9] meaning foreign exchange dealing was worth more than 15 times total world income even though the vast majority of that income would never involve foreign exchange transaction.

What this clearly implies is that there is something going on internationally and speculatively that is quite different from the description of cash transactions already noted. The savings market that fuels this speculation clearly exists as if in a parallel universe to the market used for real transactions; a real transaction as previously referred to being one which has an underlying exchange of value of real goods or services implicit in it. The implication of this is shown in Diagram 10.12.

Diagram 10.12

The circle of capacity, in this case for the economy as a whole, is the circle on the left. Partly contained within it, and partly outside it, is the dashed area of transactions undertaken in cash within that real economy. Those transactions as shown here exceed the capacity of the economy on a sustainable basis but then, way out beyond the real economy is another whole area, marked here by the bolder solid area, that represents the cash used for speculative, portfolio-based, savings activity: an activity that includes the third type of fund flow, which is transactions in cash themselves – i.e. currency speculation.

As can be seen, those transactions overlap with the real economy but the important point is that there is a vast quantity of transactions here that have no real bearing to the economy in which real wealth, real activity and real resources are generated by real people at all. It is, quite literally, a world apart, and the fact that so much of what it does is called derivatives is entirely appropriate: it is derived from something unrelated to real economic activity.

Unfortunately, that does not mean that this cash economy does not impact upon real economic activity because it clearly does, as the diagram shows. The impact is, however, strange in its impact. Although there is an overlap with the real economy that overlap does not imply this activity does not in any way meet real needs, or relieve poverty (meaning the overlap is never with the areas of absolute or relative poverty) and nor does this activity ever create societal or community well-being. What it does, because such a savings activity denominated entirely in cash demands a cash input into the real economy, is drag resources from that real economy and from those who might benefit from them towards those who manage this vast amount of cash. And leverage that cash management process to extract from the society in which real transactions take place a return to wealth the demands of excess consumption (as the diagram implies) to fuel it, for the reasons already noted, and which distributes that reward incredibly narrowly to a tiny number within society as a whole.

This is, of course, the world of banking that we have seen, in which all the related financial activities that have been undertaken have so distorted economic activity without any benefits flowing back into the real economy as a whole, and which has instead increased divisions in society, forced those who have to work for a living to sustain themselves on what have, effectively, been static wages, and which has undermined so much of the fabric of the country on which common principles of mutual governance depend. Nothing symbolises this better than the gated communities of the ultra-wealthy, or the culture of excessive, celebrity focused consumption that fuels so much of the media.

There is, however, an even more pernicious aspect to this. If the existence of this cash, floating above and beyond the real economy and capable of demanding resources from it, undermines proper resource allocation within an economy the impact is much more serious when the same cash floats above and beyond almost all economies, and between them. When that happens this cash, very often recorded in tax havens so that it is beyond apparent regulation, can be used to undermine the effectiveness of regulation and even the democratic principle within mainstream economies. This is undoubtedly done, and deliberately so. Used in this way this cash can be used, for example, by speculators who threaten to undermine the value of a currency, as happened in the UK in 1992. Alternatively it can be used to attempt to force a change in a government's policies by aggressive intervention in bond markets, as has happened in some smaller states since 2008. Not to put too fine a point on it, this cash, moving over, above and beyond the boundaries of any economy, provides the opportunity for economic blackmail, which some at least have found hard to resist.

The consequence of the cash relationships in society

The implication of these cash transactions has to be considered. To understand them the consequence they will give rise to if uncorrected has to be predicted, because if those likely patterns of behaviour are not understood then no appropriate policies to counter those consequences can be created.

In a sustainable economy the area of achievement for the population will, in an ideal scenario, be as close as possible to that which they are capable of: they will achieve as much of their potential as they can. That will, of course, also ideally happen is a way that is sustainable because people have a natural empathy not just for each other, but for the generations to come. And if that is the case then, of course, money transactions will be a subset of that hopeful area of achievement and the result will be as shown in Diagram 10.13.

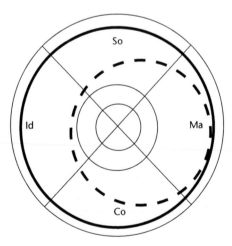

Diagram 10.13

The outer circle is the limit to sustainable potential. The inner bold circle is the area of actual achievement compared to that potential, while the dashed bold line represents the transactions undertaken using money to achieve that goal. This is an economy that is doing well, that is sustainable, is using money for proper purpose, and is delivering well-being.

That is not the outcome that would happen as a result of the activity of the imperfect markets that exist in the modern economy, however important those markets are in delivering some aspects of well-being (a point, which should be reiterated, is not disputed). Left unregulated and without government intervention of the sort noted in the next section of this book, the market would deliver an outcome as shown in Diagram 10.14.

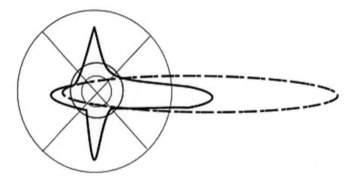

Diagram 10.14

This diagram is nothing like the ones we've seen before, and has to be drawn the way shown to really demonstrate just what is happening. What is happening here is that a small number of people in society achieve considerable material satisfaction but many do not. This would, however, if the market prevailed, not just be true for material well-being. As the diagram implies, this will also be true for the communal aspect of life, reflecting the relationships that we have. Those with material sufficiency may well be able to enjoy life well but those without will, as this diagram implies, suffer in other areas too. So relative poverty threatens relationships, harms esteem and has consequent impacts on family and broader aspects of life, not least because the safety net that the welfare state provides will be removed if the market had its way.

In the same way, in this scenario it is quite likely that the market would deny a good education to most while providing an exceptional outcome for a few.

All this is reflected in the solid bold line, which looks like a sword laid on the ground, viewed from above, and with the blade reflecting excess material consumption.

Coupled with that, and reflecting the fact that the effort of most in this society would be expended to generate wealth which would accumulate to a few, would be the illustrated imbalance of the cash resources within this economy with vast sums being held for a few having cash and savings balances way beyond any reasonable need they might have. These resources will, in the interests of preserving the wealth of the owners of this cash be excluded from productive investment in the economy. This will mean the prospects of most people achieving anything close to their potential will be stunted and not just materially, but emotionally and intellectually too, with an inevitable implication for the chances of people realising their purpose.

That might sound alarmist, except this outcome is one that reflects the vision of society put forward by a great many market-based think-tanks driven by neoliberal dogma. That dogma emanated from the Mont Pelerin Society created by the likes of Milton Friedman, Friedrich Hayek and others, all of them associated with right-wing economic thinking. Their goal was to promote the idea that the market must provide solutions in society, the state must not intervene, regulation is necessarily bad, failure must be allowed, diversity is the necessary outcome within society of differing ability, and subsidy should not be given. By creating vast networks of think-tanks to promote this idea they have left us with the impression that there is no alternative to these views.[10]

As is obvious from the analysis in this book, the situation drawn in Diagram 10.13 reflects welfare, well-being, and prosperity in a way incompatible with the situation drawn in Diagram 10.14.

My point is a simple one: there is a choice we can make when discussing economics. There is an alternative after all.

Thankfully, we are not in the position shown in Diagram 10.14: sufficient remains of the post-war consensus that we still have a welfare state, but it is under continual challenge, with a desire to privatise it, remove the subsidies within it, to abolish the safety net that ensures that all can participate in society, with the idea that failure is now to be tolerated and even encouraged within public services, at a cost to large parts of the community at large through no fault of their own. This will be enormously destructive if the ideas outlined in the previous pages are correct. That means government still has an absolutely vital role to play in the economy to ensure that we end up in a position as close as possible to Diagram 10.13, and as far away from Diagram 10.14 as possible. The policies described in Part 3 of this book are designed to achieve that goal.

1   See http://en.wikipedia.org/wiki/Thorstein_Veblen
2   Schor, J. 2010 *Plenitude: The New Economics of True Wealth*, Penguin
3   See for example a Bloomberg report of February 2011 noting US corporations were sitting on $1.8 trillion in cash and demanding further tax cuts to encourage investment even though they weren't actually already doing much with the cash they had. http://www.bloomberg.com/apps/news?pid=newsarchive&sid=a6kXsL1Q5FYc
4   http://highpaycommission.co.uk/wp-content/uploads/2011/05/HPC_interim_report2011.pdf
5   http://www.statistics.gov.uk/downloads/theme_economy/bluebook2010.pdf
6   http://ftalphaville.ft.com/blog/2011/02/10/484851/the-bank-of-englands-big-dilemma/
7   http://www.thisismoney.co.uk/money/cardsloans/article-1714095/How-personal-debt-grew-to-14-trillion.html
8   http://en.wikipedia.org/wiki/Foreign_exchange_market
9   http://en.wikipedia.org/wiki/List_of_countries_by_GDP_(nominal)
10 See http://www.bbc.co.uk/blogs/adamcurtis/2011/09/the_curse_of_tina.html for more information on this

CHAPTER 11

DELIVERING THE COURAGEOUS STATE

We now know what a sustainable economy, built on the foundation of a Courageous State would look like. It is what Diagram 10.13 shows, in the previous chapter. But we also know what the market would deliver if given free rein: that would be the outcome shown in Diagram 10.14. As is quite obvious, the two outcomes are very different.

A totally free market economy of the type shown in Diagram 10.14 is incompatible with social democracy: indeed, it is incompatible with democracy itself. Although it is obvious that people can be persuaded to act against their own self-interest, and advertising exists to ensure that they do just that, and that the same advertising and marketing processes can be used to promote economic outcomes that are clearly incompatible with the well-being of people who are persuaded to vote for them (as the current support for the Tea Party in the US amply illustrates), ultimately democracy is incompatible with a system where a tiny elite benefit at cost to the enormous poverty of the majority. It is not by chance that the post-war consensus was created so soon after universal suffrage for all adults in the UK was achieved in 1928.

Extremes of wealth and democracy are incompatible

Nor is it a surprise that greater social equality and reduced wealth and income inequality motivated people like Aneurin Bevan, who wrote in his classic book 'In Place of Fear' (page 3):

> "The issue therefore in a capitalist democracy resolves itself into this: either poverty will use democracy to win the struggle against property, or property, in fear of poverty, will destroy democracy. Of course, the issue never appears in such simple terms. Different flags will be waved in the battle in different countries and at different times. And it may not be catastrophic unemployment. There may be a slow attrition as there was in Britain before the war, but poverty, great wealth and democracy are ultimately incompatible elements in any society."

Bevan was right: Extremes of wealth and democracy are incompatible. It is a lesson that appears to have been forgotten, as evidenced by the massive increase in income and wealth disparities over the last two decades and by the rise of right-wing politics dedicated to increasing those gaps still further, but it is one that all who believe that, as Winston Churchill put it, democracy "is the worst form of government except all those other forms that have been tried from time to time"[1] would be wise to remember.

The goal of social democratic government

In that case the goal of social democratic government is obvious. If applied to Diagram 10.14 it looks as follows:

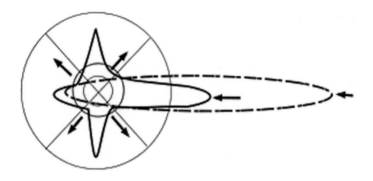

Diagram 11.1

The arrows show the direction policy must take. The excess size of the cash economy that drags resources from the real economy and distorts well-being within it has to be reduced. Excess material consumption by some in society also has to be reduced, while the opportunity for most to achieve anything like their potential with regard to meeting their material, emotional and intellectual needs so that they might realise their purpose has to be created. The result is, of course, overall a significant increase in well-being.

There is only one agency that has the potential to deliver this correction to the consequence of unfettered market activity, and that is the government. It is the undoubted duty of the government of the Courageous State to encourage markets, because when natural monopolies do not exist and universal provision is not necessary they provide (to parody Winston Churchill) the worst form of mechanism to meet many of the needs of society, except for all those other forms that have been tried and that have failed from time to time. However, government has at the same time the obligation to counter the inbuilt and inevitable tendency of markets to produce massive inequality, to fail to supply some services at all, and to destabilise democratic government if left unfettered. It is the paradox of the courage that a Courageous State would exemplify that it has to undertake these two tasks simultaneously, living with the inevitable compromises that result.

So how is the Courageous State delivered?

Clearly the Courageous State can, as described here, only be delivered democratically. That is at the core of all that follows. But to have a democratically elected government is not enough – we have had those and they have not delivered due to their enslavement by neoliberal ideology. We need a state that will deliver much more: a state that will use its power to:

- Tax to both redistribute income and wealth and to meet need;
- Compensate for the externalities created by market excesses;
- Constrain excess consumption;
- Limit interest rates;
- Constrain excessive speculation;
- Regulate markets to ensure access for all;
- Limit the asymmetry of information in markets;
- Regulate capital flows – the interaction with the rest of the world;
- Promote sustainable activity;
- Sustain money as a medium of exchange;
- Ensure access to well-being for all;
- Promote inter-generational well-being;
- Support and sustain communities and personal development in an environment of mutual understanding.

Many other requirements are implicit in that list, but what is clear is that none of this can be done without tax, and it is to tax that I turn next.

The role of tax in the economy

Tax has a special role to play in any economy, much of which I have explored in Chapter 7. However, tax is also a tool in the management of any economy. For that reason this chapter considers the issues of tax and economic management as related.

Tax is invariably a payment made in cash. It is not a payment for a consideration: there is no guarantee of perceived equal exchange of value implicit in the payment as there might be when making payment for the purchase of goods or services. It is, instead, the settlement of an obligation arising from a property right, with that property right belonging to the government but arising as a result of a conditional property right that belongs to the tax payer that results in their obligation to pay tax.

This has direct consequence of the way in which the cash impact of transactions arises in the economy. To go back to Diagram 10.1, the area of personal achievement included a sub-set (which it was later shown could also exceed it in size) relating to transactions denominated in money:

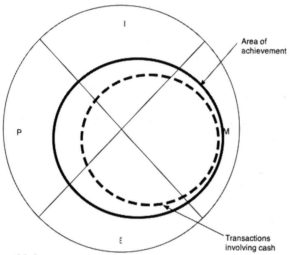

Diagram 11.2

The same diagram could, of course, also be relabelled for the economy as a whole and then looks like Diagram 10.13. As was noted in Chapter 10, cash transactions have an inevitable bias towards material transactions within the marketplace, which was the type of activity then being considered. If, however, those transactions give rise to cash property rights that are attributable to the government this outcome changes, as follows:

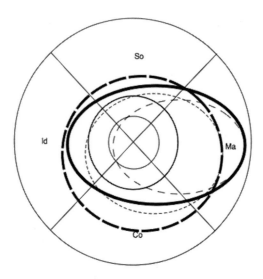

Diagram 11.3

In Diagram 11.3 the solid bold line and the dashed line that nestles against it in the material area (Ma) represent the area of achievement and the part of that relating to monetary activity prior to a tax charge.

The dashed bold line and the short dashed narrow line that in turn nestles against it in the material area represent the area of achievement and the part of that relating to monetary activity after tax is imposed.

It is clearly suggested that the amount of material consumption has reduced as a result of a tax charge: that is the consequence of the amount of cash dedicated to this activity being curtailed because the cash available for expenditure on material consumption has to be shared with the government as a consequence of the property rights acquired being conditional on doing so. But this is far from being a negative process: the cash now available to the government allows a more overall balanced outcome to be achieved because governments almost invariably use their tax resources in ways that increase communal achievement (e.g. by supporting families) (Co) and societal achievement (e.g. by providing education) (So) and they do, hopefully, also promote the sense of identity (Id) for the community as a whole through shared culture as well. This is reflected in the fact that more cash is dedicated to each of these areas.

I suggest that this has a symbiotic consequence for well-being. First, this is because in almost all current circumstances the consequence of reducing material consumption will be to reduce consumption occurring outside the sustainable area of achievement, while providing enhanced emotional and intellectual well-being will be within the sustainable limits, so helping all in society achieve their purpose. As already shown, this is automatically beneficial by delivering better balance and so enhanced well-being in society as a whole.

Second, and as importantly, there is an empathic benefit for human well-being from the redistribution of wealth that takes place. This is best explained by another diagram or two, as follows. Suppose there are just two people in society in the following situations:

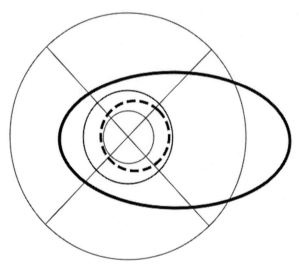

Diagram 11.4

213

The person with the solid area of achievement probably thinks they are doing rather well: they are comfortable in all areas even if their balance is out of kilter and their potential to achieve their purpose and emotional and intellectual well-being is restricted by their excess material consumption.

The person with the dashed bold line representing their area of achievement is clearly in a very different position. While they are not in absolute poverty anywhere, it is a close-run thing and they are in relative poverty everywhere – if only by comparison with the only other person in their society!

Empathy and redistribution

At this point I suggest a natural and powerful human emotion comes into play, and that is empathy, which is the ability to understand and share the feelings of another person.

Most of us are empathic. The degree to which we are so may vary: some are hardly at all, although that is considered so serious a condition it is often considered as a form of disability. Overall most of us are able to put ourselves in another person's shoes, at least to some degree, and if that other person's situation is significantly worse than our own feel compassion as a result.

As a consequence so long as the person doing rather well knows of the situation of the person who is not doing so well (and of course, knowledge is critical here) then they will feel some empathy with that other person's position. In part, this may depend on the person's own predisposition towards empathy, but there is more to it than that. Other factors include:

- First, the relative difference between their positions (the greater the difference the more likely an empathic response is going to be);

- Second, the degree of knowledge on their part of the other's situation (so, for example, people are more inclined to be empathic towards those relatively geographically close to them, not because they do not care about those further away but because they can less easily comprehend the situation of those living in places of which they know little); and

- Third, and perhaps importantly, how much they think those who are relatively worse off hold them to account for the situation they're in (this is otherwise called guilt!).

An empathic response to this situation might be charitable, and in a one-to-one situation that might be a reasonable response. It is not, however, a systemic response, and cannot now hope to provide the mechanism to reallocate significant amounts of resource from those whom the market might provide it to, towards those to whom it denies opportunity to achieve unless intervention by the state takes place. This is not to say charity has no role to play, and the special status of charitable action is reflected in much tax law for this very reason, but it is not a widespread solution to the empathic need of many in society to respond to the need of others.

Tax and redistribution

Tax provides that mechanism. My suggestion is that, as a consequence of tax playing that role, the gain from redistribution is more than that which simply results from the redistribution of resources. (Although that will invariably be positive, both by reducing over-consumption and because the benefit to those in relative or even near relative poverty from additional resources being made available to them will, for reasons of their enhanced marginal benefit from achievement compared to that of those already well off noted in Diagram 8.23, be greater than the loss to those who forego achievement to effect this purpose.)

There is also a gain to society, community and purpose over and above that because of the empathic gain that results from greater equality: a fact evidenced by more equal societies invariably performing better, as noted by Richard Wilkinson and Kate Pickett in their ground-breaking book 'The Spirit Level'.[2]

To put it another way: after redistribution as a result of tax paid this outcome may result:

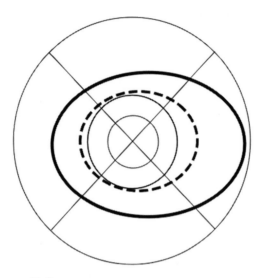

Diagram 11.5

These are the same two people as in Diagram 11.4, but now the poorer of the two is out of relative poverty, the better off of the two still achieves somewhat more than the other, but with reduced differential, and because of empathic gains the sum of the total areas in Diagram 11.5 will be greater than the sum of the total areas in Diagram 11.4: there is a symbiotic gain as well as an absolute advantage from redistribution in relieving poverty.

Note, incidentally, that as a result of the redistribution the worse-off of the two just creeps out of relative poverty. That is not a coincidence: it is likely that the point of relief from relative poverty is the point where redistribution ceases to be demanded. Of course, where that point lies is subjective and a matter for a government to decide upon, but the criteria for setting it is clear: it arises when all have the opportunity to participate fully in the opportunities that exist in the society in which they live. Courageous governments might presume that point somewhat further away from absolute poverty than cowardly ones, not least because correcting the imbalance does require that a courageous government stand up to those forces seeking to exacerbate imbalance for their own purposes, including the advertising industry and much of the media that is dependent upon it. However it is determined, I suggest that the basic objective of redistribution through tax is that all should be free of relative poverty, meaning that they can fully participate with real prospect of achieving in society. Of course, if that objective were achieved many more would be lifted way beyond the relative and even absolute poverty to which the market would consign them as shown by Diagram 10.14 than would just reach a point of basic achievement of this goal. That is why a thorough policy of proper redistribution through tax might overall take an economy to a situation closer to Diagram 10.13.

The five Rs of taxation

What this point makes clear is that the goal of taxation is more than the simple raising of revenue, which might be seen by many as its primary goal. If revenue raising is therefore the first R of taxation[3] (Raising Revenue) then the second is the Repricing of market externalities (to counter market excess and externalities), and the third is Redistribution. These goals are not determined by the market, of course, but are instead controlled through another, equally effective choice mechanism – democratic representation. This in itself indicates the fourth reason for tax: engagement by the people of a country with taxation ensures they also engage with its democratic process, in which they then have a clear and tangible stake. As such, the fourth R of taxation is Raising Representation through the democratic process. That, of course, takes us back to Nye Bevan and his point noted earlier that democracy, extreme poverty and great wealth are incompatible. Democracy is fundamental to resolving the disparities in wealth that can incapacitate societies, but tax is the delivery mechanism for doing so.

Fiscal policy – and why it's so much more useful than monetary policy

Then there is a final and fifth R of taxation. That is Reorganising the economy through what is called fiscal policy. This is the use of the balance between government revenue collection through tax and its spending to achieve its objectives to influence the overall direction of the economy.

If the government spends more than it collects, and funds the difference either by borrowing or creating cash in its own right (euphemistically 'printing money', but recently undertaken through quantitative easing), then it effectively counterbalances the stock of incomplete cash transactions that the market creates. In effect, the government 'over-completes' transactions when it does this, and does so to compensate for the cash economy over saving (which is the same, in effect, as failing to complete transactions). As a result the government creates growth in the economy as a whole. But if the economy as a whole is growing too fast because the market's own cash is being used for investment that creates current demand for goods and services in excess of the current capacity of the economy to meet it, then the government can underspend its tax receipts to deflate the economy.

As a consequence, tax plays a vital role in this overall goal of economic management, but it is important to note that so too might other measures, and to also note just what the objective of this management process is. That overall objective is, of course, to achieve the situation shown in Diagram 10.13, As we now know, the market will disrupt this outcome as an inevitable consequence of its nature. Macroeconomic management is therefore the task of achieving the goals noted in Diagram 11.1.

Fiscal policy – using tax to overcome the imbalances in the economy – is one way to do this, but the importance of the situation shown in Diagram 10.12 (reflected also in Diagram 10.14) and reproduced here cannot be overstated:

Diagram 10.12 (repeated)

The circle of capacity, in this case for the economy as a whole, is in this case the circle on the left. Partly contained within it, and partly outside it, is the dashed area of transactions undertaken in cash within that real economy – transactions that exceed the capacity of the economy on a sustainable basis in this case. And then, way out beyond the economy is another whole area, the bolder solid area, that represents the cash used for speculative, portfolio-based savings activity: an activity that includes the third type of cash transaction, which is transactions in cash itself, i.e. currency speculation.

Currently fiscal policy is one of only two choices for governments seeking to manage their economic goals. Monetary policy is the other; that is using the interest rate to manage the level of borrowing and saving in the economy (higher rates suppressing economic activity and lower ones boosting it). There are, however three problems to this preferred choice of monetary policy.

First, if it is the intention of macroeconomic policy to have impact upon the domestic economy, then monetary policy is not very helpful because it probably has greatest impact upon the relationship between the domestic economy and other economies through the impact it has upon exchange rates. When interest rates are high the exchange rate rises, imports are cheap, exports are dear and so the domestic economy makes little and consumes a lot: that's far from helpful if the rate is increased to deflate the economy, and vice versa.

Second, monetary policy can add considerably to the amount paid in interest and that simply adds to the amount stripped from the real, productive economy and transferred to those who hold cash resources outside it. The stock of incomplete transactions increases, and while this has a negative impact on growth it increases the volatility of the economy as a whole due to more money being held in the finance sector without being put to productive use. All transactions do, of course, ultimately have two impacts and it is most unwise to ignore that fact

Third, monetary policy ceases to have impact when real or notional interest rates are set at around 0% as they have been since 2009. At that point the impact of monetary policy appears negligible.

Monetary policy is therefore in general a poor alternative to fiscal policy. In any economy, the obvious desire of any government that wants to ensure that the impact of the financial sector and speculative activity is kept to a minimum on the real economy in which people actually live, work and sustain themselves, is that real interest rates be kept as low as possible. This keeps transactions within the productive economy as far as possible. That, in itself, sets another goal for fiscal policy: it has the objective of reducing the impact of the speculative, financial, economy upon the real economy. The implications of this for policy will be considered in Part 3, but for now it also opens up another opportunity for consideration, which is that if taxes are to undertake this role then other mechanisms have to be used in conjunction with it to compensate for the diminished role that monetary policy should play in macroeconomic management.

The other tools of macroeconomic management

There are at least five other mechanisms available for macroeconomic management.

The first is that regulation also has a key role to play within the economy, whether with regard to tax or otherwise. Fiscal policy is not just about setting rates, or even deciding what taxes to use; it is also about setting specific rules within the tax code to achieve specific objectives. So, for example, rules that might prevent tax relief for advertising costs being claimed for offset against profit for corporation tax purposes might be of benefit in curtailing spending on advertising for all the reasons noted desirable in this book. Some might call this a complication in the tax code, but it is not: it is about using regulation to achieve economic goals. That justifies the complication. More possibilities of this sort are considered in Part 3 of this book.

Second, and more broadly, regulation has to be used to curtail the impact of the financial / speculative sector on the real economy. So, for example, banking needs to be firmly regulated. It is not a business like any other: it is a core part of the real economy to the extent that it creates the vast majority of the cash used in that economy (a privilege for which it charges others but for which it is not itself charged) but it also manages much of the non-productive financial / speculative economy. Regulation to ensure that the privilege of creating money (giving rise to an income once claimed by the Crown, and which should now be due to the Exchequer, and which is called seigniorage) is not being used to subsidise speculative activity is essential. In principle, that is only possible if those banks that are operating in the real economy are distinct from those operating in the financial / speculative economy. Again, this is an issue I return to in Part 3 of this book.

The third scenario is when the real economy is under pressure and failing to perform (usually indicated by a lack of full employment so that people are not achieving their potential with regard to the opportunity to work, and in return, with regard the opportunity to consume the material resources which they need to avoid absolute or relative poverty). It is then obvious that more of the 'incomplete' transactions that constitute the savings made in the financial / speculative economy (that by definition have failed to complete on the implicit promise that gives value to money) must be forced to complete transactions, resulting in an exchange in the real economy and so be drawn back into productive use.

This can be done by tax policy, of course, resulting in a fiscal deficit on the government's current account, but there is another mechanism that can be used to great effect – and which was during the Second World War. That is a requirement that banks hold a part of their assets in Treasury Deposit Receipts. These are cash deposits of a bank held with the Bank of England at very low interest rates as part of the regulatory capital a bank is required to hold as a condition of trading. The impact is similar to the issue of government bonds, except the money is enforceably held by the Bank of England to withdraw it from speculation and to ensure it is available to support the productive economy. It does therefore, in effect, reclaim the benefit of seigniorage from commercial banks for the benefit of society at a time when the economy is in need of an increase in real economic activity which is being denied to it by the speculative economy. That happens because during periods when economic activity is depressed, savings tend to rise (for reasons described by Lord Keynes as 'the paradox of thrift'), with an increase in resources allocated to the unproductive savings / speculative sector as a result. The use of Treasury Deposit Receipts can overcome this tendency and make sure cash deposited with banks is returned to productive use.

In the fourth scenario regulation can ensure that tax reliefs are used to direct funds saved into productive investment and out of the speculative / financial economy. So, for example, tax relief of about £38bn a year is given in the UK to funds saved in pension funds.[4] Well over 90% of those funds are invested in 'second-hand assets', i.e. shares already in issue, existing property, and the like, all of which are then as a consequence part of the speculative economy in that their purchase does not create any new investment in the real economy.

While it is undoubtedly true that for the sake of being able to pay future pensions, some pension contributions have to be dedicated to ensuring that a market in second-hand financial assets does exist, the importance of liquidity in those markets is drastically overstated. It was claimed prior to 2008 that a major role for the speculative / financial economy was the provision of liquidity for the banking sector and that banking and other financial markets could not survive without that support, but in September 2008 that liquidity completely dried up precisely when it was needed and it was the Bank of England that had to provide the liquidity the sector needed for many months. The lesson learned is that the speculative / financial economy does not actually provide liquidity, and nor is banking or the financial market as a whole nearly so dependent upon the existence of the massive levels of trading that occur in the City of London and elsewhere for their liquidity; like so much else, it is governments that underpin that. In that case, a significant part of the £80obn or more of funds being put into pension funds in the UK each year can be compulsorily directed straight into investment in new job creation in the economy as a condition of the tax relief given to those contributions. This type of creative conditionality of tax reliefs has not yet been explored in the UK, and is well overdue for use.

And in the fifth scenario credit controls are an essential part of economic management of the economy. They must be used to limit excess consumer credit, especially that used for consumption and often issued on credit and store cards. Here, central monitoring of credit to limit supply to any person is essential. But more than that, credit for speculation must also be limited; so, for example, steps must be taken through regulation and the tax system to limit borrowing to fuel property speculation that has denied access to home ownership to far too many in the UK, and action is also needed to limit bank lending for financial speculation, including on its own account. One way to do this is, without doubt, to limit tax relief on borrowing for commercial purposes, and this is considered further in Part 3 of this book.

The attributes of a good tax system

All of this activity, whether with regard to tax or with regard to the related and additional measures a government can use to regulate the macroeconomy, assumes that a national capacity to act on these issues is available. It is obvious that a good tax system has to be:

1   Comprehensive – in other words, it is broad-based;
2   Complete – with as few loopholes as possible;
3   Comprehensible – it is as certain as is reasonably possible;
4   Compassionate – it takes into account the capacity to pay;
5   Compact – it is written as straightforwardly as possible;
6   Compliant with human rights;
7   Compensatory – it is perceived as fair and redistributes income and wealth as necessary to achieve this aim;
8   Complementary to social objectives;
9   Computable – the liability can be calculated with reason

All of which facilitate the chance that it will be:

10 Competently managed.

In combination these are key attributes of a good tax system.

It is equally obvious that this requires that it be possible to put in place a six-stage management process for a national tax system is dependent on it being possible to:

1   Define the tax base. This is the first essential step in creating progressive taxation and in promoting the better use of resources within society;

2   Find what is to be taxed. If the tax base cannot be accurately located then there is no point trying to tax it;

3   Count the tax base. Unless the tax base can be quantified it cannot be taxed;

4   Tax the tax base at the right rates of tax. In the process, making sure the inter-relationship between the various tax bases is properly managed to ensure that the essential revenue raising, repricing and redistributive qualities of a just tax system is vital;

5   Allocate the resulting revenues efficiently and to best social effect;

6   Report outcomes, because governments must be accountable for what they do with tax revenues or the democratic principle fails.

However, to achieve these goals the Courageous State has to both believe they are entitled to create such tax systems and to then enforce them. That cannot happen by chance. To achieve it, information is needed. That means all potentially taxable people, whether they are human beings or legal entities created under law, must be transparent about what they do, are, and have done, and that is true whether they choose to locate themselves within the state where their transactions occur or seek to record that they exist outside it. The latter situation is of course, a particularly prevalent problem when it comes to the use of tax havens, or secrecy jurisdictions, as I prefer to call them. This is because secrecy jurisdictions are places that intentionally create regulation for the primary benefit and use of those not resident in their geographical domain. That regulation is designed to undermine the legislation or regulation of another jurisdiction. To facilitate its use, secrecy jurisdictions also create a deliberate, legally backed veil of secrecy that ensures that those from outside the jurisdiction making use of its regulation cannot be identified to be doing so.

As a consequence, the creation of financial transparency is a vital ingredient within and beyond the state to ensure tax is collected and the problem of asymmetric information in markets is also overcome as far as is possible. Financial transparency exists when the following information is readily available to all who might need it to appraise transactions they or others might undertake or have undertaken with another natural or legal person:

1   Who that other person is;
2   Where the person is;
3   What right the person has to enter into a transaction;
4   What capacity the person has to enter into a transaction.

And with regard to entities that are not natural persons:

5   What the nature of the entity is;
6   On whose behalf the entity is managed;
7   Who manages the entity;
8   What transactions the entity has entered into;
9   Where it has entered into those transactions;
10   Who has actually benefited from the transactions;
11   Whether all obligations arising from the transactions have been properly fulfilled.

The last, of course, includes the obligation to pay tax.

There is, however, only one way to achieve this goal, and that is through international cooperation. It is, of course, the case that international trade, migration, multinational corporations, tax havens and tax evasion through fraud and tax avoidance undertaken with the assistance of the financial services industry are facts of life. Some of those are positive to well-being and some are decidedly negative, but all are potential impediments to the proper collection of tax unless there is international cooperation to achieve this objective. That is why this is an issue I return to again in Part 3 of this book. Unless there is clear, effective, and strong cooperation on these issues, or as an alternative, an equally clear policy of sanctions against those who violate the principles of financial transparency, the prospects of maintaining an effective tax system are reduced.

Capital controls

That is not, however, the end to international cooperation on economic policy. Unless there is also cooperation on the regulation of the flows of capital between the world's economies, then an unlevel playing field is created, where the enormous cash resources of the speculative / financial economy can be used to threaten the stability of exchanges taking place in the real economy for transactions relating to the exchange of goods and services in the course of trade. The impact of this is all too readily seen as currencies around the world are brought low by speculators, exchange rates fluctuate without apparent meaning and governments run scared of so called 'bond vigilantes' in the world's banks who they think will refuse to buy their debt unless and until they put into place tax and other policies on spending that the financial / speculative economy thinks in its own best interest, and that of the wealthy they serve.

This may be the point where the state has to be most courageous of all. Until 1980 there were measures in place to deal with such issues, and most particularly capital controls on foreign exchange. Then in pursuit of the aims of neoliberalism, Thatcher, Reagan and in turn the governments of most states in the world, abandoned such controls in favour of an ethos of the free movement of capital, but not (most emphatically) of labour. The result has been obvious: returns to capital have increased while those to labour have reduced. In the UK in 1980 labour enjoyed 58% of GDP according to the Office for National Statistics; the ratio is about 53% now with returns to capital rising commensurately. This, of course, explains the shift in wealth towards a few in society who locate their activities in the financial / speculative economy that exists largely beyond that of the real economy as noted in Diagram 10.12.

This shift did not happen by chance: it was the entirely deliberate and planned outcome of neoliberal economic policy, reversing a trend in favour of labour over the previous three decades of the post-war era during which Keynesian policy improved the relative lot of ordinary people. The entire structure of the offshore tax haven world was at the same time liberated by this move to free capital controls that let the offshore world become a fundamental component in the mechanisms challenging the right of states to manage their economies and collect the taxes due to them. The removal of exchange controls let money flow to tax havens unaccountably. The subsequent removal of tax withholding on most payments of income to these places – whether that payment be of be interest, royalties, dividends, licence fees or such-like that fuel the income of the financial / speculative economy behind ring fences of legal privilege, ensured that not only is the money supposedly located in such places untraceable, but untaxed in its untraceability.

Thereafter, having claimed the privilege of being untaxed and untraceable, those funds are then used – very often by hedge funds, which almost always locate themselves and their assets in tax havens – to mount attacks on the currencies and financial stability of the countries that granted tax havens almost total freedom from regulation in 1980 in what was probably the greatest act of political and economic negligence ever perpetrated without direct human suffering being involved.

The question now arises as to how control over capital flows can be reclaimed and three solutions seem clear. The first is that the whole logic of the freedom of capital to move unhindered has to be challenged. It is a very obvious assault on the real economy and the rights of real people designed to create the imbalance shown in Diagram 10.14. It is not just tax, therefore, that requires international cooperation; international cooperation is essential if this challenge to well-being is to be addressed. Second, therefore, the whole logic of tax haven/secrecy jurisdiction activity that exists almost solely to facilitate this unregaulated and unchallenged movement of capital has to be challenged. And third, the issue of transparency that would make activity traceable and therefore controllable has to be addressed.

There are several ways to do this, and each will in turn be explored a little more in Chapter 14.

First, the need for capital controls has to be recognised and cooperation will be needed to reintroduce them. There is no way that the stability desperately needed for the world's economies to meet the needs of real people can be created without this now being recognised as critical to well-being. The impact of the volatility of free-roaming capital is now far too obvious for it to be allowed to continue. Of course, such controls should not be designed to impede real trade, but the currency movements that now facilitate such real trade flows are now a tiny proportion of the trillions of dollars and other currencies traded daily when world GDP (by no means all of which crosses international borders) is only just over US$60 trillion a year according to the World Bank. Flows for other purposes – such as speculation – should be impeded, routinely, as they are likely to be harmful to trade and do not create useful liquidity.

Second, for those places refusing to participate in capital controls, withholding taxes on payments made should be the norm, meaning that tax must be deducted at source from all payments made to any location that refuses to participate in an exchange control regime unless it can be proven that payment is being made for a documented trade genuinely emanating from the place to which payment is made. However, even then distinction must be made: payment for the supply of goods to such a location may be tax-free but the payment for services should not be; since the origin of services is always hard to prove, tax deduction should be the universal in their case, although at a lower rate than that used for pure financial flows. Thankfully, existing VAT systems already more than adequately differentiate flows between goods, services and pure finance for accounting purposes, so the imposition of such charges will not be hard, but nothing else but tax withholding could better enforce a system of capital controls with sanctions attached against those states unwilling to participate.

Third, financial transactions taxes have to be introduced in the form envisaged by James Tobin with the deliberate intention of 'throwing sand in the wheels' of financial speculation, as he suggested. However, as that tax is unlikely to impede speculation, but simply raise revenue from it, what is known as the Spahn variant of this tax[5] is needed – which increases the tax rate automatically when speculative flows increase, so making such speculation uneconomic.

Fourth, multinational corporations can at present routinely hide many of their transactions and internal group trades in tax havens, providing opportunity for tax abuse as well as illicit financial flows and corrupt transactions. This opportunity is available to them because of the secrecy those places provide, where accounts are not required to be placed on public record. It is also possible because of the form of accounting currently required of such companies that only discloses to users of their accounts those trades that take place between the companies that make up a multinational group and third parties; this means that that users of those accounts are left wholly in the dark about the nature of flows in trade within multinational corporations that might make up between 40% and 60% of world trade (the OECD seems to be unsure, simply indicating yet more reason why data on these flows, many through tax havens, need to be disclosed). A new form of accounting called country-by-country reporting[6] (which I should disclose that I created) would tackle this issue and make data available on what multinational corporations do where, as it would also disclose how much tax they did and did not pay in each and every place where they traded, so holding capital to account wherever it is. Its adoption is now in the agenda of the European Union, Organisation for Economic Cooperation and Development, the International Accounting Standards Board and others, and it would transform transparency in world trade and reinforce necessary tax, trade and regulatory controls if adopted.

Fifth, the world has simply not cooperated sufficiently to ensure that each state is supplied with the information it needs from other countries around the world to ensure its own residents, whether companies, trusts, foundations or individuals, are properly taxed. Extraordinarily, until a decade or so ago the default position on tax cooperation was that states should not cooperate on such matters, exceptions being relatively rare and governed by a somewhat exclusive network of bipartisan treaties that were very difficult to use. That attitude has now, thankfully, changed a little but the automatic exchange of information on what the tax resident of one state earns in another tax jurisdiction is still very unusual, and is heavily opposed by many tax haven states. Such opposition of course, serves the interests of the financial / speculative economy very well, but it also fundamentally undermines the well-being of the vast majority of the people of the world onto whom much of the responsibility for paying taxes has been shifted as a result, since those states that refuse to cooperate have done so to deliberately drive down tax rates on unearned income such as interest, dividends, or the tax rate on corporate profits, which are highly mobile and easily hidden offshore. It is essential as a result that systems for ensuring that income earned by a tax resident of one state earned by them in another jurisdiction is reported to the state in which they reside so that the risk of tax evasion and avoidance, which is high on all international transactions, is mitigated.

These are, of course, ambitious goals. But they are not unrealistic. As the global financial crisis of 2008, and its potential recurrence in 2011 show, the economies of the world are not isolated: they are an interconnected symbiotic system. Despite that, each reflects the different cultures, aspirations, hopes and (hopefully) democratic wills of the populations that make them up. The feral nature of the financial / speculative economy, created and driven by neoliberal logic, has sought to impose a uniform economic policy on all states through the power of that market to attack any economy at will if it wishes. That was never the case before 1980. Before then states had a choice about their tax, spending, and economic policies. The neoliberal drive was to end that difference because that diversity had challenged the wealth of a minority.

The result of that challenge that was made possible by permitting freedom for capital to roam the world at will was that governments were coerced to act in acquiescence to the neoliberal wish. That has very obviously been the wrong direction of travel. It has not reflected the genuine diversity of the world, the differing economic aspirations and wishes of the economies of the world, or the different societies of the world. The result has been all too obvious tension within and between nations as far too many people's aspirations and potential have been dashed to suit the whims of the market. That is why we need to rebuild the mechanisms that let us monitor capital and to then bring it back under control, using regulation to ensure it is the servant of the state again, and not its master.

There is a solution to this. That is the solution of the Courageous State. That state has its own identity, and a confidence in it. It is a state that can and wants to manage its own economic, tax and other affairs in accordance with the will of its people. But it is also a state that recognises the right of other sovereign states to do that as well. So the Courageous State is also about cooperation between states, but cooperation in diversity rather than cooperation in uniformity. Courageous States recognise the diversity of the world and they do so for a reason. They recognise that the people of the world cannot live in their own courageous states in which they can achieve their own potential unless the diversity of each and every person on earth is also respected, encouraged and fulfilled.

That is the goal of the individual's courageous state; it is the goal of the Courageous State and through cooperation it can be the goal of the united Courageous States of the world.

1   *Hansard*, November 11, 1947
2   Wilkinson, R and Pickett, K. 2009, *The Spirit Level: Why More Equal Societies Almost Always Do Better*, Allen Lane, London.
3   The Rs of taxation were first suggested by Alex Cobham, now head of policy at Christian Aid in the UK, previously of Oxford University. He created the first four, I added the fifth.
4   See Murphy, R, 2010, *Making Pensions Work* Finance for the Future, at http://www.financeforthefuture.com/MakingPensionsWork.pdf
5   See http://en.wikipedia.org/wiki/Spahn_tax for discussion of this variant
6   See http://www.financialtaskforce.org/wp-content/uploads/2009/06/Final_CbyC_Report_Published.pdf for more information

CHAPTER 12

SUMMARY OF PART 2 ARGUMENTS

How should the thinking in this second part of this book be summarised? To do that let me suggest some relationships that need to be explicitly linked.

First of all, look at banking. It's my suggestion that the UK has considerably too much banking and financial services activity for its own good. It's my belief that it represents an excessive proportion of economic activity. More than that: I believe that this excess actually squeezes out other more productive economic activity that would be of benefit to the UK.

Let me put this idea on a graph:

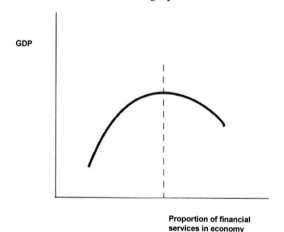

Diagram 12.1

As the proportion of financial services in an economy rises then I am clearly suggesting that benefits can arise: money is an amazing thing, with the power to release all sorts of advantages and it would be wrong to deny it.

But I am also suggesting that there comes a point over the longer term (and all that I am saying here is an analysis over time because the impacts being discussed arise over years and even decades, not days and months) when those advantages can be outweighed by the disadvantages of an excess of financial services in an economy. Too much banking can crowd out real money-making in real business that makes goods and services people want and need. This is the widely recognised economic concept of 'squeezing out' in operation.

The same can also be true of too much speculation within an economy as opposed to real wealth creation. It would appear glaringly obvious that having large numbers of intelligent people spending their lives gambling cannot be good for the generation of real well-being and yet this is encouraged in our current economy. Since speculative trading is not the same as making things, the diversion of real talent towards the moving of money around the financial system can eventually deny talent to the production of goods and services, education and art, care and creativity that any society really wants and needs.

When this happens – when squeezing out occurs – I suggest that the long-term GDP of a country actually goes down because there's too much banking going on. And that's what this graph shows: there is a tipping point beyond which too much speculative banking is not good for us. It's my suggestion that we reached that point some time ago and that we are on the right-hand side of this graph now, where the return from banking is a reduction in our national income.

I stress when saying this that this is not a criticism of what is not called High Street banking that handles payment management and finances businesses, mortgages and so on. That's a service and I am quite sure it is beneficial and no suggestion is being made it squeezes out real economic activity, precisely because it helps that activity. The banking referred to is providing excessive consumer credit, speculative banking and related financial services industry activity.

But how does this excessive speculation arise? How do we get a banking sector too big for the needs of an economy? As I've argued, advertising is the mechanism used to create the dissatisfaction that encourages people to both over-consume and to stay in debt. This characteristic of advertising can be added to the graph noted above by adding an additional right-hand axis and using the X axis in two ways:

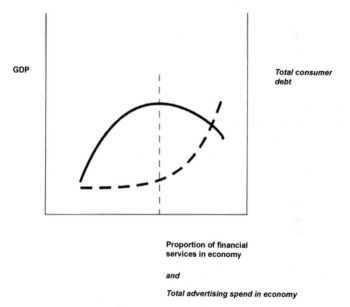

GDP

Total consumer debt

Proportion of financial services in economy

and

Total advertising spend in economy

Diagram 12.2

What the graph now shows is the relationship between long-term GDP and financial services noted above, which remains the same solid line whilst the dashed line now shows that as advertising spending rises so does the value of consumer debt. At first the relationship is weak: there is no doubt at all that some advertising does serve the purpose of supplying information and increases knowledge of the options available to individuals. Some plays a very valuable function: for example, job advertising, newspaper small ads and property sale notices. In that case it is not being suggested that all advertising has a negative impact, either at all, or on debt in particular.

However, as with banking there comes a point of inflexion where the goal of advertising changes and the returns on it change too. At that point, which is, I think, near enough where banking also reaches its natural limit in size as a service of social value, advertising begins to be used to encourage consumption beyond the capacity of either a society or the earth to support it, and the incomes of those doing the consuming to sustain it, meaning that debt is then the main driver for that increase in consumption driven by this advertising-led consumption. So debt rises, fuelling additional banking activity, but the impact on the economy as a whole may not be positive. Debt repayments reduce the capacity of the economy overall by sucking opportunity away from the relatively least well-off in society by reducing their long-tem capacity to spend as they face mounting debt, while transferring their monetary worth to those already wealthy who then save it, so denying economic activity to the economy (except bankers, who over-expand their activities as a result).

There is a further consequence. This is the impact on the wealth gap. It looks like this:

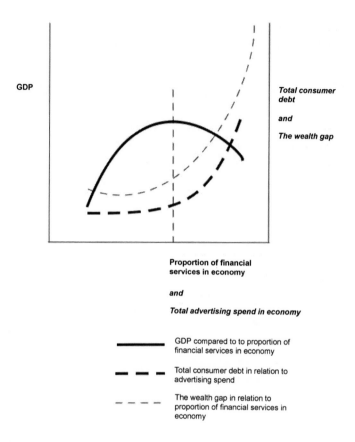

Diagram 12.3

What is now shown is that the wealth gap increases as banking takes on a dysfunctional role in society and advertising fuels excess consumption. More than that, as the share of financial services increases, a point is reached where keeping this inequality in place actually becomes policy. We see this, for example, in tax havens where the scale of financial services is very high (it is more than 50% of GDP in Jersey for example) and there are deliberate laws that intentionally exacerbate inequality, for example by attracting very wealthy people by offering them very low overall rates of tax on their income that mean they will inevitably accumulate wealth more quickly than local people resident in those tax havens possibly could. Incidentally, note that I suggest that at lower levels of activity on the left-hand side, increased advertising and banking may reduce that wealth gap: that seems intuitively obvious and is the reason why well-regulated markets do undoubtedly help real wealth generation in poorer countries.

But it's not just GDP that might actually fall as a result of this dysfunctional behaviour, although I think it might well do so: real well-being may as well. Let's add that to the graph too:

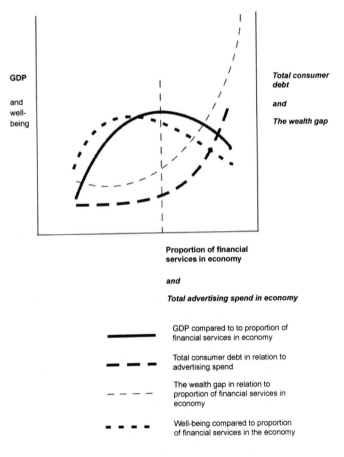

GDP

and well-being

Total consumer debt

and

The wealth gap

Proportion of financial services in economy

and

Total advertising spend in economy

——	GDP compared to to proportion of financial services in economy
– ▬ –	Total consumer debt in relation to advertising spend
— – – –	The wealth gap in relation to proportion of financial services in economy
▪ ▪ ▪ ▪	Well-being compared to proportion of financial services in the economy

Diagram 12.4

238

Well-being almost certainly peaks earlier than GDP in an economy – rising inequality will start to reduce well-being before
GDP peaks in most cases, and excess consumption can reduce the
potential of people to achieve and the prospects of sustainability
long before banks can tip GDP onto a downward trajectory, but
what is also clear is that well-being then falls faster than GDP. That
is the inevitable conclusion of the arguments in this book that
are also to be found, for example, in 'The Spirit Level' by Richard
Wilkinson and Kate Pickett, which is the best book on this thesis.

What all this means then is that beyond a certain point, further
growth in the financial services/GDP ratio becomes damaging to
a society. At this point, money market manipulation by banks
dominates their traditional role of acting for savers and borrowers and as managers of payment systems. Although there can
be short-term economic benefits, in the longer term this leads
to lower GDP. This is because the 'success' of financial services
squeezes out other, more genuinely productive sectors of the
economy; and also because putting so many of an economy's eggs
in the risky basket of financial services is likely to lead to greater
volatility over time, with successive shocks (or crashes) imposing
serious costs that destroys productivity in the rest of the economy.

But more than that, this excessive expansion has human and
social effects. As the financial services/GDP ratio passes a certain
point, the economy becomes so dependent on this sector that
policymakers risk being captured to the point that they confuse
the financial services sector's interests with the national interest
and then write regulations and policy (including those on tax)
to suit that sector, rather than society as a whole. That, almost
inevitably then gives rise directly to higher inequality, because
it supports, for example, lower taxation on capital and high
incomes, and higher taxation on consumption through taxes like
VAT, which invariably hit the poorest hardest proportionately.
Since at any level of GDP the authors of 'The Spirit Level' have
shown that higher inequality is associated with worse human and
social outcomes, it follows that long-term well-being falls with
higher levels of financial services, even before the long-run GDP
effects becomes negative, as I show above.

Overall, this analysis demonstrates the case for the Courageous State. It shows how easy it is for policymakers to go along with a status quo that is built on the dominance of the financial services sector, not least when short-term gains for GDP are put ahead of long-term well-being. It needs a Courageous State to challenge that short-term view now and for the future.

In that case, what do we need to do? That's the subject of Part 3, where the policy implications of these ideas are explored.

SOLUTIONS

CHAPTER 13
IDENTIFYING THE COURAGEOUS STATE

Based on the arguments in the first two parts of this book I hope it is now clear that the Courageous State has three goals.

First, it wants to run its own economy in accordance with its democratic mandate to achieve a balanced outcome that is sustainable and that permits as many of its resident population to achieve as much of their potential as possible.

Second, the Courageous State wants to cooperate internationally so that other states can achieve the same goal for themselves.

Third, it wants to provide as much freedom as it can to its population to explore their potential while imposing only those constraints necessary to ensure that a balanced society results. The result should be personal courageous states where individual risk-taking – not just economic, but across the whole spectrum of life – is possible.

It is important to note that these goals are fundamentally different to those of the feral, neoliberal state we now have. That state that sings to the neoliberal tune and runs its economy to primarily meet the needs of the financial / speculative economy that exists largely outside the real economy in which real people live, work and exchange. Internationally, the neoliberal state succumbs to the demands of international finance represented in popular myth as 'the bond markets'.

It is also important to say that the Courageous State is also different from the post-war consensus. In a nutshell that consensus offered a bargain with the people of the developed world, offering better material living standards for all now, and for their children thereafter. In the process it ignored the constraints of the planet. Oil found it out and led to its downfall.

In contrast to the post-war consensus, the feral neoliberal economy offered a different bargain with the people of the world: it offered (relatively) stable consumer prices, an illusion of wealth through asset inflation and cheap, readily available credit so that people could have whatever they wanted as soon as advertising succeeded in persuading them of their desire for it. The mountain of debt this created as an elite accumulated unsustainable wealth has found this model out and has led to its downfall.

The Courageous State offers a different bargain with the people of the world. It offers those people the chance to fulfil their potential, both economic and otherwise, in a world that offers them and their children sustainable hope for their future. No one has done that before, but the Courageous State is a not a twist on what we've had: it is about creating politics fit for the 21st century.

In saying that I know, of course, that the degree to which any state can be courageous depends to some degree upon the eventual extent of international cooperation there is on these goals; there is no point pretending otherwise. But for all those who say that is unlikely to happen, it is wise to recall that for many years neoliberals thought they had no hope of overturning the post-war Keynesian consensus that delivered the greatest period of sustainable increased prosperity the world has ever seen. However, they did just that. Circumstances gave them the opportunity and they took it. The current world economic crisis provides the opportunity to create the Courageous State. To put it another way: without courage, the Courageous State will not happen, but the time for it to be created is now.

All that being said, in reality Courageous States will not be built on theory; Courageous States will be built on the back of practical policies delivered by courageous governments. That's why this last part of this book looks at the policies that would identify a Courageous State. There is, after all, no point in promoting a Courageous State if you can't identify one when you see it.

Recognising the Courageous State

Courageous States are driven by principles. Of course they'll also be pragmatic sometimes – politics always is, and has to be an exercise in pragmatism. But principles matter in a Courageous State. This will be a fundamental change that will differentiate them from the neoliberal states they will replace.

Those principles are reflected in the following beliefs:

- People come first;
- People must have the opportunity to achieve their potential;
- Poverty is unacceptable;
- Sustainability is essential;
- Balance is best for human well-being;
- Government has to work well;
- Real business deserves strong support.

These are joined by concerns about issues that undermine well-being which the Courageous State will have to tackle:

- Financial speculation is always secondary to real business, the community and society at large and can harm the prospect of society achieving its potential;

- The payment of interest is the cause of considerable stress within the economy;

- Advertising seriously distorts behaviour in the economy and reduces the chance of people achieving their potential by encouraging over-consumption.

Concerns not dissimilar to these have, admittedly, been at the forefront of thinking before now: the Beveridge Report settled the five priorities on which in very many ways the post-war consensus was built, saying they were:

1 Want;
2 Idleness;

3   Ignorance;
4   Squalor;
5   Disease.

As a result, growth, full employment, education, housing and health became the focus of social policy post-1945, and rightly so. They would also be priorities for the Courageous State. They were, however, the goals from an era when poverty was so widespread that what now seems pejorative language could be used to describe the objectives the state set when seeking to improve the conditions of a great many people. Of course they remain relevant: absolute and relative poverty remain pressing issues in the UK, and yet the Courageous State needs to aim for more than their relief. The Courageous State has to set itself the goal of ensuring people's potential can be achieved. That can only happen if the following are available:

1   Rewarding work;
2   Safe banking;
3   A sustainable environment;
4   Affordable homes;
5   Security in old age;
6   Nurturing environments;
7   Communities where we belong;
8   Healthcare;
9   A work–life balance;
10   Opportunity for meaningful leisure.[1]

These are the objectives, but objectives require practical policies if they are to be fulfilled. The result is that the Courageous State needs to have policies to:

1   Constrain the world of feral finance that has so dominated the economies of the world in the last thirty years;

2   Rebuild the role of the state in supporting real business activity;

3   Encouraged a balanced, sustainable economy;

4   Support the broader goals of family, community and society and the achievement of purpose through identity;

5   Cooperate internationally to support the rights of Courageous States.

These are the issues that would drive policy in the Courageous State. Since there is no chance in the space available of outlining all the policies that the Courageous State might want to promote to deal with these concerns, an outline under these five broad headings must suffice. Each policy is listed in the area of concern where it might fit best for description purposes, but in very many cases there will be overlap and straightforward complementarity. A little jumping around may therefore be needed to find the answer on particular issues.

---

1   My thanks to Larry Elliott, Neal Lawson, Andrew Simms and Tony Greenham for input into preparing this list

CHAPTER 14

CONSTRAINING THE WORLD OF

FERAL FINANCE

If the feral world of neoliberal finance worked there would be no reason to discuss the Courageous State. As the evidence of 2007 and onwards has shown however, economies based on neo-liberal economics do not work.

The stock of financial assets in the world is, according to some reports (and these figures are always going to be estimates) some $220 trillion,[1] of which about $150 trillion is believed to be debt of various sorts. World GDP is about $63 trillion.[2] Meanwhile, the total flow of financial speculative trades in the world each trading day is approximately $4 trillion[3] – or a staggering (approximate) $1 quadrillion a year. That is sixteen times more than total world income – the vast majority of which, of course, is entirely unrelated to any such trades.

As importantly, if interest at just 6% were on average charged on the total debts outstanding in the world (and of course, some rates will be much more and some a bit less) then some $9 trillion of interest would be paid a year, reallocating almost 15% of total world income from those without resources, which means they are borrowing, to those already wealthy, which means they can lend.

These are enormous numbers. These flows have the capacity to enormously distort trade and the allocation of income in the world and to put massive pressure on government to behave as the financial markets want even if against the common good.

Feral finance has to be constrained as a result. The following proposals are all designed to assist that objective.

Create financial transaction taxes

Financial transaction taxes (FTT) were first proposed by Nobel Laureate economist James Tobin in 1972. His aim was then, as I still think appropriate now, to put 'sand in the wheels of international finance', so slowing its processes down. He proposed to do this by putting a tax – a tiny tax – on all transactions converting one currency to another. Since the vast majority of these are speculative and undertaken in enormous sums to make what appear to be tiny profit margins, the intention of a financial transaction tax is to prevent a great deal of that speculation by making it unprofitable, because even if it supposedly makes money for the organisation undertaking it, the impact on the world at large is harmful.

This issue has been much discussed over recent years, not least as a result of the global financial crisis that emerged in 2008 which resulted in the emergence of the Robin Hood Tax campaign in the UK and elsewhere demanding such a tax. How much the tax would raise is open to speculation – not least because many of the variants so far proposed have had the deliberate intention of making the tax small enough to ensure that significant sums were raised from the tax to benefit development but without the intention as a result of seriously reducing the volume of trade, which would otherwise reduce the tax yield.

I do not share the logic of those proposing the tax in this form. I do not think a financial transaction tax should be viewed as a serious revenue-raising tax. I think it has the purpose of repricing activity that the market encourages but which is fundamentally harmful to human well-being until such time as that abuse is eliminated. In the case of financial transactions this would mean those relating to real trades would continue, while those for speculative purposes would almost certainly cease. As such I would suggest that higher rates should be used than those proposed by organisations seeking to raise revenue. So, for example, the rate of 0.05% proposed by the Robin Hood Tax campaign[4] is too low precisely because it will not restrict trade sufficiently.

It is, of course, true that higher rates will restrict the volume of trading. Opponents of the move say this will harm the world economy, but the exact opposite would be true. We cannot afford this speculation.

Those opponents of such a tax also say the trade will continue and the cost of the tax will be passed on to other bank users or world trade: I dispute that. First, as I note below, banks should be split so that this trade cannot take place in high street institutions; and second, if this trade were slowed down considerably there would be much greater certainty in currency prices – enhancing real world trade to its obvious benefit.

A Spahn tax

A Spahn tax is a form of financial transaction tax. Proposed by proposed by Paul Bernd Spahn in 1995, it changes the basic form of FTT by providing that in periods of high trading volatility or serious price volatility, the tax rate increases considerably. This immediately increases the price of trading to the point where in most cases it will not be worthwhile. The intention is not that tax is raised but that excessive volatility that is almost invariably both irrational and harmful is avoided. In effect, the tax puts an automatic brake on market excess and lets people take a break for a quiet reappraisal of reality, which is almost always beneficial. Such a tax has to therefore be of benefit in taming feral capitalism.

A ban on short selling

Short selling is a practice on many trading exchanges where goods are sold but the person selling them does not actually own what it is selling at the time that the sale is made. So, for example, on a stock exchange a sale is made of shares that the vendor does not own. They make the sale in the hope that by selling they force the price down so that before they have to complete the transaction they can acquire the shares they need to complete the transaction at a lower price than they sold them for, so making a profit on the deal. This is blatant speculative abuse for no end goal and as such should be banned.

Loan of shares

Some anti-speculation regulation requires that those undertaking it appear to have title to the shares they are dealing in. This is overcome by the practice of lending shares. Pension funds and other institutional investors are paid a fee by speculators to 'lend' their shares to the speculator who can then, for example, actually appear to sell them and reacquire them before returning them to the person from whom they were borrowed now worth less than when they were lent. This whole process is not only wholly unproductive: it also appears completely contrary to the fiduciary duty of fund managers to act in the best interests of those who save with them, and as such this practice should be banned.

Splitting banks

Until the 1980s many of the functions of the City of London were heavily demarcated. So, for example, stock market trading was split between those managing client relationships and those actually trading on the exchanges. Banking was also split: high street banks handled deposits and payments and lent to businesses and homeowners (by and large), while investment or merchant banks (as they were then called) dealt with takeovers and mergers and speculative trading.

As a result of the reform processes set in train by Margaret Thatcher this all changed. Stock market trading could, after her so-called 'Big Bang', all be undertaken by one firm, while banks were integrated, with one organisation able to spread itself across the entire spectrum of banking activity – including trading on its own account and that of others, at its own will. This was intended to liberate markets from regulation – and to let markets develop at will.

That is exactly what has happened, and the results have probably been much as those who promoted this market liberalisation intended. Wealth has been concentrated, and for a few has increased enormously. Banks, once minor players in the stock exchange indices, have come to dominate the FTSE indices while competition has reduced, with the result being an increase in monopoly profits captured by a few for their own benefit, as the pay of senior banking executives evidences.

There is no doubt that this enormously harmful move to concentrate power has been detrimental to well-being as a result of the over-promotion of the financial / speculative economy, both for the sake of capturing that economy for the benefit of a few senior bankers and market traders and because the combined institutions so conspicuously under-invested in the real economy, in which they had no real interest. Therefore a Courageous State must now split banks in two so that no bank involved in the processing of transactions, managing customer deposits or in routine business and household lending, including mortgages, can engage in speculative market trading; and nor can such entities themselves or through related entities rely on bulk money markets for funds as, for example, Northern Rock did. Only by doing this can the security of our money be ensured, and the massive risk to society from speculation be reduced.

Such a split would also be characterised by a considerable increase in investment in the regulation of banks. Never again must banks be allowed to assume their behaviour is so rational it cannot go wrong (which was the basis of UK regulation until 2009, as the Financial Services Authority retrospectively agreed). The reality is that banks can, and do, very obviously make mistakes – which is precisely why they must be well regulated in the future, and much more so than in the past.

State ownership of the payment platforms used by clearing banks

As this book has explained, money is made by banks and yet it gets its credibility from governments. It is because a government demands that taxes be paid in the currency it creates that the currency in question has to be used in the country it governs.

There is a massive risk in this split between the creation of money and responsibility for the credibility of money. Making money – the process by which banks create the money they lend – is intensely profitable. That is why they have become so powerful. The profit in question once belonged to the state and was called seignorage and it belonged to the state. Banks have now claimed this for themselves and yet when things go wrong – as they did in 2008 – the state picks up the bill. This is obviously wrong.

Some suggest as a result that banks should have to borrow the money they lend on from the Bank of England and pay for it. It's an interesting idea but it does not secure risk in the event of a banking failure. My suggestion is different. I suggest that the state should take over control of the various bank clearing systems operating in the UK and then licence their use to the banks in exchange for a fee in lieu of seigniorage. They should additionally have the right to take over the activity of a bank in risk of failure without compensation to ensure that its function in the bank clearing system can continue without interruption. That means the cost of failure to the state is reduced as the critical payment functions of a bank could continue without all its liabilities having to be assumed by the state. This is vital. Of course, protections on data would be needed: that would be important, but protection of society as a whole from the activities of reckless bankers is also essential, while banks should only profit from the value they really add, which is not the case at present.

Taxing banks

The reality is that even when split, as suggested above, much banking activity will be excessively profitable and distorting for the real economy. There is a remedy for this – and curiously, it comes from the tax haven world. In the UK Crown Dependencies of Jersey, Guernsey and the Isle of Man they have for a number of years (and it has to be said, for all the wrong reasons) had a policy of charging banks and other financial institutions to an additional 10% tax on their profits. The idea is worth copying, not for their reasons but because such a tax would also, or in alternative way to the previous suggestion, compensate society for the right to seigniorage on the creation of money that we have passed over to banks. That right to the profit on the creation of money belongs to society, not banks, and it is time a Courageous State reclaimed it for the common good.

Stopping tax relief on the excess incomes of those speculating

This additional tax on banks and the financial transaction taxes already referred to will not though be enough to prevent the harm banking (and related sectors in financial services) have caused: the banks have passed considerable wealth on, unaccountably, to their senior staff as their control of economic power has increased. This has been enormously harmful. It has distorted the labour market. It has denied talent to more productive uses. It has distorted housing markets. It has made the UK a much more unequal society. It has fuelled the excess consumption of a few which has then been used as a base for incentivising others to consume excessively through the use of debt. This has in turn destabilised the economy and promoted the financial / speculative economy to grow excessively. Measures have to be taken to stop this harm.

One way to do this is to make it considerably more expensive to pay high salaries in the UK. If, for example, all salary and related costs paid to a person in the UK that exceeded a sum ten times average pay (which would mean any payment in excess of about £250,000 at present) were denied tax relief when computing the employing company's tax liability, then the cost of paying such salaries would increase considerably. This does not mean that paying that salary would not be not allowed; it would still be possible for a company to pay what it liked. However, the cost of excessive salaries would not then be subsidised by the UK tax payer. Because this measure would increase the cost of paying excessive salaries, there is a good chance that the level of such salaries and the total sums involved in their payment would be reduced.

Taming tax havens

There is little prospect of taming banks if they can at any time simply relocate their transactions to tax havens, or secrecy jurisdictions as I prefer to call them. Secrecy jurisdictions are places that intentionally create regulation for the primary benefit and use of those not resident in their geographical domain. That regulation is designed to undermine the legislation or regulation of another jurisdiction. To facilitate its use, secrecy jurisdictions also create a deliberate, legally-backed veil of secrecy that ensures that those from outside the jurisdiction making use of its regulation cannot be identified to be doing so.

There are now ample established criteria available for identifying secrecy jurisdictions and their pernicious effect is well known, not least because it is obvious they have a primary role in moving money in the financial / speculative economy beyond the reach of regulation. They of course argue that the capital they supply to the UK and other world economies more than makes up for the costs they impose. That is not true: they supply no capital at all, since there is no capital in tax havens. Secrecy jurisdictions are simple conduits through which unregulated money flows and that unregulated money is a key element in the feral financial / speculative economy.

It is argued by some that the UK and other states have no power to stop tax haven activity in other sovereign states, but that is not true. Nearly half the world's major tax havens are under British protection of some form and we unambiguously have liability and responsibility for these places that are ultimately regulated by Westminster even if, rather genteelly, that control is structure is of a Governor reporting to the Crown in Privy Council of some similar such antiquated but nonetheless effective control relationship. These places can therefore be stopped from undertaking their abusive practices, even if we have then to provide for their economic transition to new activities. They might squeal in protest, but all those denied the opportunity to abuse tend to do that.

For other locations we can still do a great deal, as detailed by me elsewhere,[5] of which just a few ideas can be repeated here.

For example, if a tax haven promotes secrecy we can simply declare contracts made with it illegal. Alternatively, for those that offer zero tax rates, with those taking advantage of them being hidden behind a near-perfect veil of secrecy, we can require that all payments made to that place have tax deducted from them at source at a penal rate – so effectively destroying their tax-free status. And for all involved in the financial services industry we can deny UK operating licences unless they bring their offshore operations under UK regulation (or the equivalent elsewhere). To put it bluntly: sanctions will work against those seeking to undermine our economies, our tax base and our democracy, and we will have to use them if necessary.

Capital controls

The issue of capital controls is a vexed one. Holding capital to account for where it is, demanding that it pay tax where it is due, putting in place measures to tackle tax havens and reducing the number of banks likely to be involved in speculative financial flows all reduce the potential harm to the world economy from free-floating capital. Financial transaction taxes have the same impact. All these measures can then rightly be seen as actions taken to control the harmful flows of capital that have so characterised the economies of the world, and their collective failures, over the last thirty years.

This may not, however, be enough to keep speculative capital under control. There are massive resources, such as hedge funds, that might still seek to use their power to abuse – which is the basis on which they make profit, so no gainful productivity results from their activity. Additional measures are needed to tackle such flows in that case.

The first thing to do is ensure that as far as possible these activities are brought within the control of those states able to regulate them. So, for example, the nonsensical situation where the management of a hedge fund sits in London but it is claimed that the hedge fund itself is resident in the Cayman Islands because it has a token board of directors that sits there has to be stopped. Reform of corporate residence rules has to be reformed so that where ultimate control of any company rests (in management terms) determines where it is resident, unless very clear evidence of local productive activity can be demonstrated. This would deny many funds the chance to act as they now do, effectively beyond the remit of regulation.

Second, the free movement of capital has also to be challenged. Clearly, it would be absurd for small trades of foreign currency to be regulated: the days when people had to get permission to buy currency to go on holiday have long gone. Nor is any move that hinders real trade useful: automatic approval of payment for goods when payment is made to the country from which they really originate has to be part of any system of capital controls. But that said, the payment for services to countries on designated 'black lists' (basically tax havens) and the movement of funds to such places must now be regulated if the stability of the world economy is to be secured, with a right of veto at times of instability being permitted. Normal approval would require four things: identification of the originator; identification of the recipient; identification of the relationship between the two, in full, and disclosure of motivation. Without such records being established and maintained in full, no approval for the transaction could take place. Usually this could be delegated to participatory banks, subject to substantial payments for failure, but the right to intervene by the state would have to exist. National economic security might require it and a state has a right to defend itself from attack, including economic attack which in many cases represents the greatest risk to it. Capital controls therefore are an essential component of the future management of the economy.

Tax on investment income

The tax structures that have encouraged the over-expansion of the financial / speculative economy have not existed solely in the corporate sector of banking and financial services. The entire UK tax system favours the financial / speculative sector of the economy while imposing the highest tax rates on income from work.

So, for example, while national insurance (a tax in all but name) is paid on all income from work except for a modest allowance, there is no equivalent charge on any source of income paid from the financial / speculative economy. That national insurance charge (which includes for all practical purposes the employer's contribution which is usually hidden from view but which when combined with the employee's contribution brings the total national insurance rate to in excess of 20% of much declared gross pay[6]) represents a significant part of the total tax take on income in the UK, meaning the whole system is heavily biased against labour as a result.

There is no excuse for this bias and implicit subsidy to those who can engineer that their income arises from the financial / speculative economy. As a result a Courageous State would tackle this issue by imposing an investment income surcharge on all income earned from the financial / speculative economy, whether it be interest, dividends or of other sort, including rents. That surcharge, of say 15%, would be payable above a modest agreed annual allowance for such income of, say, £3,000 per annum (which would require wealth of way above national average before such a charge would be made) and would help to seriously redress this imbalance in the UK economy and bring the inappropriate tax subsidy to the financial / speculative economy under control.

Equal taxation of capital gains

Of similar importance to the proper taxation treatment of income derived from the financial / speculative economy is the proper taxation of capital gains. Capital gains arise on the sale of investments and other assets held in the long term. Until the late 1980s these were always taxed at lower rates than income. Then, rather surprisingly, the then Conservative government had the courage to set the tax rate on capital gains at the same rate as that which would be due on them if they had been treated as a person's income, albeit after the offset of some quite generous allowances and reliefs. This lasted until Labour returned to office, when again rather surprisingly, the link between income tax rates and capital gains tax rates was broken, with much lower rates being offered on capital gains. This situation has only recently and very partially been corrected so that at present capital gains tax rates are higher than income tax rates for 90% of all tax payers, but much lower than income tax rates for those most likely to have such gains, who are in the top 10% of income earners and wealth holders – a situation that is wholly illogical.

Indeed, this differential in favour of capital gains makes no economic sense: it encourages tax avoidance, it encourages artificial mechanisms for the recognition of income, it encourages excessive investment in those assets that enjoy these low rates of tax and it distorts the whole economy in favour of the financial / speculative sector that is so harmful to the overall balance of activity and well-being.

The necessary policy change is obvious, and requires reintroduction of similar rates of tax on income and capital gains, with only very modest allowances for untaxed capital gains each year and that for the sole reason of preventing excessive taxation reporting.

Close the tax loopholes that encourage excess saving

The whole tax system is also geared to provide incentives to people to save excessively in the financial / speculative economy without there being any necessary consequent investment of funds in real economic activity..

So, for example, one of the most popular tax reliefs available in the UK is the ISA (Individual Savings Account) through which an individual can save a set annual sum either in cash or in stock market-based investments with the resulting income being tax-free, and free of capital gains. There are some 15.3m such accounts with more than £53.7bn saved in them, almost £38bn of that being held in cash.[7] The result is that a significant annual tax subsidy is given to encourage people to hold assets in the financial / speculative sector economy in a way that almost certainly yields no net benefit to the real economy. This makes no sense at all.

There are, of course, good reasons to encourage people to save and the tax system can and should be used to change behaviour, but the ideal change in behaviour is one that ensures that long-term savings are used to create investment in the real economy that generate well-being for everyone. This can be achieved through ISAs, but only if a condition is attached to the whole ISA arrangement that stipulates that the funds saved are used to either directly fund loans to (for example) the small business sector, or that the cash saved must be used to fund investment in new infrastructure that generates employment in the UK. This then relates the grant of tax relief for saving to the generation of real benefit for society, and that is an indication of a desirable policy in a Courageous State.

Other tax reliefs are saving are as inappropriate: Venture Capital Trust investments, Enterprise Investment Schemes and much else all have the simple effect of subsidising the savings of the wealthy without, in most cases, guaranteeing any real net benefit to the economy, but the most egregious example of such misdirected tax relief for savings is that of pension tax relief, and that is referred to separately later in this chapter.

Restrictions on buy-to-let speculation

The provision of good quality housing to everyone in an economy is a fundamental task for a Courageous State. It is obviously impossible to live well without good housing that forms the basis for stable, long-term, involvement in a community in which a person can flourish.

Throughout much of the 20th century the UK's housing policy was to assist people to either own their own homes or to build social housing, owned by the state, to let to those who could not or (less likely) did not want to own their own homes. The outcome was (in the main) high quality housing provided on secure tenancies.

Margaret Thatcher changed this policy: she encouraged the sale of council houses by local authorities throughout the UK, and refused to let them invest the proceeds in new social housing. The consequences been the rise of the buy-to-let market, where rental property has been used as an investment, transferring its ownership into the financial / speculative sector, with rent being paid by those who have effectively been priced out of the house buying market by the excessive prices that have resulted from the speculative fever that this use of domestic housing for investment purposes has created.

The purchase of property for buy-to-let purposes has been tax subsidised because the full cost of interest paid on the acquisition price of such properties can be offset against rent paid on the property. That means that many of those who have participated in this market have purchased their property at prices that are in effect considerably lower than those paid by those who bought property for their own use, who have enjoyed no equivalent tax relief on any interest they have paid. The result is that a significant tax subsidy has been given to the financial / speculative sector amounting to billions of pounds a year when this money would clearly have been better used actually meeting housing need through the provision of housing in which people could enjoy long-term secure tenancies. This subsidy has also denied access to the housing market to millions of people and has at the same time fuelled the cash circulating in the financial / speculative sector of the economy wholly unproductively.

There is an obvious policy to deal with this issue, and that is to reduce the amount of interest relief available to those acquiring properties for use on a buy-to-let basis steadily, but nonetheless quite aggressively over time to ensure that residential housing property is brought back into the owner-occupied market at prices that people can afford to pay. Addressing this form of speculation on behalf of the majority of people to ensure that those people's hopes of securing their own long-term place to live is a sign of a Courageous State.

That Courageous State will at the same time recognise something that is glaringly obvious and which has been ignored for far too long, which is that some people will never, for their own very good reasons, participate in the owner-occupied housing market. The outsourcing of these people's housing needs to the buy-to-let housing market has been a cowardly act by successive governments in recent years. The result has been the provision of mean housing, often too small for a family's needs, designed around viewing television and not the community of interest that a family must develop that is focused around the kitchen, the sharing of meals and eating together. It is the duty of the Courageous State to build houses fit for families to live in, and it should do so using the sources of funding explained in the next part of this chapter.

Treasury Deposit Receipts

Finally in this particular policy area it is important to note that there are measures available to any government that they might use to enhance their management of the macro economy which are not solely related to interest rates and to tax rates.

So, for example, it was always open to a government in the era prior to Margaret Thatcher's liberalisation of the banking sector to demand that banks held a certain proportion of their capital that regulators require that they hold with the Treasury. Government bonds, or gilts, still play this role, but obviously at rates of interest that are not always so favourable to the government. By acting in this way the government could readily reduce the availability of credit in the economy to reduce demand, or conversely increase it if there was a shortage of economic activity.

During the Second World War, when there was a period of excess inflationary pressure because of the high level of government spending to achieve the crucial social objective of the security of the state and beating fascism, the need to keep the financial / speculative sector under control was addressed by demanding that banks kept part of their funds with the Bank of England in the form of what were called Treasury Deposit Receipts. These accounts, which they were not allowed to draw upon without permission of the Bank of England, paid exceptionally low rates of interest. What they effectively did was withdraw cash from the financial / speculative sector of the economy (which was, of course, in those days much smaller than it is now). This compensated for the otherwise excessive inflationary pressure on the economy which would have resulted from there being income paid in the economy to the armed forces and wartime workers that was not matched by the production of consumer goods on which they might wish to spend those incomes.

The creation of a Courageous State, and the transition to sustainability, may well create some similar inflationary pressures.

There is an urgent need for investment in infrastructure, while at the same time there will, necessarily, be a reduction in consumption expenditure that will be encouraged by the policy proposals outlined later in this chapter. This combination of factors could result in inflationary pressure as the economy adjusts to a new long-term approach to sustainable investment and sustainable living with sustainable levels of consumption. It would be folly for this to be a prevented by the limitations of both monetary policy and fiscal policy, both of which have been found wanting at various times. The reintroduction of Treasury Deposit Receipts to manage this situation is, therefore, an essential step to ensure that the government can regulate credit within the economy to ensure that social objectives are fulfilled and that banks behave responsibly in accordance with that policy.

1   http://www.guardian.co.uk/commentisfree/2011/aug/07/observer-editorial-economic-crisis
2   http://en.wikipedia.org/wiki/List_of_countries_by_GDP_(nominal)
3   http://en.wikipedia.org/wiki/Foreign_exchange_market
4   http://robinhoodtax.org/how-it-works/everything-you-need-to-know
5   http://www.pcs.org.uk/taxhavens
6   http://www.hmrc.gov.uk/rates/nic.htm
7   http://www.hmrc.gov.uk/stats/isa/table9-4-2010-11.pdf

CHAPTER 15

REBUILDING THE ROLE OF THE STATE

One of the central theses of this book is that politicians have lost confidence in the state, and the power it has to do good. They have as a result backed off from their responsibility to both manage the state and the economy in the interests of all in society. The policy proposals that follow are designed to address these issues.

Close the tax gap

As has been noted, tax is a central and vital tool for any government in the management of the economy for which it is responsible. It does, of course, raise revenue but it does much more than that. However, the objectives of raising revenue fairly, redistributing income, repricing externalities created by the marketplace, reorganising the economy and raising representation in the democratic process can only be fulfilled if the tax system of the state is properly managed.

Every country the world over suffers from a tax gap; that is, the difference between the amount of tax that should be collected by a government on the basis of the legislation that it has in place and the amount that is actually collected by it. The tax gap is made up of three, or possibly four, parts. The first and biggest part is tax evasion. Tax evasion is criminal non-payment of taxes because income is not declared to a tax authority or

265

expenses are claimed to which the taxpayer is not entitled. I have estimated that this activity costs the UK up to £70bn a year, although HM Revenue & Customs suggest it is less than £35bn a year.[1]

The second part of the tax gap is tax avoidance. This is a legal activity but is designed to ensure that taxpayers get round the requirements of the law, rather than comply with them. So it exploits loopholes within tax law, or between the tax laws of different states, or between tax law and other legislation, e.g. accounting requirements and company law. This issue is contentious, with the tax profession defending its right to undertake this activity. I estimate that it costs the UK £25bn a year, while HM Revenue & Customs think it is somewhat lower at perhaps £7bn a year.

The third component of the tax gap is tax paid late: this is money that taxpayers have declared that they owe but which has not been paid to the relevant tax authority. On average, about £25bn is outstanding to HM Revenue & Customs at any point in time. Of course, a significant part of this is eventually collected, but some is not, and the longer that the amount is left outstanding, the greater is the risk that it will never be paid at all.

The final part of the tax gap is unquantified, but might be classed as innocent error. It is, of course, possible for both a tax authority and taxpayers to make such errors. They generally arise because of the complexity of the tax system. Some issues with regard to that complexity are noted below.

The important issue about the tax gap is not that it exists because that is a matter of fact. The real issue is whether it is managed or not. Until 2008, when my work for the UK's Trades Union Congress[2] put this issue onto the political agenda, it was hardly recognised as having any significance in the management of the UK economy or the affairs of the UK government. It is now, just three years later, said to be the number one objective of HM Revenue & Customs but evidence of action does not support that claim. In a decade starting in 2005 and predicted to end in 2015 the number of staff at HM Revenue & Customs is expected to halve from 100,000 to 50,000.

It is impossible to collect tax without engaging skilled and motivated staff who work in the communities from which tax is to be collected. Tax is a key component in the social contract: it is, if you like, the consideration in the relationship between the government and the people who are governed. Tax does, therefore, have to be seen to be not only fair, but to be fairly collected and those who have concern about their tax payments, the calculation of what they owe, or the sums demanded of them must have access to local tax offices so that they can resolve these questions in one-to-one relationships where trust can be created. This is not happening at present and a Courageous State would invest heavily in its tax authority for three reasons.

The first is that a Courageous State would believe that it had better right to and use for the sums that are presently evaded, avoided or paid late than those who are cheating the state of them at present.

Second, a Courageous State believes in the creation of a level playing field, where all play their part and accept their responsibilities so that all can lay claim to their rights. Deliberate failure to collect tax, which is what is happening at present, means that a decidedly unlevel playing field exists, particularly in the field of small business where those businesses that are cheating the tax authorities of money due to them are obtaining an unfair, illegitimate, and wholly inappropriate competitive advantage over those businesses that are seeking to comply with the law. This undermines the whole credibility of law-abiding business and threatens the well-being and efficiency of markets at potential cost to the whole of society.

Finally, unless the state is seen to uphold its claim to property rights then it has great difficulty in upholding the rule of law at large. Given that democracy is dependent upon the credibility of the rule of law, it is vital that taxation is seen to be well managed.

As a result the Courageous State would employ sufficient staff to seriously tackle tax evasion, would put a general anti-avoidance principle into operation in law with instruction being made to the courts that such a provision should be interpreted to uphold the spirit of the law, and would ensure that tax was seen to be collected in all the major communities of the UK by ensuring that a very visible presence of HM Revenue & Customs is to be found in each and every one of them.

Regulate business properly

The state is the foundation of a strong economy, but as the cappuccino metaphor noted earlier in this book emphasises, it can only undertake certain tasks; it has always to work in partnership with private sector business if the economy is to flourish as a whole. However, the state must set the terms on which private sector business operates. It establishes, for example, the right to limited liability. It defines the law of contract and the right to own property. It sets accounting rules that define profit and loss. It protects the creditor, and defines bankruptcy that provides those who make a mistake with a second chance. Many of these issues are addressed in the policy recommendations that follow, but perhaps the most important of all regulations created by the state with regard to business is that concerning limited liability companies.

It isn't true that the limited liability company is as important as the wheel in the creation of the modern commercial state, but it might be a close-run thing. Limited liability companies allow those with capital to promote, without liability to each other, an organisation that can then trade without those providing its capital having responsibility for the losses that it incurs if those losses arise honestly as a consequence of genuine trading error. That reduction in risk represented by the freedom from responsibility for the debts of the company that the limited liability entity provided encouraged the formation the companies that built the UK's railways, and then in turn its large industries, and now all the major private enterprises and a great many of the small businesses that operate in multitudinous ways to meet the needs of the UK's population, and that of many other countries too. As a result it is quite fair to say that without limited liability companies the modern economy would look very different from that we see all around us.

That said, the privilege of not being liable for a company's debts means that the limited liability company that shareholders create has to accept specific and onerous responsibilities to ensure that the privilege in question is not abused at cost to society at large. Those responsibilities include placing an accurate statement on public record of who genuinely owns the enterprise, those who manage it and the rules that govern their behaviour, plus a set of accounts that fully explain the transactions that it has undertaken and the assets and liabilities of the enterprise so that anyone engaging with it can truly understand who it is that they are dealing with, who benefits from the transactions that arise, what risks they take and whether or not the company is profitable and therefore likely to be in a position to settle its debts.

Unfortunately my research[3] shows that, while the UK has laws approximating to these requirements, they are at present largely ignored. At best only 80% of companies file their accounts each year and the agency responsible for enforcing the law simply ignores this non-compliance in almost every case. Instead it removes the company that has failed to comply with its requirements from the register of companies without pursuing any further action, thereby exonerating the directors and shareholders from all responsibility, and leaving those who might have lost through trading with the errant company without any effective recourse for the loss they might have suffered. This is an act of significant negligence on the part of the government. If the UK government is not willing to regulate limited liability then they should not allow it to exist. If on the other hand it believes that limited liability is important then it must invest sufficiently, and charge those who use limited liability enough for using it, to ensure that the regulation of trade through limited liability companies is properly enforced.

If that use of limited liability is not regulated properly then there are massive consequences, including significant asymmetries in the supply of information to those undertaking trade, substantially increasing the risk of trading activity increasing the cost to society as a consequence, as well as significant risk of fraud and blatant abuse arising which no society can tolerate. There is also the significant cost of tax evasion that also, inevitably, follows from this failure that I estimate to amount to maybe £16bn a year and which forms part of the tax gap, noted already.

A Courageous State would, of course, support the existence of limited liability companies: they do bring benefit. But it would not only enforce regulation with regard to the use of that privilege, it would demand that other countries uphold the same standard in their commercial affairs. This would be particularly true with regard to its relations with tax havens where abuse of these privileges is actively encouraged by the governments of those places, most of which deliberately ensure that no information is available on the limited liability entities that they allow to be incorporated within their jurisdictions. That abuse results in an unquantifiable loss in terms of tax evasion, corrupt flows of funds, bribery, criminality of all sorts and abuses such as drug trading and people trafficking, the proceeds of all of which can be hidden through secrecy jurisdiction companies.

No society, no system of government and no trade can eventually survive abuse on this scale. That is why urgent action is needed to regulate limited liability, now.

Stop the privatisation of natural monopolies

As a result of neoliberal thinking governments have for the last thirty years believed that any action they take is inferior to that which the market might ordain. The consequence has been all too clear: from Thatcher onwards governments have privatised the natural monopolies that were brought under state control after the Second World War to prevent abuse of consumers in British society.

The utility companies providing water, gas and electricity were privatised, as was the telecommunications infrastructure upon which the whole of our modern electronic economy is based. Railways were wholly inappropriately privatised using a model that anyone with experience of that industry knew could not work. Then there was the Private Finance Initiative that financed state assets at a price far in excess of the cost that the state needed to pay for them, while the mass outsourcing of contracts for services has resulted in many vulnerable and low-paid former state employees, in particular, being exposed to much worse conditions of employment than they once enjoyed.

Now the government proposes the effective privatisation of the National Health Service.

For all the reasons explained in this book these privatisation exercises are contrary to the best interests of the people of this country. They increase costs and do not create real competition, but allow private companies to enjoy the benefit of capturing a significant part of the taxation income stream of the government for their own private gain at cost to the majority of people in the UK. For that reason a Courageous State would not pursue this policy but would instead cancel all PFI contracts (buying them back in with new state debt issued at very low cost if no other option is available), and prevent further outsourcing while terminating all existing contracts as soon as possible. It would cancel rail franchises as soon as feasible, would end all pretence of there being a healthcare market, and would instead ensure there was a system where healthcare professionals can manage their service for optimal outcomes for patients.

A Courageous State would also, without hesitation, nationalise any core supply industry that fails to deliver the services that the people of the UK need at reasonable prices where regulation to achieve that goal can be shown to have failed. Just as firmly as a Courageous State believes in the importance of markets when markets can best meet need, it believes that monopoly can lead to abuse for private gain, and would take all necessary steps to prevent that.

All these suggestions are not anti-market activity; they are action to support the right of markets when markets are appropriate by ensuring that the population at large acquires the services it needs at reasonable prices, so minimising the costs to those businesses that operate in genuine marketplaces in the UK at the same time.

Create country-by-country reporting so multinational corporations are accountable

No state is an economic island, and multinational corporations are a fact of life.

It is also true that, quite remarkably, multinational corporations are not required at present to report in their accounts on the activity they undertake in each country in which they operate. They are simply required to present accounts for their operations as a whole plus whatever geographical information on the breakdown of their activities that they alone, in their own discretion, think appropriate.

No government can effectively manage its economy if some of the most important players in that economy are not accountable for what they do within it, including banks, other companies in the financial services sector, major manufacturers, the suppliers of energy and other essential services, and the largest retailers. That is the case in the UK at present. As such it is essential that an accounting initiative (that I should declare I created) called country-by-country reporting be adopted by a Courageous State so that all multinational corporations operating within its domain are required to account for precisely what they do in each and every country in which they operate. That will assist macroeconomic management. It will also assist tax collection. And it will assist the appraisal of risk, which as recent economic events has shown, is too often under-appreciated in the world economy.

Only procure from companies with acceptable business policies

A Courageous State would be pro-business but on very specific terms: it would want to engage with good business pursuing sound business practices when procuring goods and services for its own use to ensure best practice is encouraged universally. Being pro good business would be the policy of the Courageous State, but that requires a clear understanding of just what a good business might be. I am not seeking to offer a definitive guide here to what a good business might be, but take the following as examples. A good business:

1) Makes clear who it is so people know who they are dealing with;
2) Makes clear who runs it;
3) Makes clear who owns it;
4) Makes clear the rules by which it is managed;
5) Puts its accounts on public record if it enjoys limited liability, and does so wherever it is incorporated whether required to by law or not;
6) Seeks to comply with all regulation that applies to it;
7) Seeks to pay the right amount of tax due on the profits it makes in the place where they are really earned and at the time they really arise;
8) Seeks to pay a living wage or more to all who work for it;
9) Recognises trade union rights;
10) Operates a fair pay policy so that the pay differential between highest and lowest paid in the company cannot exceed an agreed ratio that should never exceed twenty;
11) Makes fair pension provision for all employees;
12) Does not discriminate between employees on the basis of race, nationality, national origin, gender, sexual orientation, age, disability and similar such issues;
13) Does not abuse the environment;
14) Has a clear code of ethics that it publishes and is seen to uphold;
15) Is transparent in its dealings with customers;
16) Seeks at all times to minimise risk to those it deals with and takes all steps to ensure they know what those risks are;
17) Accepts responsibility for its failings and remedies them;
18) Works in partnership with its suppliers and does not abuse them;
19) Advertises responsibly;
20) Creates and supplies products meeting real human need.

I could readily add to that list but the gist is obvious. What this list clearly implies is the need for country-by-country reporting.

Only with it would the data to assess whether a company is a good corporate citizen using these criteria be available for assessment.

How would those criteria be judged? In some cases this will, again, be obvious from the suggestions made. For example, it might be expected that a company either recognises a union or it does not. However, things are rarely that simple. Different subsidiaries in different countries may or may not recognise unions so composite scores are possible.

Other indicators can be prepared using this data. For example, explainable and unexplainable presence in tax havens becomes an issue when the number of subsidiaries in such places is known. The proportion of trade through or assets in such places also become significant assessment criteria if country-by-country accounting data is available. The likelihood of tax compliance can also be assessed properly when country-by-country reporting data is available.

'So what?' might then be the question. What would be the point of all this? Simply that, as the government is a major purchaser from many companies, if its procurement policy was based on the requirement that a company meet a minimum standard or no contract could be issued then this assessment methodology would become a very powerful tool indeed for encouraging good business practice. A Courageous State would use its purchasing power to encourage good practice.

Create a green investment bank

Government not only has the job of encouraging and regulating business in the economy, it also has the job of supporting new enterprise. For far too long the UK economy has been dependent upon the pursuit of profit in the speculative / financial sector and on consumption as the basis for its apparent prosperity. As a result, the government now has the responsibility of ensuring that new private sector activity can be created in the UK economy to fulfil the promise that a Courageous State has to offer. Anyone who thinks a Courageous State would not be pro-business is wrong: it would be very strongly in favour of business, but would be biased to those meeting real need.

The most effective way to do this is to ensure that the funds that are needed to build a sustainable, long-term focused business sector are available to those who want to rise to the challenge of building that opportunity. Banks, venture capitalists and others whose activities have been focused almost entirely on the speculative / financial sector of the economy have failed to rise to this challenge in the past, which is a major reason for the problems we now have, and as such this task has to fall to the state, at least for the time being.

The obvious need that we have is for a state investment bank, led not just by those with experience of banking but by a combination of politicians, senior civil servants, bankers and those with proven vision in the new economy that can invest in those new enterprises that can fulfil the industrial and commercial vision of a Courageous State. Some of those enterprises will be majority privately owned and some may be mainly state owned: differentiation on the grounds of ownership would be pointless if they can achieve the objective that is desired. What is essential is that they are capable of delivering a new economy suitable for the 21st century.

That new economy will focus upon building the infrastructure that supports communities and the development of society in the UK. It will build in sustainability, both from the viewpoint of energy generation, and from the perspective of durability. It will develop new sources of energy, whether from wind, wave, sun or other sources and make the necessary technology and equipment here in the UK. It will deliver energy sustainability for the households and offices and factories of the UK, so providing us with a long-term future, reduced energy consumption and greater financial security from external supply sources with unknown long-term prices. It will build new transport systems to replace our carbon dependency on the car. It will increase our electronic communications capacity. But it will also invest in local agriculture, new small-scale manufacturing, better facilities for the care of the elderly both in their own homes and communally, and in those services that will support people in realising their potential, whether in learning, leisure, play or simple communal time. It will also support the building of the new housing that this country desperately needs for the sake of its many families currently living in mean, unsuitable accommodation.

This vision can be created, and funded, by a Courageous State: indeed, it has the duty to do that, and for this reason a new investment bank will be an essential component within its planning, financed as explained next.

Funding the new economy

A new economy needs finance. That money is available to a Courageous State. First, it can raise money if it needs it from banks at very low rates of interest using Treasury Deposit Receipts. This cash can then be used to fund an investment bank.

Second, the state can create its own money. Why this is considered shocking in a modern economy is hard to imagine: banks do it every day, which is how they have ended up creating 97% of all money in circulation using the simple and effective method described in this book that means they literally conjure that cash out of thin air. No one expresses horror at privately owned banks doing this, and yet the idea that the state might create money in the same way is considered abhorrent, precisely because, I suspect, this would challenge the enormous monopoly profits private banks make from this exercise. The state can do this by the Bank of England simply lending money to the Treasury at its official base rate. This does, unfortunately, at present break the laws of the European Union: a Courageous State would have to challenge that law which at present requires these loans to be routed through commercial banks through the process known as quantitative easing, which wholly inappropriately profits those private banks while did not delivering the benefit the economy needs at the low cost that is appropriate. The process my colleague Colin Hines and I have called green quantitative easing could be the way to overcome these issues.[4]

Third and importantly, pension reform could deliver the cash needed for necessary investment in the economy of the UK. At present approximately £80bn a year is invested by UK employers, employees and self-employed people in UK pension funds.[5]

This investment attracts about £38bn a year in tax relief when the combined costs of income tax, national insurance and corporation tax reliefs are considered. The private pension sector at present manages to pay pensions of approximately £35bn a year out of the resulting pension funds. This curious combination of statistics shows a number of things. The first is that, in effect, at present all pensions paid in the UK are paid at cost to the state. Second, it shows that pension tax relief is an item of government spending that swamps in size total government spending on such issues as public order and safety.[6] Lastly, it suggests that the use of that tax subsidy to support pensions saving that is almost entirely used to purchase shares already in issue, bonds already in issue and buildings that are already in existence adds almost no value to the real economy but does provide enormous support to the financial / speculative economy and those people who most benefit from it through their employment in the financial services sector. That therefore appears a most inappropriate use of the state's resources at a time when it is seeking to constrain activity in that financial / speculative sector and promote it in the real economy.

The result is that I suggest that a Courageous State should demand that at least 25% of all funds invested in private pension funds qualifying for tax relief should be required to be invested in activity in the real economy that results in the creation of new investment that delivers long-term value and job creation for the UK. Most obviously, that obligation could be fulfilled by investing those resources in a new state investment bank or in new social housing and other dedicated infrastructure bonds issued by the Courageous State or local authorities within it, for example to fund new transport systems. In this way, the funding required to regenerate the UK economy should be readily available, and in the process that investment should ensure that those making pension savings might actually have jobs for long enough to take them through their eventual retirement age – something the current economy seems very unlikely to do.

There would, of course, be no coercion on this issue: any pension fund could decide it did not want to comply. It would simply lose tax relief as a result. The benefit of tax relief carries an obligation with it to use funds for the benefit of the economy as a whole: that is all this policy says.

1   See http://www.taxresearch.org.uk/Documents/PCSTaxGap.pdf
2   http://www.tuc.org.uk/touchstone/Missingbillions/1missingbillions.pdf
3   http://www.taxresearch.org.uk/Documents/500000Final.pdf
4   http://www.financeforthefuture.com/GreenQuEasing.pdf
5   http://www.financeforthefuture.com/MakingPensionsWork.pdf
6   http://cdn.hm-treasury.gov.uk/2011budget_complete.pdf page 6

CHAPTER 16

BUILDING A BALANCED, SUSTAINABLE ECONOMY

A balanced and sustainable economy requires that the government move beyond the measures identified in the previous section. It has to positively promote better balance, between people and between parts of the economy. It has to help communities. It has to promote achievement within society. And it must provide opportunity for people to achieve their purpose, which is so much more than the act of consuming that seems to be the sole current goal that the state can imagine people have. The policies that follow are intended to achieve these aims.

Progressive taxation

Our society is extraordinarily imbalanced. A tiny minority owns most wealth and our income distribution is skewed so that a few people earn much more than the vast majority. These trends have become significantly more marked over the last thirty years. Inequality reduced until about 1980, and thereafter it increased, although the Labour government after 1997 slowed that process.

These inequalities are not addressed through the tax system. The group with the highest overall tax rate (taking into account indirect taxes including council tax, alcohol, cigarettes and other duties) is the poorest 10% in society. Perversely, those with the lowest overall rate of tax are in the top 10% of income earners.

In between those groups those on middle incomes with earnings between about £20,000 and £40,000 have broadly similar overall tax rates that exceed the overall rate of those on higher incomes.[1]

This phenomenon is easily explained: the poorest in society spend all (and more) of their income and as a result pay high levels of consumption taxes in proportion to their incomes. The rich face low levels of consumption tax as a proportion of their income because they do not spend all their income, can readily avoid their taxes due to loopholes in the tax system, have many incentives offered to them to save (which by definition only they can really afford to do) and also tend to have control over their income streams meaning they can divert them through structures like limited companies that tend to reduce the tax and national insurance rates. In addition, some taxes like national insurance are blatantly regressive, with very low rates (just 2%) for those in the top decile of income earners. The wealthiest also, of course, enjoy high levels of income from the financial / speculative economy which, as noted in the previous section are not subject to a national insurance charge unlike income from employment which dominates the earnings of those with overall lower levels of income. This creates an enormous tax imbalance in their favour.

This is not the place to entirely redesign the tax system: that is an exercise needing a book of its own, but suggestions on tackling this issue to ensure we have a progressive tax system in the UK that creates better balance in society include:

- Reduce the level of income at which a 50% tax rate is charged on income in the UK to, say, £100,000;

- Create a 30% tax bracket for those earning approximately £40,000–70,000 a year but at the same time remove the ceiling on charging National Insurance at full rates. This does as a result not penalise those in the higher echelons of middle income, but does mean that National Insurance ceases to be a regressive tax and does at least become something approximating to a flat tax;

- Create an investment income surcharge on all sorts of investment income, as already noted;

- Close the tax incentives for saving noted previously;

- Restrict the availability of all allowances and reliefs for those earning over £100,000 a year so that at most they can claim £5,000 of such allowances and reliefs over and above their annual personal allowance (which they do not receive at present, but whose absence seems curiously contrary to basic human rights). So, for example, a taxpayer with this level of income might allocate this £5,000 entirely towards tax relief on gifts to charities or to pension relief, but they could not allot £5,000 to both: their total reliefs would be capped at £5,000. It is absurd that at present a person in the 50% tax bracket can claim £50,000 of pension relief a year and so get actual tax relief in cash terms of £25,000, a sum greater then the take-home pay of the average UK household.

Such measures, and these changes are only indicative, would begin to create a progressive tax system in the UK.

Simpler taxation

Many taxpayers complain about the complexity of taxation in the UK and it is undoubtedly true that we have a complex taxation system. In no small part that reflects the complexity of the modern commercial environment and as such it is unavoidable. However, steps can be taken to prevent some of the abuses of that complexity. First, as noted above, caps could be placed upon the use of allowances and reliefs by those with the greatest resources in society who are most likely to seek to avoid their tax liabilities.

Second, a general anti-avoidance principle could be introduced in tax law to ensure that whenever a person puts an artificial step into a transaction wholly or mainly to secure a tax advantage which, while in itself legal was not intended to be used by parliament in the circumstances in which it was claimed, then that tax advantage would be cancelled. This would, of course, also require a presumption that the onus of proof that the transaction was commercially motivated should fall upon the taxpayer and that the courts should interpret the law in accordance with the spirit in which they thought that law was passed into legislation.

In addition, much of the current complexity complained about by those who are operating in the real economy arises from the anachronistic nature of the limited liability company, which was created in the 19th century and is wholly inappropriate for use by small business in the 21st century. This has resulted in multiple layers of taxation for those using these companies, matched on occasion by significant tax advantages, and this whole area of complexity and abuse needs to be swept away in most cases, as is addressed further below.

Wealth taxes

None of these moves will, however, by themselves create the necessary redistribution of wealth within society that is a prerequisite of creating the better balance that is needed if a more equal, just and sustainable society is to be created.

Serious attempts at creating an effective system of wealth taxation were undertaken in the UK in the 1960s and 1970s, but since the 1980s these have been progressively undermined. Capital gains tax is now charged at low tax rates compared to those due on the incomes of those most likely to pay it, and it is as a result widely used as a mechanism for income tax avoidance, as noted previously. Capital gains tax is also effectively charged, unlike most taxes, on the family unit basis because spouses and civil partners can pass assets between them without tax charge arising, giving enormous scope for avoidance. Steps to prevent this abuse should now be introduced.

Inheritance taxes are also now largely ineffective because of a paranoia whipped up by the press about charging tax on the passing of family homes from generation to generation, even when in many cases such a supposed transfer of the family home does not take place until the recipient is well into late middle age and therefore already firmly ensconced in their own home, long ago acquired. As a result the value of estates on which inheritance tax is charged have now risen to the point where the vast majority of estates fall out of tax. In addition those with very high asset worth almost invariably avoid inheritance tax charges because, as with their income, they have excess capital available to them which they can pass on well before death, so avoiding any liability to inheritance tax, or they can afford to pass wealth on through trusts or by manipulation of the loopholes available in inheritance tax law allowing avoidance of liability.

This means that at a time when we need effective wealth taxation to redress the imbalances in the UK we have two wealth taxes that have more holes in them than the average Swiss cheese. This makes no sense at all, especially when we have an ageing population in need of greater social care, a reducing population of those able to provide that care, and the need for the realisation of assets to pay those from the next generation who must look after the elderly out of the income they generate themselves.

The result is that we must have effective inheritance and capital gains taxes in operation in the UK, even if a wealth tax as such is unlikely to be introduced simply because this is usually very hard to enforce. Capital gains taxes should be charged at the same rates as income tax, allowances for capital gains taxes should be low and should not be transferable at least in the period immediately prior to the sale of an asset, and inheritance taxes should be charged even if it does mean family homes must be sold after the death of the last occupier of the generation that owned them (taking into account the fact that provision for carers, sibling relationships, and other such arrangements can always be incorporated in law to prevent hardship in such circumstances).

In addition, the extraordinarily generous allowances and reliefs for business property that both capital gains tax and inheritance tax laws share must be reviewed. There is little or no evidence that business people are motivated by eventually realising substantial capital gains: entrepreneurial activity is a lifestyle choice that genuine entrepreneurs take irrespective of taxes but the allowances and reliefs included for inheritance tax in particular are open to widespread abuse. There is a need for redistribution of wealth in our society. That is only possible if tax charges on wealth are effective and enforced.

There is one further tax that could contribute significantly to this necessary redistribution, and that is land value taxation. There are, I think, problems in imposing land value taxation universally but that is not true of high-value property. The current council tax system in the UK is regressive because the highest band of tax now applies to relatively modest properties, and this has the effect of trivial rates of tax being charged on properties of considerable worth. This situation must be corrected through the operation of a land value tax on high-value domestic property with additional charges being rendered if those are second properties, or are owned by those not normally resident in the UK, and which therefore impose a charge on the community through being left vacant for considerable periods meaning that those who own a property play no part in the communities in which they own property but do not live.

Redistribution

However, redistribution of income, which is the most pressing priority, cannot take place only through the operation of a progressive taxation system. There are limits to the effectiveness of any such system and as a result an effective benefit system must also be in operation.

Benefits must, as far as possible, be universal. Controversial as this might be, there is a strong argument for suggesting payment of a national minimum income to everyone, compensated for by higher taxation charges that recover the sum from those who are in no need of it. Such incomes might also be paid for the benefit of all children, but with those parents on higher levels of income having negative tax allowances with regard to their children, to ensure that the payment made is recovered from them through the taxation system when it would be inappropriate for them to benefit.

Universality of benefit payments ensures, as far as possible, completeness of payment to those in need. It is cost-effective to operate and it is an essential mechanism for ensuring that bare minimum incomes for survival are made available to all. Of course, such an allowance cannot cover all circumstances and needs.

There will, therefore, continue to be need for extra payment to those who are unemployed and in search of work to ensure that they do not suffer hardship during unavoidable short-term periods of unemployment, and there will also be an obvious need to support the disabled and others with special needs. In addition payments will be needed to reflect particular need, such as for housing in areas where this is costly.

However, by far the greatest necessity is to ensure that all participate, at least potentially, in a system where all are bound into the process of ensuring that poverty is tackled mutually for the benefit of society as a whole. This will have the greatest prospect of reducing imbalances in society, and so the gap between the areas of achievement of those in poverty and those with opportunity to achieve as much of their potential as they choose to fulfil. It is that opportunity of choice that has been denied to so many that universal benefits must seek, as far as possible, to overcome so that all can participate in society with equal opportunity. It is that logic must underpin the payment of benefits in the future.

Tax and interest

As this book has explained, interest payments on loans quite literally created out of thin air have created massive distortions in the real economy while overly promoting the growth of the financial / speculative economy. The resulting loans have also led to massive instability in households and corporations as the burden of debt has accumulated. This has been a particular problem in many businesses.

This growth in interest payments, the resulting instability and the consequent increase in inequality in society have all been encouraged by the fact that the tax system has favoured the accumulation of debt finance by business and has discouraged the use of new share capital, which should be the mechanism that bears risk within companies and so prevents catastrophic business collapse. This has happened because most businesses can usually offset the interest they pay on all their loans against their taxable profits and reduce their tax bills as a result. The outcome is all too obvious: a tax subsidy to the financial / speculative sector has contributed to its excessive and harmful growth while increasing inequality and denying revenue to the government that it has urgently needed and which would have been paid if businesses had been appropriately funded using share capital.

There is an obvious solution to this problem. The assumption now inherent in the tax system that interest paid by businesses is tax allowable must be removed. That should cease to be the case with one exception, and that is intended to favour the small business sector that has always had problems in securing adequate share capital and has as a consequence had to rely on borrowed funds instead. To support these businesses I suggest that the first £50,000 of interest paid by any business or group of companies should be tax allowable. Thereafter, no relief should be given with related restrictions on lease payments that include interest payments within their charges also applying.

The impact would be significant. The financial / speculative economy would shrink in size – and that is the intention. More important, the attraction of share capital might increase, which would increase the stability of many companies as they would have a greater buffer against financial shocks available to them. That is also intentional. The tax system should not encourage excessive risk taking that threatens the durability of the UK business sector, and yet that is what it does. This is why many informed commentators from across the political spectrum now believe that reform is overdue and that denial of tax relief on interest paid is vital if stronger businesses are to be created in the long-term interests of the UK economy.

Taxes on advertising

Advertising is, as has been noted, designed to deliberately create feelings of dissatisfaction. Adverts are intended to undermine the prospect of a person achieving their purpose by encouraging a sense of inadequacy among their target audience because they do not have the promoted products or services, whether or not they have a real need for them. This is immensely harmful to society, not least by denying hope to those who have no prospect of acquiring the products advertised, and by breeding discontent even among those who can afford them, because so soon after they acquire such products they are informed that they must now acquire another in a continual process of artificially manufactured dissatisfaction fuelled by advertising.

Advertising is pervasive in the modern economy, but pernicious. A Courageous State will have to tackle this issue and there is no doubt that one way to do this would be through the tax system. There is, of course, advertising that is of benefit, including small advertisements in local media, job advertisements and such other announcements. Most of these could be exempted from any tax penalty on advertising simply by setting a monetary limit per advertisement below which such penalty would not apply. Above that limit, where the advertising in question would be designed to fuel demand for products and services whether or not they were a benefit to the consumer in society, there must be a radical overhaul of our tax system as it relates to advertising.

First, no tax relief on such advertising should be available within the tax system, so that the cost of advertising cannot be offset against the profits generated from trade to reduce a taxpayer's profit on which they owe tax.

Second, any value-added tax charged on the supply of advertising services to a business should be disallowed as an input in the VAT reclaims it makes from HM Revenue & Customs. In other words, that VAT then becomes a business cost of advertising.

The impact of these two moves is obvious: it is to increase the cost of advertising, and that would be deliberate. Tax has to be used to counter the harmful externalities created by the market, and the feelings of inadequacy, indifference, and alienation promoted by advertising in very many sections of society are almost universally harmful.

There would, however, be a cost to such arrangements: the media would of course suffer from a loss of income. The media has, however, itself been under scrutiny of late, and has not always emerged with its reputation intact. While media independence is vital, so is its objectivity and in that case there appears to be strong merit in using some, or all, of the additional tax revenue raised by government as a result of these proposed taxation changes on advertising to fund the media, both nationally and as important locally, but only if it agrees to act with political impartiality in the way that the BBC is obliged to do. If it did that then I think funding to compensate the media for some of the loss of revenue it will suffer as a result the loss of advertising revenue would be appropriate.

But also note that what is being suggested here is hardly without precedent: when it became obvious that business entertaining was giving rise to abuse, tax and VAT relief on it was stopped in much the same way as I now suggest for advertising. Many said that the restaurant and other trades would collapse as a result. They did not, of course, do so.

Ban advertising to children

A type of advertising that is particularly pernicious is that aimed at children. There is no parent that cannot recount the nagging of a child who wants a product that is either beyond the parent's means or that is wholly inappropriate to the child's needs who cannot also directly attribute that demand from their child to advertising aimed solely at children.

There is only one solution to this problem and that is to ban all advertising aimed at children. This will not stop children enjoying their lives to the full; indeed, as almost any parent will tell you, a cardboard box is one of the best toys ever invented, with the stick a close-run second choice. And of course, any parent will be at liberty to take their child to any toy shop whenever they like with a child able to make a better, more informed, and freer choice if advertising does not distort their prior decision-making. Creating young people able to form their own opinion is one of the strongest objectives of the Courageous State. Banning advertising aimed at children is one way to achieve this.

Multiple rates of VAT

Such measures aimed at advertising will not, however, correct the whole environment of overconsumption from which much of the western world currently suffers at cost to its long-term sustainability. There have to be some more direct measures to achieve this goal. One of these is to introduce differential VAT rates.

There is, of course, a European constraint on behaviour in this area and this, therefore, would have to be negotiated, but the problems the UK faces are ones that are universal across the whole of that community, and the Courageous State must stand up for reform that is in the best interest of people whether within or beyond its own borders.

The UK does, to its credit, already operate systems of zero rating for VAT on some essential items which are usually subject to VAT in Europe including, for example, books and children's clothing. When Margaret Thatcher was in office she also introduced differential VAT rates, with additional VAT being charged on what were considered luxury items, such as consumer electronic goods and jewellery. The same could obviously be done now. So, cars above a certain size or price point, items of consumer excess such as yachts (including those bought by British resident people outside the UK, which they would have a duty to declare for these purposes) and many of those items that Margaret Thatcher thought appropriate to charge higher rates of VAT on should now suffer the same additional charge so that excessive, conspicuous consumption is curtailed.

Of course it is true that such a move will have some implications for employment and the businesses producing such products but so be it, this is a price worth paying. Any such impact will be more than compensated for by the measures already proposed for job creation.

Promote repair and recycling

One of the problems with our current consumer society is that many of the products we buy are designed to have short product lives and to be disposed of not long after their acquisition. So, for example, the volume of clothing we acquire has increased enormously in recent years and much of that clothing is worn only occasionally before being disposed of. In addition, we dispose of many items of consumer electronics within a year or so of acquiring them, while model product life cycles in most consumer sectors have been shortened deliberately to encourage increased consumption. Worse still, far too many products cannot be repaired either by the consumer or even by the manufacturer. They are simply designed to be thrown away when they go wrong.

Recycling is, of course, an important part of sustainability, but so is repairability, as is reuse. Among the VAT incentives that must be given should be reduced rates of VAT on products that can be shown to have a high degree of repairability. Reduced rates of VAT should also be charged on repair services.

And we must realise that, far from being the scourge of the high street, charity and other shops that recycle consumer products should be seen as being at the forefront of modern retailing and they should be given incentives to extend their operations to ensure that products have the longest possible lives in use, however many owners are involved.

In combination, these policies will reduce our overall level of consumption, but they would also do something else: they would create skilled employment opportunities and increase the range of local economic activity. Both are vital the building of effective communities and societies in which a strong local skill base helps meet local need.

Increasing the minimum wage

The desire to work to maintain one's self, or to maintain one's family, is core to the human condition. The provision of employment opportunities for all who want them must be a fundamental objective of the Courageous State and a condition for the achievement of potential for most who live in it.

Ways of creating new employment in the UK through the creation of an investment bank that will build new infrastructure to support a long-term sustainable economy have already been discussed but it is as important that the employment created sustains those who are engaged in it. That means that at a minimum a person should be able to live without suffering relative poverty on the reward of their employment.

The minimum wage was one of the great successes of the Labour governments between 1997 and 2010. It was universally condemned when proposed, with claims being made that it would create mass unemployment and harm business, but neither happened. The real wages of many were increased as a result of that legislation, but it remains the case that a minimum wage of only just over £6 an hour is far too little to ensure most people, even people living by themselves, can sustain themselves without risk of being in relative, and sometimes absolute, poverty. As a consequence those employers paying at this rate at present receive a massive effective subsidy from the state because their employees must apply for benefits to ensure that they can live at the most basic standard of living. That is ludicrous: to support business to pay wages that are below poverty levels makes no sense at all and the minimum wage must be increased to reflect the real cost of living, if necessary with regional variations to reflect the fact that, for example, living in London is more expensive than in some other areas.

Protecting union rights

A minimum wage is a basic prerequisite for ensuring that an employee can sustain themselves as a result of their own efforts, but it is not enough to protect them from all situations that might arise during the course of their employment. The employer/employee relationship is a perfect example of an asymmetric relationship, with the employee almost always having the weaker negotiating hand. It is not by chance that the trade union movement helped employees throughout the UK achieve some of the most basic advances in employment rights ever seen. So, for example, they helped secured legislation on health and safety, paid holidays, equal pay, protection from dismissal and much more.

It is now popular to dismiss union power on the basis of some excesses in the 1970s, and there is no doubt that unions must not be in a position to influence the economy in the way that banks do now, but to deny employees the right to collective bargaining, protection in industrial disputes, and representation in the workplace is to deny them fundamental human rights and as such the role of unions in the workplace must be supported by a Courageous State.

Industry wages boards

Collective bargaining is powerful: it has almost invariably improved the lot of those workers whose conditions are negotiated in this way, to their own benefit, and although many will only grudgingly admit it, to the long-term benefit of their employers as well. There are, however, many situations where collective bargaining cannot be applied. This is, for example, the case when the place of employment is small or the workforce is widely dispersed. This happens in retailing, restaurants, agriculture, and many small businesses. In these cases there has been too prevalent a tendency for business to offer the minimum wage as if it was the de facto basis for employment, whatever the skills a person has to offer and whatever their worth to the enterprise. That is wrong, and was recognised to be wrong in the past when industrial wages boards set minimum pay levels for particular skills in specified sectors to ensure that people would not exploited whatever their particular employment circumstance. The restoration of these boards with the task of setting minimum standards for pay and conditions of employment seems a basic necessity to ensure that all employees are properly rewarded without the difficulty and embarrassment of complicated negotiation having to take place in situations which inevitably favour the employer.

Of course such boards cannot provide an ideal solution for all employment situations, all skills and all environments but they can offer clear guidelines, empower employees and ensure that people can advance their claim for rightful reward against pre-established benchmarks which should make reaching fair agreement easier for all.

Apprenticeships

Fair pay is an important part of the workplace relationship, but it is by no means the only component of a successful working relationship in which both employee and employer benefit.

There is widespread recognition that the UK has a skills shortage and that this is particularly prevalent among the young, where currently education is heavily focused on academic achievement even if that has little bearing upon the needs of an eventual employer.

It is obvious the UK needs more skilled employees, and not just those with academic qualifications. Apprenticeships were at one time the foundation upon which the skills of our economy were built. Those who would master a trade, prove their skills and demonstrate their worth were rightly rewarded for doing so. This fostered the skills that society needed while training in the workplace built a strong sense of community and provided the skills needed in the local economy to meet local demand. Apprenticeship is an essential way of delivering this opportunity to young people and as such financial incentives, support and if necessary tax encouragement must be given to both employees and employers to participate in these arrangements, with the inherent long-term relationship that they also imply.

Industrial training boards

Apprenticeships are vital but the skills a person needs change during their life, as do the jobs that people undertake. Skilled employees add value and yet far too few employers invest anything at all in the skills of their staff. This results in a loss in productivity, profit and opportunity for advancement on the part of those they employ. This is a scandalous waste of resources that must be corrected.

In more enlightened times industrial training boards existed in the UK to ensure that those who worked in a wide variety of industries, from the service sector to heavy manufacturing and construction had access to training appropriate to their needs at reasonable cost that ensured that they could fulfil their potential at work. A Courageous State would reintroduce such boards and provide employees with a statutory right to training during the course of their employment, for which their employers would make only modest payment.

Extra tax relief for employing people

Our tax system is biased towards the creation of capital intensity, whether that be the capital intensity of the banks and other financial institutions that populate the financial / speculative economy, or the capital intensity that produces many of the goods produced to meet the artificial, advertising-stimulated, demand for excess consumption. Specific tax reliefs are given to encourage that capital intensity through advance tax deduction for what are called capital allowances on expenditure on equipment that in very many cases is designed to replace employees in the workplace.

Now of course the Courageous State would not be Luddite, for there is good reason to embrace much technology including that which can deliver sustainability, but there is equally good reason to encourage employment to the greatest degree possible because no society can flourish when those who wish to work are denied that opportunity. It is absurd that tax incentives are given to replace employees but the incentive given to engage employees is so limited.

New incentives to encourage employment are necessary. For these to be effective it is almost certainly the case that the headline corporation tax rate will need to increase. The tax bills of those companies that make profit from speculation without creating employment should be high. Those who add value by creating employment in the community or by providing training in society and who help people as a result to achieve their potential must have the opportunity to offset the costs they incur in doing so, and more besides (probably by applying a multiplier of cost incurred for offset against profit) so that their effective tax rate is much lower than that of the speculator or of the company that survives on technology alone when so much of that technology will almost certainly be directed at excess consumption.

This is a complex area for new tax incentives, and few have offered such an incentive yet anywhere in the world economy because neoliberalism has always had a bias against the employee. That bias has to change, and as such policy in this vital area development of taxation is essential, and the Courageous State would embrace it.

Reorganising the structure of the workplace

Far too much commercial policy in the UK and elsewhere has been designed to meet the needs of large and multinational corporations. Of course they are important and have a vital role to play in the world economy, but at least half the people employed by the commercial sector in the UK are engaged by small and medium-sized enterprises, and given the policies that a Courageous State would pursue, that proportion is likely to increase. This is unsurprising; bar the US, the UK has one of the lowest ratios of staff employed in small companies in the developed world. However, there is an impediment to progress in such companies for those employees who show clear ability to lead that prevents them from moving from the status of employee to becoming a participant in profit and risk-taking, as many should and could do.

The major impediment to this progress is the current structure of the limited company used by so many small businesses to organise their affairs. While the limited company may have suited the needs of the 19th century economy for which it was designed, it is wholly inappropriate for the 21st century economy where many would hope that staff could join in the ownership of their enterprise to take a share of profit when appropriate, and to eventually reach positions of senior management. This is almost impossible in small, privately owned companies where the possibility of giving an ownership stake to employees is exceptionally difficult without serious, and often insurmountable, taxation consequences arising. In addition, limited companies impose massive administrative costs on those who use them because of the divide between the entity and its owners implicit within them and the separation of taxation liabilities between the two, which adds enormously to the complexity of running small business.

All of these impediments to small business are inappropriate and the time has come for there to be major reform of the structures available for the management of such enterprises, including a revamp of the current limited liability partnership rules so that many more small businesses can be organised on this basis. Businesses organised in a limited liability partnership basis can reduce their administration costs substantially. Their tax affairs are also easier as the owners of the business are taxed on the profit it makes without further complication arising. But most importantly these structures allow for the easy transition of employees into partnership so that they can become fully-fledged owners of the enterprise in their own right. This provides the necessary flexibility of arrangement needed for community-based enterprises that could develop the skills that society needs and that can deliver the goods and services required by people living in sustainable economies if they are to fulfil their purpose. It is a reform long overdue that could be aided by reducing the availability of limited liability companies and this is something that a Courageous State would undertake.

1   See http://clients.squareeye.net/uploads/compass/documents/Compass%20in%20 place%20of%20cuts%20WEB.pdf page 15

CHAPTER 17

SUPPORTING THE BROADER GOALS
OF THE COURAGEOUS STATE

The goals of the Courageous State are not just limited to the economy, important as that is. It is essential that the needs of communities, such as families and extended social networks be met and that social infrastructure be supported. It is also vital that the integration of individuals in society be supported by providing them with appropriate educational skills and lifelong learning they need so that they can fulfil their own intellectual potential for the benefit of themselves and society at large. As importantly, the Courageous State has to support those who are elected in fulfilling their purpose. This part of this chapter looks at these goals.

Reforming education

The UK's education system works well, for a few. Unsurprisingly, large numbers of those for whom it works well end up in the financial / speculative economy, adding little or no value to the country as a whole. This disastrous scenario, where education is biased towards the needs of a sector of the economy whose main purpose is to extract value from the real economy while promoting excess consumption to fuel the accumulation of wealth by a few, has to be changed. The travesty of justice where far too many young people in this country are forced to follow a curriculum that offers nothing to them, and which can only hinder their achievement of their potential, has to be addressed.

It is as unjust that far too many young people are being forced to pursue university-based academic qualifications at enormous personal cost and financial indebtedness (which leaves them forever enslaved to the financial / speculative economy) when there is no prospect of the economy at large using the skills that they have been forced to acquire simply to secure a job to which they are not relevant.

It is, therefore, essential that the education system in this country be reorganised so that the needs of all young people are met, whatever latent ability they bring into the system with them and whatever their aspirations might be when they have finished full-time education, but with both situations being respected to the full. That means, of course, that academic education must continue to be offered to those who want and need it, but so must the full range of vocational, technical and life skills be taught and examined in ways suitable to the skills of those partaking in education. No one should be alienated by school: all should be motivated by learning and all should have the chance to leave full time education with a statement of their achievement of their potential, knowing what they wish to achieve in the future, and with the skills to deliver both.

Of course this is a challenge, and no one should pretend otherwise, but because the entire UK education system has been suited to the needs of a tiny group of universities for the last seventy years or more, it has left us with a population of young people alienated by the entire education system, with all the social consequences that we have seen arising in communities throughout the UK. Unless the challenge of reform is accepted there is no chance of building the Courageous State for everyone who lives in it.

Higher education should be free

Higher education is now assumed to involve a university, but that is untrue. Higher education should be available to anybody after their school career has finished who needs it to fulfil their potential, whether that is in an academic sphere or not.

Investment by one generation in the education of the next is probably the most important single activity it can undertake. Unless the next generation is able, and willing, to take on the tasks of running the economy, there is no prospect of a previous generation having a secure old age. It is as blunt as that. Saving alone is an utterly useless exercise when it comes to providing for a pension because, unless there is someone to buy things from and something to buy, no amount of savings will help a person survive in retirement. Since it is the next generation that will make the goods and services that the old will rely upon after their own working lives are over, ensuring that younger generation can supply what is needed is a vital part of pension saving.

In that case, nothing can be more important than ensuring that there is adequate investment in all types of higher education to meet the needs of young people, and that those young people can have access to that education without fear of financial penalty. Despite this we have instead loaded those who want access to education with almost insurmountable debt; a debt that enslaves them to the financial / speculative economy just as much as does our refusal to let them have access to housing at reasonable cost. Furthermore, our refusal to provide them with secure state old-age pensions also enslaves them to that economy beyond our economy.

It is therefore very obvious that society should do three things. The first is to ensure that it invests in appropriate higher education for all. The second is to ensure that those who need access to it can have it. The third is to provide that education free of charge because we are all dependent on its success.

Lifelong learning

Education is not something that ends on the day a person leaves school or college. It is a lifelong occupation and many of the skills that a person will need to best equip them for the challenges that they will face during life simply cannot be anticipated in their youth. Lifelong education has, therefore, to be available.

This issue has already been dealt with in the workplace in recommendations made above, but there is so much more than that to lifelong education, which in itself is something more much more than the many classes currently offered under that banner, good as many of those are.

So, we need training for parenthood, training for caring for the elderly, training to help children with homework, training for some of the most basic things in life like cooking, all of which can transform a person's life in community.

Of course none of these things can be compulsory but when we currently force children to learn skills 99.5% of them simply don't need (like algebra and trigonometry) then surely there is time to do these much more important things as well?

Maximum working hours

Work is important. Fair pay is important. But so too is life beyond work. The simple fact is that when people work less they also consume less, their carbon footprint is smaller, but their quality of life is usually higher. Of course, for some working too long is about avoiding poverty and that is why measures to improve benefits and to reduce tax on the poorest are essential and that is why an increase in the minimum wage is also vital. For others, though, working too long is about excess hours to consume more goods that they really do not need.

In both cases the impact is extraordinarily harmful. Family life, relationships, interaction with the wider community, any participation in society, and an opportunity to realise a person's meaning are all foregone to the sacrifice of time to work for cash.

Few countries, bar the French, have really addressed this issue properly, which is why the French example of setting a maximum number of hours that a person may work is so refreshing. A Courageous State has to say that work is vital, but you can always have too much of a good thing and that working for too long is harmful: a cap on working hours is essential.

Local democracy

As described in this book, communities are about our social relationships, while society is the infrastructure that supports them.

In both cases, and for the vast majority of people, both are local. In other words, the people most people know live nearby in the main and the infrastructure that supports their lives is that of the city, town or village in which they live. That may not be the view from Westminster, or even the view from London, but for the vast majority this is the case and there is nothing wrong with that.

However, while most people's lives are local, their democracy is not. Local democracy has a proud history in the UK. As the 19th century turned into the 20th century it was the UK's local authorities that led the way in social reform. They built sewers, the greatest single contribution to health the UK has ever had. They pioneered social housing. They built local transport systems. Electricity and gas were supplied by local authority-owned power stations and gasworks. School boards transformed the lives of many. Local markets were built. And all this was done without the hint of a profit motive: communities were transformed because people believed in them. There is something quite astonishing to think about in that fact.

That faith continued into the post-Second World War era. Of course mistakes were made: no one can say that all social housing built in the 1960s was desirable, but the intentions were clear, and right: local authorities, based on appropriate civic pride, provided for their communities and in the vast majority of cases they did so well, and efficiently.

Margaret Thatcher destroyed that. She detested the challenge that the Greater London Council posed to her authority. She left London as the only major capital city in the world without its own local authority for many years. She demanded central control of funding and borrowing, and in the process destroyed local autonomy. Authorities no longer had the right to tax as they saw fit and their right to borrow was curtailed. The result was obvious. Local democracy withered as local autonomy failed.

Local authorities have become the agents of central government. Their power to supply housing was stripped from them. Local education authorities have had their authority removed. As providers of social services local authorities simply represent government; they now have only minor input into transport and it is only in the areas of waste management, planning, the police and fire service management that they really have very much authority left. Peripherally, they run some sports and leisure and arts activities, but the reality is that this is too limited an agenda, with too much of their funding being provided by central government for people to believe that local democracy is worthwhile, or worth voting for, let alone investing their time in.

This has been a disaster for democracy in the UK. Indifference to voting locally has led to indifference to voting at all. The remoteness of Westminster from local people has led to an indifference to the whole political process. And the failure of the Westminster power system to believe in local democracy has led to a dangerous centralisation that is symptomatic of alienation.

A Courageous State would have to do overcome this centralised fear of local autonomy. It has to restore the right to local authorities to raise funds to build social housing, and to encourage them to do so. It has to give them control of local energy so that appropriate innovation can take place, including combined heat and power schemes, local generation and local energy saving. They must have power to borrow to raise capital for these projects.

Local authorities must the able to influence local education to meet local needs, while their role in the delivery of the arts is vital, and must be funded. And they also have a critical role in the development of local enterprise. Just as social housing is vital to provide security of tenure to people in local communities, local authorities having an incredibly important potential role in providing high quality, local, and flexible business accommodation to local enterprises that need access to a similar security of tenure so that they can develop knowing that they have a landlord they can rely upon.

But none of this is possible unless local authorities have the power to tax more than they do now. The council tax is already an archaic, outdated and inefficient tax that is highly regressive because the amount due is strictly capped at a relatively modest valuation of property. Innovation in local taxation and in land value taxation has to be explored to help local authorities exercise a local mandate. At the same time it is vital that central government ensures that those in wealthy areas do not enjoy lower overall tax rates as a consequence of the fortune of their circumstance compared to those who live in poor communities with local authorities which have greater obligation to compensate for need as a consequence. Formulas for redistribution are, therefore, essential, but local decision-making must drive this process so that local democracy once more has the opportunity provide a powerful, not-for-profit, force for good in the local economy.

Social housing

It was an act of cowardice when central government demanded that local authorities walk away from their responsibility to provide high-quality social housing. It was negligent of government to outsource the management of the social housing that remained, effectively putting many tenants under quasi-private sector control that was supposedly (but not actually in many cases) more efficient than the local authority management it replaced. The hopes of many were dashed when social housing was put beyond the reach of those who cannot afford their own homes, but are not in the category of those requiring emergency housing, sometimes in situations that are engineered to achieve that purpose. Opportunity the long-term, stable housing for many was denied as a consequence and that is a cause of fundamental social injustice.

I have already noted that local authorities must be given the power to become major supplies of social housing once again, and must also have the opportunity to raise funding to finance it. If there is one thing the Courageous State should do, then this is it.

Healthcare

I discussed in Part 1 why it is impossible for the UK to provide healthcare on a market basis. I will not repeat the arguments now. All that needs reinforcing is that healthcare must not only be provided by the Courageous State to all who need it, but that there must be no pretence of the marketplace having a role in its provision. In other words, the competing structures that have been created within the NHS are themselves harmful and create a breakdown in the unity of provision that is essential inside what must be a coordinated, professionally coherent, and seamless supply of service to those who need it. All marketisation damages this potential outcome and must therefore be eliminated from the management of the NHS in a Courageous State.

Pensions

The issue of pensions has already been discussed in Part 1 and again the arguments do not need to be repeated here. It would, however, be essential for the Courageous State to play an active role in the supply of pensions to all in society.

These pensions would not be backstops of last resort since, as I have already noted, suitable savings media to transfer wealth from one generation to another in the volume required to meet the demand for pensions simply do not exist and attempts to use markets for this purpose have been highly destructive due to the massive and inappropriate expansion of the financial / speculative economy that has resulted as a consequence. The private pensions sector has also failed in effect to deliver pensions, since at present tax subsidies to pension funds exceed the value of all private pensions paid in the UK, meaning the entire cost of them is effectively born by the state.

The result is that a Courageous State will have to move towards comprehensive payment of earnings-related pay-as-you-go pensions for all in society because no other form of pension provision eventually makes sense financially or economically. Of course, anyone will be at liberty to increase their income in retirement by saving, but in the long term providing pension subsidies for this process makes no sense: cash, if it is to be used for pension provision, must go to pensioners and not towards inflating the financial / speculative sector as is the case at present.

This will be an enormous change in direction in policy by a Courageous State, but it essential: the whole current pension industry is in many ways little more than a giant Ponzi scheme with the capacity to explode at any moment, and unless action is taken to address this fact serious hardship for those in old age will arise. The Courageous State has no choice as a result but to act on this issue.

Care for the elderly

The UK has an ageing population: that is a fact. It is also true that a great many people cannot work for a great deal longer than they do at present: the simple reality is that the human frame is fragile. While medicine might let us live longer, it does not necessarily make us more durable as we progress through our 60s and into our 70s. For some, working into old age maybe possible, and exactly what they desire. For others, that will never be the case. As there are practical physical and social constraints on the number of people who can come to live in the UK at any point in time this does, inevitably, mean that in the future there will be more old people in the future who will be maintained by a smaller cohorts of younger people, at least in proportion.

We have to be realistic about the fact that this means three things. The first is that we might all have to consume less in the future, but that is almost inevitable in a sustainable economy and something we will have to embrace anyway.

Second, it means we will dedicate more resources to looking after those in old age in the future. Again, that is an inevitability we will have to embrace.

The third inevitability is that this will have to be paid for, and there is only one way to do that, and it will be through more taxation. This is inescapable. However, this poses problems if the resistance to people having to sell their houses at the time they go into care that generates so much emotion at present is to be avoided. The inevitable consequent policy is a simple one and is that when people have no further need for their houses, which will inevitably occur when they reach the end of their lives, or when those with whom they cohabit reach the end of their lives, then tax must be paid.

It is only through the operation of an inheritance tax at a realistic level, which will require that many people will eventually sell their homes to ensure that tax is paid, that we can make provision for the old in society in the future.

However, that fact is not by any means all bad news. A tax that means that homes have to be sold may well have a secondary impact. It will force more houses onto the market and that in itself will increase the supply of housing and so will in due course reduce the cost of houses. That is desirable. House prices are too high in proportion to incomes in the UK and their current concentration of ownership is rapidly narrowing so that a few now own a great deal of such property at relative cost to the rest in society, with the housing they own being moved into the financial / speculative economy which has additional social impact, the most important being reduced security of tenure which has long-term implications for the stability of communities. As a result, taxes that ensure properties are sold on when members of a generation cease to have use for them are, in fact, welcome and increase overall well-being. People might want to walk around this issue (and many politicians have done just that), but ensuring we can pay for the care of the elderly is vital.

There is one other aspect of this matter that is also important. In the UK we have already seen that relying upon commercial companies to provide care for the elderly is dangerous: one has failed and far too many are making marginal profits. In addition, care is by no means what is desired in some cases and that is because too many of these companies have speculated in the underlying value of the land and buildings that they own and have not invested in the provision of care. That is because we have built provision of care for the elderly on an investment model driven by the financial / speculative economy and not on the needs that real people have.

The reality is that we can only ensure that people can enjoy long-term stable care in the communities in which they wish to live if we empower local authorities to invest in care homes that they will own and manage on behalf of the communities they represent. Those authorities did this until the 1990s when this sector became one of the first to be outsourced by the state. Local councils must, of course, be accountable in that process, but if the capital costs of the provision of care for the elderly are kept as low as possible (and that is only achievable by using the states' low cost of capital as the basis for its supply) then the overall cost to society of providing for the elderly will be reduced to the minimum possible, with the lowest possible leakage into the financial / speculative sector, and that means that resources will be released for what we really need – which is care services.

Youth services

If care for the elderly is vital, provision for the young is essential. In a material sense it is probably true that the young in our society are now better off than any of their predecessors have ever been before and yet there are clear signs of discontent. The relationship between the young and community is strained in far too many cases. Far too much of their interaction is ephemeral, electronic, and fails to recognise the responsibility that goes with relationships. Alienation from family, school and the community is too commonplace. Too little activity is demanded of too many young people and we have a problem with obesity as a result. There is an obvious need to engage young men in particular in activity that encourages their responsibility.

There are, it has to be acknowledged, no simple solutions to these problems but when in far too many places the cost of leisure and in particular sporting activities are beyond the realistic financial means of young people on benefits or the minimum wage, then the risk of people being alienated from their communities increases, and the interaction between young people in proactively beneficial ways is diminished.

Local authorities as a result have a vital role to play in the provision facilities for young people that encourage above all else commitment in communities, because these qualities are vital to the development of a sustainable economy.

Relocating work

There is one last point to note with regard to many of these proposals and that is that each of them requires that work is available in the place where people actually are.

It is easy to ask what many communities make in the modern world because it is sometimes very difficult to discern what they export to pay for the goods and services that they so obviously import into their retail outlets and from society at large through the provision of central government services. And yet, this ignores the fact that the vast majority of people's needs are met by other people living in their locality and that unless we re-empha-sise the importance of local economies that build and replenish themselves through local interaction then we ignore the greatest possible source of development of a sustainable economy within a Courageous State.

Investing locally to ensure that local need is met is one of the most important functions that local authorities can undertake in the UK, using resources that they can secure through local taxa-tion and through the issue of bonds. Local currencies may also have a role to play that has been ignored by government to date.

Bonds are particularly important though, not least because they are precisely the sort of investment most people will want to acquire underpin their own pensions because they pay an imme-diate, and obvious, rate of return in the local community in which the funds are invested, while providing a secure and stable finan-cial return that can underpin a person's own security in old age. In this sense they provide a double return, both now and in the future, for any such investor that almost nothing else can provide. There is a virtuous local economic cycle within this process that has to be explored and developed further if we are to build effec-tive communities in the 21st century.

CHAPTER 18

COOPERATING INTERNATIONALLY

The Courageous State cannot exist in isolation: it must, of course, cooperate internationally to achieve its objectives. However, at present far too much of the interaction that takes place in the world economy is prejudicial to the best interests of any state. That is not accident: that is the case by design. The financial / speculative economy has promoted the use of tax havens in particular to further its stranglehold on the world economy precisely because tax havens can be used to challenge any nation state that might seek to constraint the financial sectors supposed right to claim resources for itself. This last chapter is on the policies that the Courageous State might pursue to address this particularly important issue.

Closing down tax havens

Tax havens should properly be described as secrecy jurisdictions. Secrecy jurisdictions are places that intentionally create regulation for the primary benefit and use of those not resident in their geographical domain. That regulation is designed to undermine the legislation or regulation of another jurisdiction. Secrecy jurisdictions also create a deliberate, legally backed veil of secrecy that ensures that those from outside the jurisdiction making use of its regulation cannot be identified to be doing so.

There have been international initiatives to tackle tax haven abuse, most particularly that started by the Organisation for

Economic Cooperation and Development in 1998 and the successful initiatives put in place by the European Union starting at about the same time. All of these are in the course of being developed further at present, and the moves being made by the European Union to tackle tax evasion are welcome, and overdue. A Courageous State would need to support such initiatives and demand they be taken further.

In particular, enhanced transparency of tax haven companies, trusts, foundations and charities is vital if tax, commercial and economic abuse is not to be hidden behind them and therefore measures, some already discussed, need to be taken through the tax system to ensure that those places that refuse to cooperate on the issue of disclosure of the ownership and accounts of these bodies must be taken to prevent international fraud and abuse.

There is no doubt, for example, that tax haven abuse could be massively curtailed if there was international cooperation to require these places to automatically exchange information with countries such as the UK so that if any tax resident of the UK operated a facility in a tax haven then at least once a year that tax haven would be obliged to tell the UK tax authorities that this was the case. For these purposes a 'facility' would be any interest a UK-resident person had in a tax haven bank account, company, trust, foundation, charity, partnership or other structure. Each and every tax haven must have this information because they are universally required by international money-laundering rules. These rules now operate in all tax havens as a result of international pressure to tackle terrorist financing. They must, therefore, know the beneficial owners of all the accounts that they maintain on behalf of any person in the world, and this can therefore form the basis of that information exchange process without imposing any significant additional cost upon them. If the existence of such arrangements was automatically notified to the tax authorities of the UK, then firstly there would be many fewer such arrangements in existence because, quite clearly, the risk of discovery would discourage their use, and secondly the tax authorities would have all the necessary information they need to pursue the collection of tax arising. This would represent a massive step forward in tackling the tax fraud that tax havens facilitate that I have esti-mated might cost the UK as much as £18bn a year in total.[1]

Country-by-country reporting

The financial / speculative economy is populated by wealthy indi-viduals, many of whom maintain their wealth through tax havens, and by multinational corporations, many of which use such loca-tions extensively to reallocate profit from those places like the UK where they might otherwise be taxed.

The use of tax havens by individuals can be tackled using the measures noted above but their use by multinational corpora-tions requires something a little different. Country-by-country reporting, which would require multinational incorporation to include profit and loss accounts in their annual report for each and every individual location in which they or their subsidiaries work would necessarily require that they disclose the transactions that they undertake in such places, and this would help to hold them to account for their use of these places.

It is argued by some that international cooperation would be required to introduce country-by-country reporting, but that is not true, although moves in that direction are already underway. The UK could undertake this move in isolation if it so wished, and if it wanted to hold its financial services industry and other multinational corporations to account for the use they make a tax havens; a use that is in no small part motivated by their desire to avoid their obligation to pay tax in the UK, and which therefore necessitates this action to bring them to account.

International tax agreements – unitary taxation

If country-by-country reporting were to be introduced to make multinational corporations accountable, whether they were quoted on a stock exchange or not, then a new method for the allocation of profits between states that would ensure that there was fair taxation of the profits of multinational corporations between countries could also be introduced. Country-by-country reporting would provide the essential data to check the credibility of such a system which would allocate the total profits made by a company for a year to each and every one of the jurisdictions in which it operates on the basis of a formula. The normal formula used is called the Massachusetts formula and it allocates one-third of the profit on the basis of the state where sales take place, one-third on the basis of the state where staff are engaged and one-third on the basis of where physical assets owned by the corporation are located. Since it is impossible to make a profit without customers, and it is impossible for a company to make profit without engaging people, and every company, without exception, must make use of physical assets at some point, then this formula is in itself complete and allocates profit as fairly as possible on the basis of the true factors of production that generate it. Adding another factor to allow for the use of natural resources would add to the credibility of the formula, as would allocating the tax bill on the basis of head count in a country and not the cost of paying staff in a jurisdiction.

This system of taxation is, inevitably, prejudicial to tax havens. It is rare that there are any physical assets located in these places: the average tax haven company only requires a slot in a filing cabinet in the lawyer's office to support its existence. It is also rare that any tax haven company employs real staff while very few sales actually take place to the population of tax havens, meaning that the overall allocation of profits to such places will be tiny if this system of allocation of profits were to be used to apportion income between states so that each could, in accordance with its own democratic mandate, then decide what rate of tax should be applied to them in the course of collecting its own taxation revenue.

The system is fair, it is democratic, it defeats one of the principal weapons of the financial / speculative economy in its attempt to withhold taxation payments from all states, whether Courageous or not, and the mechanisms to deliver this system of allocation of profits for taxation purposes can be put in place. That is precisely why Courageous States should support this method of taxation for all multinational corporations.

Fair trade

Country-by-country reporting of profits and the necessary mechanisms that support it also help another objective that should be endorsed by any Courageous State. This is a policy that all trade should be undertaken fairly. In other words, those with rightful claim on the profits of an enterprise should be able to enjoy the benefit arising from them.

There is significant evidence that at the present point in time a great many of the world's multinational corporations reallocate their profits from the locations where they really arise to location such as tax havens, where they are recorded but not earned so that taxes are avoided as a consequence. This is particularly prejudicial to the developing countries of the world. Many of those countries are as a result dependent upon aid because they cannot collect tax on the profits that should be recorded in their countries. This is believed to be especially true in the case of the extractive industries that operate mines, drill for oil and extract gas in many developing countries. This abuse arises because multinational corporations can abuse the principles of what is called 'transfer pricing'. Transfer pricing is the mechanism multinational corporations are meant to use when they sell goods and services between companies that they own across international borders. If it worked properly it would mean profits would be taxed where they really arise, as would be the case with unitary taxation, but it clearly does not work, especially because many developing countries cannot secure the data they need for multinational corporations to ensure that such prices are properly calculated. The result is that profits are all too easily transferred in the resulting conditions of secrecy from the places where profits are really earned to places where they are not, such as tax havens, or secrecy jurisdictions as I prefer to call them.

No one knows precisely how much this transfer mispricing activity costs the developing countries of the world, but all estimates suggest that it is significant; Christian Aid has suggested that the total loss might exceed $160bn in year,[2] a sum substantially in excess of the annual aid budget, which is generally believed to be approximately $100bn a year.

A Courageous State would commit itself to fair trade, a process it would support by demanding country-by-country reporting, even if it reduced the profits available for taxation in its own country, because this act would provide the real basis for economic development for those most vulnerable countries in the world where the poorest people live so that their poverty, whether absolute or relative, is relieved for the benefit of humankind at large.

Capital controls

The measures suggested in this chapter are forms of capital control: they are intended to make sure that capital is accountable wherever it is. This is essential if the inevitable increase in the rate of return to capital that has been a characteristic of the last thirty years, and which has been so harmful to the world economy, is to be corrected. The proportion of the world's income paid to labour has to increase if people are to have any prospect at all of realising their potential, meeting their needs and even of paying their debts, which in itself makes this a matter of self-interest for capital itself.

I believe that tackling tax haven abuse, demanding that capital owns up to who owns it, making capital account for where it is and what it does there and changing tax systems to ensure tax is paid in the right place at the right time will have an enormous impact on the way in which capital behaves. You cannot make capital transparent without changing its behaviour. We know this to be true. Measuring and reporting something changes behaviour in the physical world: it will do the same in the world of finance.

But that does not mean that the changes suggested will be willingly acceded to. I realise that will not be the case. Tax havens and multinational corporations will resist these changes. In that case, given the threat such abusive activities pose to the stability of the world economy and to the well-being of the people of the world the Courageous State will have no choice but to suggest sanctions on those states and those companies that refuse to cooperate with the process of transparent accountability which will assist the process of making capital accountable to people once more.

There are steps in this process. The first is one of active engagement in research on these issues and promotion of the alternatives. The Norwegian government is a current exemplar of good practice on this issue through its work on tax havens and its promotion of the Task Force on Financial Integrity and Economic Development, of which I should declare I am a committee member. It is a truism, and sometimes an annoying one, to say more work is needed in this area, but on this occasion that is true.

Second, the governments of Courageous States have to be willing to join together to tackle this issue. We saw that this was possible in April 2009 when the London Summit of the G20 said it was willing to impose sanctions on those states that refused to cooperate to end tax haven abuse. The rhetoric was sound and the threat was appropriate. Unfortunately, the OECD failed to deliver an appropriate standard for assessment of tax haven abuse and as yet the sanctions have not needed to be used. However, the important point was that a precedent was set: the possibility of action was at least anticipated.

Third, the measures to enforce capital controls have to be designed. This is no small task. It has been thirty years since we have had effective capital controls and the knowledge and experience of their operation has largely been lost. That means lessons have to be learned again. This is not the place to suggest all the measures that might be required: however, it is clear that measures that might include the following are needed:

- Creation of lists of 'black' and 'white' states: white states being those to which it is presumed payment is acceptable. To achieve that status a jurisdiction would be required to have matching capital controls in place and appropriate accounting and taxation systems.

- A presumption that all payments for goods might be made without objection – but that banks arranging payments must have evidential support that the payment is for this purpose.

- Payments for services will be subject to tax withholding at source by default with payment being approved without such deduction only if paid to white list states and for agreed types of genuine services, which would always exclude payments for royalties, licence fees, interest, leasing, management charges and such services that are easily subject to transfer mispricing.

- Payments for investment purposes, whether for direct investment or portfolio investment will all require prior consent for payment.
- Payments for speculation will be subject to quota allocation, which could be withdrawn at any time.

Of course, the reality of capital controls will be complex: that is not denied. And of course they will impose cost. But that cost will be a price worth paying. Thirty years of the free flow of capital has resulted in at least 5% of world GDP shifting from labour to capital. And that shift has massively destabilised the world. The recreation of a stable environment in which people can achieve their potential is the goal of the Courageous State. That is unlikely to be possible without capital controls. Unpopular as they will be with the owners of unfettered capital, they are essential if order is to be restored to markets, economic stability is to be recreated and world peace is to be preserved. I suspect they are as significant as that. For which reason capital will have to be taken on in its own best interests to create the controls which will also let it prosper, which is vey unlikely in the current situation where it is all too obvious that the absence of controls has allowed situations to develop that are utterly disorderly and where massive loss of value for capital is the likely outcome. Surely capital controls are better than that?

Peace-keeping – not war

This brings me to the final recommendation on the policies that a Courageous State should adopt. The UK has historically been a warmongering nation, and that tradition has continued to the present day. It is, of course, the duty of any state to protect its citizens against threats, and any state must invest in the necessary resources to do that. This obligation cannot be compromised. But

x WTO rules

the capacity to defend is not the same as the capacity to attack. And the capacity to defend does not also require that the state produce offensive weapons for sale on the international market where they can create international instability. The UK has done just that. It is prejudicial to long-term stability and sustainability to do so, and the impact is always to reallocate resources that could be used for the benefit of humankind at large to totally destructive activity.

It is also important to note that there has always also been a substantial link between the financial / speculative economy and the defence industry, with significant profit being made from warmongering as a consequence of over-investment in aggression. The extraction of this profit from the economy in which people must meet their needs has been another harmful consequence of our policy on war.

A Courageous State would have the courage to declare that a peaceable solution to conflict is always desirable. It would most certainly avoid ill-considered intervention in the internal affairs of other states where there is almost no prospect of military victory but high probability of long-term chaos as a consequence of action.

It was hoped that when the Iron Curtain fell there would be a long-term peace dividend. We have yet to see it, but that is because of political choice, not because of lack of opportunity. The duty to pursue peace is one that the Courageous State must embrace. In the interests of balance, in the interests of sustainability, and in the interests of all people the search for international harmony is paramount and the UK must follow the lead of countries like Norway in negotiating for itself a new role in the international community where it leads the path to reconciliation, and not aggression. The dividend for all would be enormous.

1   http://www.taxresearch.org.uk/Documents/TaxHavenCostTRLLP.pdf
2   http://www.christianaid.org.uk/images/deathandtaxes.pdf

Lightning Source UK Ltd.
Milton Keynes UK
UKOW051816150212

187371UK00003B/14/P